IDENTITY THEFT, INC.

disinformation®

IDENTITY THEFT, INC.

A Wild Ride with the World's #1 Identity Thief

Glenn Hastings and Richard Marcus

© 2006 Glenn Hastings and Richard Marcus

Published by The Disinformation Company Ltd.
163 Third Avenue, Suite 108
New York, NY 10003
Tel.: +1.212.691.1605
Fax: +1.212.691.1606
www.disinfo.com

Library of Congress Control Number: 2006932334
ISBN-13: 978-1-932857-41-2
ISBN-10: 1-932857-41-9

Printed in USA

10 9 8 7 6 5 4 3 2 1

Text design: Maya Geist
Cover illustration: anlända
Cover design: Jacob Rosette
Editorial director: Ralph Bernardo

Distributed in the USA and Canada by:
Consortium Book Sales and Distribution
1045 Westgate Drive, Suite 90
St Paul, MN 55114
Toll Free: +1.800.283.3572 Local: +1.651.221.9035
Fax: +1.651.221.0124
www.cbsd.com

Distributed in the United Kingdom and Eire by:
Virgin Books
Thames Wharf Studios, Rainville Road
London W6 9HA
Tel.: +44.(0)20.7386.3300 Fax: +44.(0)20.7386.3360
E-Mail: sales@virgin-books.co.uk

Distributed in Australia by:
Tower Books
Unit 2/17 Rodborough Road
Frenchs Forest NSW 2086
Tel.: +61.2.9975.5566 Fax: +61.2.9975.5599
E-Mail: towerbks@zip.com.au

For my mother

CONTENTS:

FOREWORD

Upon reading this book, you may come to dislike me. If so, I understand. However, I must write as myself, or, more to the point, as who I was while committing the thousands of felonious acts described in these pages. I am not trying to win a popularity contest. I am merely telling you my story as it happened.

When I submitted my proposal to publishing houses, not one out of two dozen expressed disinterest. The story, they all chimed, was fascinating. It was as outrageous as it was unbelievable. The book world consensus was that an insider's book about identity theft would make a big splash at the Frankfurt Book Fair. One editor called it "groundbreaking." It would be the first of its kind.

But she, along with twenty-two other publishers, ended up rejecting my proposal, even if it did introduce one of the most amazing, mind-boggling chronicles of true crime ever put forth to the media.

Why? Because the main character was not sympathetic. No, he was glib, unapologetic. Simply put: not likable.

That main character is, of course, me, so I wasn't thrilled with the judgment. Though it did not jolt me to be called glib and unsympathetic. After all, what kind of personality would one expect from someone who pulled off perhaps the greatest white-collar crime of the century, and got away with it? Certainly not the shy, introverted type. Would anyone really anticipate the helmsman of a tremendous fraud to be lacking self-esteem or suffering from image problems?

But to be called unapologetic did not sit well with me. That adjective might fit the crimes I committed, but not their aftermath. Am I not, after all, repenting by teaching in this book how people can protect themselves against scores of rampant ID thieves? And, I'll have you know, I am donating a fair share of my royalties from this book to a special fund created to aid victims of identity theft.

But this wasn't enough for those faultfinding publishers. They seemed more interested in finding a palatable character than a one-in-a-million life story. In arguing this quandary with inflexible editors I remember saying things like: "Do readers really care if the character is someone they wouldn't want to be best buddies with? Are they going to, in the middle of a chapter about his fantastic escapades, suddenly in disgust toss aside the book while muttering, 'I can't bear this excitement any longer because I don't feel Glenn is a nice guy'?"

One frumpy editor had the gall to respond "Yes." He even made the audacious statement, "If you can *nicen* up the character, then we can make an offer on the book."

"What would you like me to do?" I asked him, (deciding I was better off speaking about myself in the third person) "make him into a Robin Hood? I can have Glenn stealing everyone's identity, establishing credit in their names, and then walk along the Bowery bestowing handouts on both sides of the street."

Needless to say, the meeting with that particular editor didn't last long.

Much the same scene unfolded at meetings with the three remaining editors who did not reject *Identity Theft, Inc.* out of hand, but wanted a closer look. One said that he could deal with my not being sympathetic but not with the fact that I had never been caught. For *that* I apologized. There really wasn't much I could do about it, I told him.

So after many false starts, I had a decision to make. I had to choose whether to compromise and fictionalize the character (myself) or tell the big publishers to shove it and take a much smaller advance from a much smaller publisher and write the damn book how I saw fit. At least that way it would be a genuine book about me, the real father of modern identity theft. Whether or not I am proud of that is not the issue. Neither is my "likeability." The crux of the matter is what I did and my *accountability* for it. So with that in mind, I decided to do the book on my terms. I will tell you my story, and I will tell it to you as if you were standing next to me in a noisy watering hole blasting with music. When it's all said and done, if you don't like me, so be it. If you don't like what I've done, so be it also. But that second "so be it" is much less standoffish than the first.

But I promise you one thing: In spite of your feelings toward me, you will certainly appreciate what I've done. If not the resourcefulness of it, then certainly its sheer enormity.

PROLOGUE

Welcome to Identity Theft, Incorporated. My name's Hastings; I'm the chairman of the dishonest board here. If my corporation were in fact above board and actually traded legitimately on the world's financial markets, I couldn't tell you that IDT, Inc. would make either *Fortune*'s or *Forbes*' list of top 500 companies, but let me whisper in your ear that we're still pretty darn big! I'll let you peek at our financial statements in later chapters, maybe even allow you to sit in at an IDT board meeting. You'd probably be amused to see how my company operates.

But now, if you'll indulge me, please, I'd like to acquaint you with a hypothetical scenario: You have no money, no credit, no job and are also, in passing, a fugitive from justice. What do you do? How in the world can you possibly solve all these problems and make your life worth living again? Think about that for a minute, I mean *really* think about it. If the solution comes to you easily, then I guess you can put this book down and go back to whatever you were doing five minutes ago. No need to continue. But, on the other hand, if I've left you at sea feel free to go on to the next paragraph.

Okay. You've thought it over but you're not sure. So let me tell you what I'd do if ever bogged down in all that muck: simply become someone else. Yes, I mean another real living person—and I'd do it fast. With everything stacked against me like that, I wouldn't think the rest of my life had much potential. I'd prefer shedding my skin for someone else's, at least virtually, in the eyes of computers, where it counts most. So how, then, you must be wondering, do you go about becoming someone else—if not in the flesh, at least in plastic? And once you've succeeded your cyber makeover, how do you earn enough money to sustain the rest of your phony life?

Well, I'll tell you one thing right off the bat: you can forget the job. If you're willing to go through the trouble of switching identities, which, I might point out, is as easy as it is illegal, why bother toiling an honest day's work for a living? You might as well go all the way, cruise down the yellow brick road to illicit fame and fortune. Remember: You're a fugitive anyway, probably with nothing to lose.

Wait a minute! I've gone too far. Let's forget all that hogwash about being on the lam with no cash or credit. I gave you that down-in-the-dumps scenario just to get your attention. Now that I've got it, I'm going to tell you the truth about identity theft. First of all, it's already at the top of the financial crime heap. It's bigger than stock and securities fraud. Bigger than conventional bank fraud. Bigger than illegal kickback scams, pyramid schemes, misappropriations of funds or any other form of fiscal finagling. Bigger even than tax evasion and money laundering. Simply put, it's downright huge! Billions and billions of dollars are bilked annually from banks and other financial institutions by crafty identity thieves who have very selective tastes. They steal only identities of people with excellent credit histories and then use them to secure billions in loans, which, as you might have guessed, never get paid back. So if you don't pay *your* bills, don't worry, no one's gonna be stealing your identity any time soon.

Stealing identities (as I learned before the FBI did) is so easy that the only prerequisite is a first-grade ability to read and write. Sure, you assumed you had to be one of those geek computer hackers capable of breaking into confidential credit-data files and other heavily guarded personal-information banks. Not so. Computer literacy helps, of course, but the first time I stole another person's identity and credit history, I thought the term "dot" was an acronym for "daring outrageous thief" and "com" a simple misspelling of the word "con." I may have been both, but during most of my career as a purloiner of identities, a good library stocked with shelves of good books was the only source I needed to gather the information necessary to my craft.

In this book I'm going to take you on a step-by-step journey through my career as one of the world's biggest identity and credit thieves. We're going to make stops together in some of the world's most important financial centers. You'll see exactly how I stole several hundred identities in the furtherance of a meticulously planned and highly organized swindle aimed at banks, credit card companies, airlines, casinos and even big department store chains. Never once did I fleece an individual person or small shopkeeper, of which I'm very proud. As far as banks, airlines and casinos go, who likes them anyway?

I will, when we take time off from all the fun stuff, show you how I set up phony but real business entities in all fifty states, some of which grew into national corporations, and some of those into multinational conglomerates that did business around the globe and employed a thousand *honest* people, not one of whom ever suspected his job was as fictitious as everything else in my worldwide sham network.

I promise you a lot of laughs along the way, like my experience in Las Vegas as a fake high roller. You're going to absolutely love how the casinos, taking me for a real sucker, wined and dined me in their lavish hotel suites and restaurants, all the while thinking I was some wealthy industrialist who possessed more gold and platinum credit cards than they did gaming chips. In the end, I got their chips while they got stiffed for the millions in markers I signed.

And the shopping sprees! Have you ever had the fantasy of strolling into the world's most expensive retail shops, gathering up clothes, jewelry and bulks of whatever merchandise you fancied and then just lumping it all on the counter at the sales register and taking it home by the stroke of your pen—without ever having to worry about a bill? I used to do that in reality every week, until finally I had so many designer suits, gold watches, TVs and stereo hi-fi equipment that I began giving it away. But not all of it. You'll get a good chuckle when you read how I opened my own retail outlets to get rid of the excess merchandise I signed for at department stores. One particular scam for buying and then reselling giant-screen TVs, a few, by the way, to unwitting police officials, was quite hilarious!

But all that merchandising was penny-ante stuff, more fun and games than anything else. What you'll appreciate most is how I built my identity theft business into a little empire that was buffered from the FBI, Secret Service and Interpol by strata of clever frauds laid over more clever frauds. Which is not to say I never got heat from the feds or interfeds; I certainly did, which you'll see, but the difference between me and every other grand scammer whose book you've already read is that I never got convicted. In fact, I was never even charged. In reading this book, however, I don't ask you to admire me, nor do I ask for your respect. I only want you to enjoy yourself while hanging out with me for a decade or so. And when it's over and you *really* put the book down, please—*please*—don't go out and steal your boss's or next-door neighbor's identity.

Almost the end

Chicago, Illinois, 1998

ON THE FATEFUL SPRING AFTERNOON IN 1998 THAT MY PARTNER Bones entered the Sears Tower in Chicago, it was unusually cool and windy. The collar of his camelhair overcoat was snugly turned up to ward off the gusts shrieking through the glass panes in the revolving door. Once he stepped into the lobby and felt a rush of warm air, Bones exhaled with relief and put his collar down.

In the elevator, he seemed indistinguishable from the pack of businessmen who filled the car. Like them, he was coming back from lunch. Like them, he had matters urgent and not so urgent waiting on his desk. Like them, he had the latest shrinking version of a cell phone in his pocket. And like them, he had never heard the term "identity theft," although he was as guilty as sin of it.

Passengers trickled out of the elevator in twos and threes as the car hiked up the building's core. Bones recollected a few specific affairs needing his attention before the day was out, then nodded goodbye as the lit golden numeral above the doors indicated his stop.

On the twenty-second floor was headquarters. Each time during the past few years that Bones pushed through the double glass doors and swept into the empty reception area, he felt proud and simultaneously had the urge to laugh. Engraved on the glass in handsome silver-trimmed letters was IDT CORP. To everyone's knowledge but ours, including the State of Illinois and the Internal Revenue Service, IDT stood for "International Design Technology." We, of course, knew better. The real company name was "Identity Theft, Inc."

Bones passed through the anteroom and continued on to his inner office. He removed his coat, tossed it on the sofa across from his desk, and comfortably ensconced himself in his black leather swivel chair. He slid over to face the glass façade overlooking Chicago and looked down on the Windy City as if he owned it.

The next load of men pouring into that elevator car in the lobby was quite distinguishable from the one that had preceded it. They did not wear gray business suits and polished black shoes. Instead they wore blue windbreakers and stonewashed jeans. Most had on sneakers or rubber-soled shoes. Emblazoned in distinct yellow on the backs of half these men's windbreakers were the block letters FBI. The second half of the rush sported the words US SECRET SERVICE in the same yellow lettering.

For the people coming and going inside the lobby, confusion—if not curiosity—reigned. Certainly this was not a football game between the FBI and Secret Service. Nor was it some kind of training drill. What probably aroused marvel amongst the onlookers was the presence of the Secret Service team. Was the president in town? What was he doing in the Sears Building?

Or perhaps it was some other dignitary, American or foreign born, who commanded the protection of the enforcement arm of the United States Treasury Department.

There was only one person in the entire tower who could know why that joint team of federal agencies was currently storming into the elevator. That person was Bones, whose real name at birth was nearly as distant as that birth itself. But for the moment, the last thing on his mind was that the faint ding outside in the corridor signaled the FBI and Secret Service agents' arrival within a hundred feet of IDT, Inc.'s front doors.

When they crashed through the glass, knocking the doors off their hinges and square into the reception area, Bones knew it was not the building's window cleaners entering the suite by mistake. His angular face, sheathed in a thick crop of salt-and-pepper hair, showed surprise even if he didn't move in his chair.

He heard a joint cacophony of "FBI!" and "US Secret Service!" Everyone who'd crashed inside was now in his office barking at him not to move.

He was told to stay in his chair, where he'd been parked so tranquilly just moments before. When he felt his butt sink deeper into the plush cushion, Bones registered that a clothesline of handguns was pointed his way.

There were twenty men wearing blue-and-yellow windbreakers standing menacingly in his office. The man closest to him on the other side of the desk wearing the insignia of the Secret Service spoke in a calm, even voice as soon as the shouting had finished.

"Who are you?" he asked Bones in a tone suggesting he was face to face with a creature from outer space.

Bones hesitated a second as his eyes scanned the eager clan of agents. "I'm Bones," he responded at length.

The lead Secret Service agent exchanged a look with the lead FBI agent. They both focused back on Bones.

The FBI head said, with a strange grimace that conveyed bewilderment, "*Bones?* Do you have a real name?"

Bones nodded, then somehow broke into a laugh. "I have about a thousand real names."

There was no second look between the agents. "Do you have a real name for which you have *real* photo ID?" asked the FBI man.

Bones was not stumped by the question. "I have *real* photo ID for all thousand names," he said simply. "Which one would you like?"

The FBI and Secret Service heads exchanged another glance. The Secret Service man puckered his lips, then said ominously, "Looks like this is gonna be a long investigation."

A land of enchantment

Taos, New Mexico, 1987-1988

IT ALL STARTED IN THE LEAST LIKELY OF VENUES. BUT BEFORE I got there, I was living in San Diego with my girlfriend, Robin, an artsy chick from Manhattan with big-time sex appeal who, despite her protestations to the contrary, was more into cash than artwork. At the time, I was between scams, hanging around the beaches doing basically nothing. Robin was usually off to this art class or that one when she wasn't hanging out with me.

Robin, by nature, was quite an exuberant lady. One typically sunny and warm Southern California day, she toppled over me in a burst of that excitement as I lay tanning on Mission Beach.

"I have a whim," she said. "Will you fancy it?"

"How much does it cost?" I said with not an iota of doubt.

"You ever hear of Taos, New Mexico?" By this time she had gotten off me and was sitting cross-legged on the edge of my towel. In fact, it wasn't really cross-legged but one of those yoga positions with one leg folded and crunched atop the other. One of those semi-contortionist poses I could never twist into.

"Taos? You mean like 'Laos'?" Obviously I'd never heard of the place. I remembered Laos because I'd connected it to Vietnam during my draft resistance days.

Robin laughed. "It's really a cool place. It's got great Southwestern art, its own Indian reservation and a beautiful gorge. Some people call the gorge Taos Canyon." She added that some people jumped.

"Sounds like you've been there."

"I had an artist friend from Brooklyn named Eddie who took me there. Stayed a week and fell in love with the landscape. I think Eddie never left it."

I was thinking that Taos's landscape and a Brooklyn native wasn't a good mix, even though I had been to neither.

"And," Robin went on, "since you like skiing you'd be enthralled there."

This got my attention.

"It just so happens that Taos Mountain is one of the best ski resorts in the country. It's got terrain as good as Aspen or Vail, without the crowds. Not many people know of it."

I guess the visions of steep slopes and virgin snow was all it took. I was getting kind of sick of watching the surfers, so a trek to Taos Mountain sounded appetizing if not adventurous. Within a week we were on our way.

Taos really was the land of enchantment. It was situated seventy or so miles to the north of Santa Fe and, as Robin had said, was known for its magnificent Southwestern art museums, Navajo rugs and Taos Pueblo, its Native American reservation. She'd repeated on the drive through New Mexico that Taos was a land of great spiritual mystery and that many great writers had lived or were still living there. She mentioned D.H. Lawrence and the current novelist Tony Hillerman. This was true, although I later found out that there were more fugitives packed into Taos's crevices and canyons than writers sitting in its tea and coffee shops. Moreover, the only things *I* was capable of writing were bad checks and forged signatures.

We would end up spending a year in Taos, and I never regretted it. And that's apart from what I'd unexpectedly learned there about credit card fraud, which I later applied to identity theft. Taos is beautiful and indeed spiritual, even if the only spiritual inspiration I inhaled in its serenity was how to get rich.

We rented a spacious adobe house with vigas, those smooth wooden beams running across the ceilings so distinctive to New Mexican homes. It sat on a greatwide-open plain across a gravel road from the regionally famous Ellis Travers Museum. Besides the museum and our house, there were no manmade structures of any kind in any direction for two miles. The closest one to us was a gas station where the gravel road finally met up with a paved county thoroughfare.

The landscape surrounding our house was spectacular. All around were flat bushy fields that suddenly rushed up against jagged mountains with snow-capped peaks. Off to one side was Taos Canyon, a starkly impressive rocky gorge with a bridge spanning its expanse through the middle. Some of those writers Robin had mentioned, apparently not very happy with their manuscripts, had taken the leap off the bridge over the years.

Closer to the house we had the daytime company of cattle, prairie dogs and snakes, most of them poisonous. Nighttime brought coyotes, raccoons and other critters difficult to identify because it was often too dark to see. Occasionally a lone wolf, stranded by its pack, drifted across the prairie. Once I even caught sight of a big brown bear. The next day I bought a pair of Siberian huskies and let them grow up outside the house to guard the place.

I grew to like my new home. I fancied my *séjour* in New Mexico would be more of a cultural and spiritual awakening than anything else. Certainly nothing related to my past illicit activities. Soon I likened myself to a professor on sabbatical in a foreign land. Perhaps, I thought with a touch of self-mockery, I'd even experience a cleansing of my soul and then get on with some kind of more conventional life.

Robin was very much into Southwestern and Native American culture. She was especially fascinated by the art and the dazzling Navajo rugs with their beautiful color patterns. She greatly appreciated the two, sometimes three generations of Navajo families it took to yarn a single rug. I, too, would become enamored of these rugs, but for entirely different reasons, ones having nothing to do with aesthetics.

Before our year in Taos was out, we were out of money. Somebody had to get a job quickly. It was quite natural that the first place Robin went looking for work was across the street at the Ellis Travers Museum. They hired her right away. She was good-looking, well-educated and gave the place a touch of East Coast sophistication, which it needed because a high percentage of the tourists visiting its exhibits and buying up merchandise in the souvenir shop came from big eastern cities. She started as the cashier in the souvenir shop.

I looked for work, too. I found out quickly that if you weren't into Southwestern art and culture and wanted to find some other kind of job in Taos, New Mexico, not many types of employment were available. You had your choice between becoming a waiter and a hotel clerk. The restaurants weren't hiring so I ended up as the night front desk clerk at the Hopi Lodge, a 150-room motel complex that was proudly called a hotel by its staff. It was sprawled over a dozen acres near Taos Plaza, the small Old West-flavored town square filled with souvenir shops, coffee shops and, of course, a chain (but not fast-food) restaurant. Those were grouped along the highway on the outskirts of town.

I came in at midnight and worked until eight the following morning. There wasn't much going on during those hours, so I spent most of the time lounging around the front desk bullshitting with the security guard, the only other employee working the premises on graveyard shift. He was a Taos Indian with the typically Mexican name of Raul Martinez. He was big and pudgy, and for some reason everyone called him Martinez instead of his given name. Even his wife, when she telephoned the front desk to speak with him, asked for "Martinez." And this was a bit odd because the most common family name among the Taos Indians was Martinez. There were seven employed on the Hopi Lodge's day shift, three more on swing.

After I'd been working the front desk for a week, the manager, who was usually leaving when I came on, asked if I could handle the daily night audit. I told him I didn't think it would be a problem. I had minored in accounting at UC Berkeley (majored in reefer), although I never worked a single day as an accountant. The thought of performing what I considered such a boring task never appealed to me, and besides, counting other people's money attracted me even less.

He agreed to add the audit to my job duties, which hadn't consisted of anything more than late check-ins, early checkouts and bullshitting with Martinez. Each night upon arrival I would find the day's room vouchers neatly stacked on my desk. There were also the checks from the bar and restaurant, which I had to tally as well. First everything had to be counted, then recounted and the figures posted to ledger sheets. Then I'd have to verify the cash totals and determine if any money was missing. Usually some was, but it was just a matter of cents. When the discrepancy was in the motel's favor, I threw the extra loose change in the drawer.

The one thing bar and restaurant checks had in common with hotel vouchers was that they were more often than not paid by credit cards. The imprints of the cards were attached to the vouchers. There were Visas, MasterCards, American Expresses, even Discovery and Diners Club cards. Everything under the plastic sun. At first I paid no special attention to the dozens of credit card vouchers I went through each night. I dutifully verified the numbers, ran the adding-machine tapes, posted the figures to the ledger and bullshitted with Martinez.

The first dishonest thing I did at the Hopi Lodge was instigated by Martinez. He told me about the lack of a consistent physical inventory being conducted in the restaurant's kitchen. He even admitted that he occasionally sneaked inside it with his flashlight and pilfered a few steaks from the freezer. He'd been doing so for years.

One late night, at three a.m., I asked to borrow his flashlight. I had just finished the audit and become rather hungry. I figured I'd sneak into the kitchen and help myself to a melon or whatever fruit happened to be in the refrigerator. Martinez, in his blue security uniform, smiled at me with a twinkle in his eye and said I didn't need his flashlight. There was one deep inside the bottom drawer behind my counter.

I found the flashlight and told him to keep an eye on the front desk while I took a little tour of the kitchen. There was always the small chance of a check-in at that hour, or even worse, the surprise visit of the Hopi Lodge's owner, a mean old widow from Amarillo who, I'd been told, every so often arrived unannounced in the middle of the night to check on her hotel employees. It wouldn't be great for me if she arrived one night to find the front desk devoid of a clerk or, worse, if she found that clerk skulking around the darkness of the kitchen with a flashlight in hand.

I couldn't believe the goodies I found there. Forget the cantaloupe and honeydew melons and the rest of the fruit. There were dozens of Idaho steaks in the freezer. Packets of lobster tails, king crab and shrimp as well. Not to mention the racks of beefy ribs just dying to find their way to the barbecue on my patio. In the pantry I found a delicious assortment of bread and pastries. There were also bottles of sauce for the steaks and ribs.

I nibbled away on the pastries and fruit but did not steal anything to take home. But I couldn't hold out forever. Each night when I went for my snack, Martinez faithfully guarding the front desk like a trusted watchdog, I couldn't help thinking of what I could purloin from that treasure chest of Epicurean delights. Robin and I didn't have much money to begin with, and we were both being paid in the neighborhood of six bucks an hour, basic non-skilled wages in Taos, New Mexico, in the late eighties. If I could steal a little food here and there, the burden of our monthly grocery bill would lighten.

After three days of nibbling and torn thoughts, I took a steak. The next night I took two. The night after that I went back to stealing one steak but increased the load with two packets of crab and one of shrimp. I would run out to the parking lot and stash everything in the trunk of my MG, always just before the end of my shift so that nothing would begin defrosting. I also began eating my early breakfast of pastries and bread every morning before leaving.

Martinez was getting edgy. I started sensing that he couldn't take the heat I was causing in the kitchen. Literally. He began frowning at me when I made second and third trips each night for snacks and breakfasts. Sometimes when I returned to the desk, I noticed he was sweating. Finally one night he couldn't bear it anymore. As I came through the front doors from the parking lot, having just loaded up my car with the latest haul, he said, "Man, I think you'd better cool it. That old witch is gonna come in here one night and catch you. Then we'll both be out of jobs."

"Don't worry about it," I told him coolly. "By the time that happens, we'll both be long gone from here. Voluntarily!"

Martinez didn't know what to make of that. He'd been working there ten years and had a family. I didn't know what I'd meant, either, but sensed that he and I would eventually do something much grander than stealing packaged steaks and lobster tails from the Hopi Lodge's kitchen.

A week later, the manager was waiting at the front desk when I arrived. By the look on his face I knew he wanted to see me. I figured Martinez had been right and I was about to be canned, but he only wanted to ask me if I'd mind changing shifts for a few days. One of the day shift people had quit the Thursday preceding Memorial Day weekend, and now the manager desperately needed to fill that vacated position. I told him, with a fair amount of relief, that I'd do it gladly.

It was that quirk of fate—the employee quitting his job at the front desk—that turned me on to credit card fraud.

What got me thinking about it was the credit cards themselves. The ones I was constantly being handed across the counter as people flooded inside the lobby and checked in. Practically all the Visas and MasterCards were gold. Half the American Expresses were platinum. The guests were all very well dressed and smacked of money, and lots of it. Their cards reeked of respectability and importance. They bespoke the prestigious addresses in Beverly Hills, Shaker Heights and Palm Beach that appeared on registration cards. I began wondering what kinds of limits these credit cards had. Then I began wondering how I could find out. Finally, I decided, I *would* find out.

A Wild Ride with the World's #1 Identity Thief

A few nights after my first day shift at the Hopi, I was lying in bed with Robin. There was a feathery Navajo dreamcatcher hanging from the ceiling. Robin's employer at the museum had given it to her as a welcoming gift. Well, that night I had a dream that the catcher held on to, and I remembered it the next morning. I'd dreamed that I made a wild journey across the United States in a shiny red Corvette with a trunk full of gold and platinum credit cards, all stolen from the Hopi Lodge. My spending increased outrageously each time I crossed the border into another state. I bought anything and everything during the spree: clothes, diamond jewelry, even some very expensive Navajo rugs. I stopped along the way to dine in expensive restaurants and lodge in five-star hotels. I charged up everything on the cards. Unfortunately, when the dream ended and I woke up, I had to go back to the Hopi Lodge, without credit cards, and work for six bucks an hour.

The dream was so cool I had to tell Robin. One thing about her: despite her constant craving of culture, she also craved material things, and had a larcenous heart. Which is to say that if the dream had been reality, she would have been the first person to hop into the passenger seat of that Corvette.

After I recounted it, Robin told me something that piqued my interest. Lying seductively on her pillow, she said, "You know, practically everyone who buys souvenirs at the museum pays for them with credit cards. They're all gold or platinum. Seems like only rich people visit Taos. And you should see how the curator caters to them and kisses their asses."

Hearing that tickled my funny bone, but it was more what she said about the curator's catering to cardholders that captured my interest. I went to work, and again welcomed, greeted and bid farewell to the scores of gold and platinum credit card-packing tourists checking in and out of the hotel. They all signed the vouchers like a harried novelist in a bookstore signing copies of his bestseller. I'd slide their cards through the authorization device, get the approvals and then have them sign. Never once did a card come back unauthorized, or refused for whatever reason, and there were some hefty amounts charged up.

One bejeweled man had reserved ten rooms for the three-day weekend. He checked in with his party on Friday, ten couples celebrating his sixtieth birthday, and opened an account for all ten rooms with his gold Visa. When he checked out on Memorial Day, he advised me to leave all charges for the entire party on his credit card. The bill came to nearly $11,000 with all their meals and champagne. I obliged, slid his card through the device, and, like always, got approval. He signed the voucher and left, even gave me a $10 tip, though that was in cash.

That night I did not dream. Mainly because I couldn't sleep. An idea had been hatching in the back of my brain, and before morning it had pushed forward and taken shape. It was crazy, borderline stupid, but I knew just as well that harebrained schemes were often the first to work. I'd had lots of experience and plenty of success with various ridiculous stunts I pulled over the years.

I impatiently waited for Robin to awaken. The moment she did, I asked her, "Do you ever get phone orders to buy merchandise with credit cards?" I was thinking how people use their credit cards over the telephone to buy things seen on television.

"No," she said without hesitating to think. That did not, however, dampen my hopes.

"Remember what you told me about the curator kissing the museum's visitors' asses?"

"Yeah, sure." She looked at me funnily. She knew I was leading somewhere on the road to a scam, but wasn't quite sure at which fraudulent exit I'd get off.

"What do you think that curator would do if he received a phone call from a supposedly wealthy individual who had visited the museum and decided he wanted to buy something he'd seen in its souvenir shop? Let's say the most expensive item."

"You mean like a Navajo rug?"

"Now that you mention it, yes. How much is the most expensive one on display there?"

"There's one on sale for twelve thousand, another for eight, and then several for two and three thousand, give or take."

"Okay. If someone phoned into your shop and said they wanted to buy a twelve thousand dollar rug on his credit card and have it shipped out, would the curator accept the sale over the telephone?"

This time Robin took a moment to consider the question. Then she shrugged and said, "Maybe… probably, if he got approval from this person's bank." She cocked her head at me and smiled impishly. "What are you dreaming up, Glenn?"

"I'm not exactly sure, but as soon as I know it I'll tell you."

The next night I was back on the late shift. This time, while I did the audit, I paid special attention to the credit card imprints on the vouchers.

I searched out the ones I remembered were from gold or platinum cards, whose holders were prone to have very high limits. Then I waited for Martinez to go off and make his rounds, at which time I slipped into the little office behind the front desk and made photocopies of the imprints. As soon as my audit was done, I began secretly studying the imprints and then matching them to the cardholders' registration cards.

The information I gleaned from guest registration cards always contained their home addresses and sometimes, when their vehicles were not rented, the model and make of their personal automobiles, more often than not luxury vehicles. I could identify rented cars right away because they usually had New Mexico tags, or at least tags that didn't match up with the hotel guests' home states. If, for example, a registration card indicated an automobile from Colorado and a home address from the same state, this would undoubtedly mean that the vehicle belonged to the registering guest. Naturally I searched out people with Mercedes and Cadillacs, more reassurance that the person was rich and had good credit.

The person I finally settled on was named William Finch III. Looking at the Roman numerals after his name cinched that decision. I figured that anyone's name carrying "III" at the end of it had to be creditworthy, and then, laughed at the idea that maybe such a person would have a credit line three times larger than most.

I discussed my findings with Robin, who was becoming more and more hip. She was beginning to tire of her job at the museum, and without money all that passion she had for art and culture was disintegrating into shit. She quickly agreed to be my co-conspirator in my first credit card swindle. Our first victim was going to be the Ellis Travers Museum where she worked. Or at least indirectly, because at the end it would either be a bank or an insurance company that took the loss.

If the plan worked.

We chose ten o'clock in the morning for the coup. Robin knew the curator would be in the museum at that hour and that her colleague would be alone in the souvenir shop, covering it while Robin went on her coffee break. I called the museum's main number and reached the operator.

"Ellis Travers Museum, good morning," she answered.

"Hello," I said crisply. "Please give me your souvenir shop."

"Surely, one moment."

A second later, a female voice pleasantly answered, "Souvenir shop, how can I help you?" I recognized it instantly as not belonging to Robin, as I knew the woman I'd be speaking with had never before heard my voice. I knew as well that Robin was in earshot of her colleague and would serve as my eyes and ears while this very dangerous phone call transpired.

I had a prepared script in front of me. Just in case anyone at the museum became suspicious and questioned me on the phone, I wanted to be sure everything sounded as credible as possible. I spoke with a stuffy, almost British accent. "Yes, my name is William Finch," I said, leaving out the "III" so I wouldn't sound too snobby. "I was recently in your wonderful museum. I saw a beautiful Navajo rug in your shop. I believe it was a Ganado eyedazzler (term for a certain design woven into the rug), and if I remember correctly, its price was thirty-two hundred dollars." We'd decided not to go for the most expensive rug in the museum, not the first time when testing out such a delicate scam.

"Yes, Mr. Finch," the woman said, as she would to any other client she did not know. "Your memory is correct. We do have an eyedazzler on sale for thirty-two hundred dollars. It's one of our most beautiful rugs. Would you be interested in purchasing it?"

"Yes, ma'am, that's the purpose of my call. Unfortunately, though, I've left Taos and am at the airport in Albuquerque. My flight back to Boston leaves in thirty minutes. I don't have time to return to the museum to purchase the Navajo." Mr. Finch was indeed a resident of Boston, according to the registration card he'd filled out at the Hopi Lodge.

"I'm sorry," the woman said in a tone suggesting her regret that no sale would be possible.

"Yes, how foolish of me. But I was thinking that maybe the purchase could be arranged somehow," I pressed on. "If I gave you my credit card number, could you then run it through for verification and approval so that I might use it to make the purchase?"

"I don't know, sir," she said with some hesitation. "As far as I know, we've never done that before. However, I can ask the curator if it would be possible."

"Please do," I said.

She put me on hold and I waited nervously. If a serious problem developed, Robin would break the connection on their end as soon as she could. She couldn't very well pick up an extension and tell me something was wrong, like a possible setup in the works, so her cutting off the call in the case of danger was our best course of action. The safest. She could always say she'd done it accidentally. At the time, caller ID was not in use.

There was no risk of the police later tracing the origin of the call.

The wait seemed interminable, and I had to fight off compulsions to hang up on my own and forget the whole damned thing. But the woman was back on the line in less than three minutes. "Mr. Finch?"

I didn't immediately respond, so she repeated it.

"Yes, I'm here."

"The curator is phoning the director of the museum in Santa Fe. He has no problem with a credit card purchase over the phone, but for that amount he must get the director's approval."

"I understand," I said, trying to maintain my calm and phony British accent, in spite of my being scared shitless.

"It won't take long," she advised me. "Would you like to hold on, or perhaps you'd prefer giving me your number and I'll phone you back?"

I certainly was not giving her the number that led to the house across the street from her countertop, not more than a hundred yards away. "That's all right, I'll hold."

I did for five excruciating minutes, during which I concocted every plausible scene of disaster. First and foremost was the fear that the curator had not called the director of the Ellis Travers Museum, but the FBI office in Albuquerque, and a few special agents were already heading north to Taos to nab me. (The US Secret Service investigates credit card crime, which I didn't know at the time.) But when the woman came back on the line, she said in a cheery tone, "Our director has approved the transaction, sir, so if you'll give me your name exactly as it appears on the card and the number and expiration date, please."

I read from the photocopy of the imprint: "William A. Finch the Third. The card number is 4857 2130 5885 1964. It's a Visa. The expiration date is February 1990."

"Thank you." She advised me that she'd be a minute. I knew she would have to call a live person in some kind of central credit card clearinghouse. At the time, I had no knowledge of how this was actually done but knew enough to know that she had no credit card to slide through a reading device. Even if she had the ability to punch the information in manually, I was certain that would not be done. Approval would have to come from a human being somewhere, one who would probably get my story about being at the airport secondhand. If that person got suspicious and told the woman at the museum to call the police, hopefully Robin would intervene in time to prevent a real disaster.

"Mr. Finch," she came back on the line with no change in her cheery attitude. "I've got approval for the purchase. Do you want us to ship the Navajo to your home address? Generally we use United Parcel."

Here was the zinger. I'd knocked myself out time and again trying to find the solution to that problem. Of course I couldn't have the rug shipped anywhere. Taking delivery of it was as dangerous as picking up a kidnapping ransom. If, during the time the parcel was en route, a red flag popped up somewhere in the central credit system, the authorities would have the chance to set me up at whatever address I gave the woman. So the solution I'd finally decided on was as bold as it was stupid—two good reasons why it would probably work.

"That won't be necessary," I said to her with a slightly stronger tone in order to take control of the situation. That skill I'd learned from my partner in crime, Bones, who at the time was back relaxing at his home in California. He knew I was in Taos but was unaware of my doings there.

"I'm going to send a personal courier to pick it up for me," I explained. Now that was ballsy! Only problem was that I didn't know who the courier would be. Certainly not me, as I'd risk being tied to the crime through my employment at the Hopi Lodge. I imagined that an ensuing investigation would lead the feds everywhere Finch had recently used his gold Visa card. Then all they'd have to do is gather employee information and finally show my photograph to the woman at the Ellis Travers Museum, who'd be able to identify me as the courier who picked up the rug bought with Finch's Visa.

No thanks. I wasn't that dumb.

I held my breath. I highly doubted that personal couriers had ever showed up at the museum's souvenir shop to pick up Navajo rugs. I hoped she wouldn't have to go get approval from the director for this as well.

"That'll be fine," she said without the slightest trace of surprise. "Just have your courier come into the souvenir shop and ask for either Eileen or Robin. The museum is open from ten a.m. to six p.m. every day but Sunday."

I hung up the phone and marveled at what had just transpired. If this was not a setup—and my confidence grew rapidly that it wasn't—the Ellis Travers Museum was going to hand my courier a Navajo rug it was retailing for $3,200. I would later learn that Navajo rugs had a certain real value, with markups not prohibitive. In fact, in the stolen merchandise business, after diamonds and rare coins, Navajo rugs were the easiest hot items to get rid of at a better than halfway-decent price.

But for now, back to the problem of who would be my courier. The list wasn't very long. In fact, it wasn't a list at all because it contained just one name: Martinez.

I broached the subject as soon as we were alone on the night shift. "Martinez," I said as he leaned against the countertop at the front desk. "How'd you like to make five hundred bucks?"

"Depends what I gotta do," he answered with quick smartness.

"It's simple. You gotta go to the Ellis Travers Museum with a fake license plate on your truck and pick up a Navajo rug from their souvenir shop."

Martinez almost fell over my side of the counter. "Are you nuts, man? Everyone knows me there, including your wife."

"She's not my wife." Not yet, anyway, I thought.

"What difference does it make?"

"Wait a minute, Martinez!" I protested. Obviously he guessed that one way or the other the rug would be stolen. "You haven't heard any details yet."

"I don't need to," he said. But I noticed a twinkle in his eye. The same one I'd seen when he first told me about raiding the Hopi Lodge's kitchen.

"Listen, it's simple. They'll be expecting you in the souvenir shop. If anything goes wrong, my girlfriend will know it in advance and I'll warn you off."

"Just how did you arrange all this?" He knew as well as any Taos native how expensive Navajo rugs were. He also knew I didn't exactly have the available funds to be out buying them.

I told him as little as possible. Telling him the truth, that I had copied a credit card imprint from the Hopi Lodge front desk files on his watch might send him into an orange New Mexican rage. When I'd finished, he still refused to do it, but he had an idea of his own.

"My brother," he said. "He's spent most of his life away from Taos. Nobody knows him around here anymore." It was true that among the Taos Indians everyone knew everyone, so if his brother had been away, he would've been quickly forgotten about.

"You want your brother to do it?" I asked.

"For five hundred bucks he'll do it. He ain't never seen that kind of money."

"What's his name?"

"Martinez."

"I mean his first name."

"He doesn't use it. Anyone who knows him here calls him Martinez, just like me."

I didn't ask the obvious, and decided that I'd refer to Martinez's brother simply as "Martinez's brother." "When can you talk to him? I want to do this as soon as possible."

Martinez reached over and grabbed the phone off the countertop. He dialed a number and waited. He looked at me and shrugged, then hung up. "Must be out drinking," he said. One o'clock in the morning was prime drinking time, unfortunately, for too many Taos Indians.

At eight o'clock that morning I met Martinez's brother. He looked a lot like Martinez, and had the same beer belly, though the rest of him was less paunchy. He lived with Martinez, and it was the first time I visited their little adobe house, which sat alone at the base of Taos Mountain. In spite of it being the first week of June, the early morning air packed an icy chill. The three of us huddled around the warmth of the wood stove, which Martinez had grated, filled with logs and fired up.

"Where do I gotta deliver the rug?" Martinez's brother asked, a second after I gave him the $500 in cash, which, by the way, depleted my financial reserves.

"Actually, not very far," I said with a humorous smirk.

"He lives across the street from the museum," Martinez said.

His brother looked at both of us with a very confused expression.

"Yeah, but you're gonna have to take a roundabout route," I told him. "You pick up the rug at ten minutes to six, just before they close. Then drive somewhere and hang out for a few hours until it gets dark. Once it does, you come right over to my house with it. There's no night security guard at the museum, so no one will see you come back. The sheriff's patrols pass it by every hour, but that's no problem, either." We knew this because Martinez's uncle, another Martinez, was the sheriff. And another cousin with the same last name, at twenty-one years old, was a district court judge who'd just sat on the bench overseeing a capital murder case. He'd been duly elected by the citizens of Taos County. Taos, as you might suspect, was indeed a very unique place.

Having Martinez's brother pick up the rug just before closing time was strategic. Robin had told me that the curator always left at five. She'd be alone in the museum with her colleague in the souvenir shop and two or three other unimportant employees in offices or on the floor. The pickup could be made without the slightest notice.

Martinez's brother already possessed half a dozen stolen or expired license plates. Half of those, I learned, had come from his uncle, the sheriff. He slapped one on the back of Martinez's pickup and was parking in front of the museum at ten to six. Robin watched as her colleague carefully wrapped the rug in cellophane and then had Martinez's brother sign the receipt. He did so with some phony name, probably another Mexican one, and the woman put the rug in his arms with a smile. She'd be splitting the commission with Robin. How was that for irony? Robin would get a commission from the victim of her first grand theft!

Martinez's brother arrived at my house with Martinez and the rug just after nine. He pulled their pickup into my garage. We closed the exterior door, unloaded the Navajo and brought it inside. We spread it on the floor of my living room. The thing really was dazzling to the eye; I understood why it was called an eyedazzler. It was intricately woven, with eye-catching but not-too-loud red and gray threads with little multicolored design patterns running throughout. Robin bent over it and ran her hand along its surface, as if it were a long-desired object that finally belonged to her. Well, maybe it did, but not for long.

Martinez had schooled me on the prosperous and widespread Navajo rug trade in the Southwest. There were hundreds of reputable dealers throughout Arizona and New Mexico, and hundreds more disreputable ones. The trade had been flourishing since the Old West. People bought, sold and traded their Navajos just as city slickers did their rare coins or antique furniture. There weren't many auctions with Navajo rugs as the prize, though the most expensive ones did rival some precious artworks, with values climbing into the millions.

Although Martinez and his brother had proved to be good cohorts in obtaining the rug, I knew I couldn't use either to sell it. Problem was, these Navajo rug dealers were seldom Navajos or from any other Native American tribe. Most were art enthusiasts or just plain businesspeople from the East Coast or California. They didn't much like or trust Indians, and became suspicious when one came into their shops looking to sell a Navajo rug. Indians buying was okay, but not if they were selling. I reflected how it was an ironic tragedy that Native Americans drew suspicion when trading Native American goods.

I called Bones. He'd been my faithful partner in crime. I was just a confused and rebellious, doper college kid when we met. We'd been together a decade during which we frolicked around the country committing a host of non-violent, sometimes humorous crimes.

Bones was the ultimate con man, as polished as a flawless diamond. I knew he'd be a natural for posing as a Navajo rug dealer. On the phone, I gave him a quick rundown about what I'd done. The next day he was at my house in Taos.

"Very clever, my son," he said as he admired the pretty rug on the living room floor. "We ought to be able to obtain scores of 'em with credit card imprints."

"First let's make sure we have an avenue to get rid of them," I said, but without skepticism.

"You're right. We'll do that right away."

We didn't waste much time. We rolled up the rug, put it back into the cellophane and loaded it into Bones's rental car—a station wagon that I'd told him would be necessary. Robin was sad to see the rug go, but I promised her that if our scam grew she would have her own Navajo to keep on our living room floor. She could even bring it back to California once we left Taos. We would end up bringing back two, one for her apartment, and the other for mine.

Bones and I drove down to Santa Fe. We scouted out two dozen Navajo rug dealers. Some we found in small souvenir shops selling Kachina dolls amongst other Native American handcrafted items and artifacts. Others, in bigger stores, only dealt with the rugs. A handful traded them from private homes.

We chose the largest dealer in Santa Fe, figuring his shop would be the most prone to come up with fast cash for a rug. It was smack on the main square of the artsy town. I went inside first and made like I was a customer browsing. My real purpose was to watch and listen to whomever Bones would be dealing with when that person was out of his sight and earshot.

It was the first time I saw a host of Navajos like that, and they really were stunning. They blew Persian and Oriental rugs right off the marble. A ticket identifying the type and price was knotted to the edge of each rug. I couldn't help but notice the steep prices.

A salesgirl asked if I needed any additional information on the rugs I was looking at and touching. I told her no, thank you. Then Bones came in, schlepping our Navajo over his shoulder. He looked comical with it. I noticed the girl's eyes go right to it. His met hers with a smile. Bones had perhaps the most ingratiating fake smile I'd ever seen. And that included in the movies. He could turn it on faster than Cary Grant.

"Good day," he said in delightful tones. "How are you, young lady?"

She smiled at the warm reception. It probably *was* delightful being greeted like that. A good con man knows how to instantly put his victims at ease. Make them feel special. "I'm fine," she answered. "And you?"

"Couldn't be better." Bones gently laid the rug on the counter and stripped off the cellophane.

"That's a pretty one," she said, touching its fringes.

"Yes, it is," Bones agreed. "But unfortunately I need to sell it. The wife and I have decided to move back east, and we just don't want to pack up everything. Besides, you know how East Coast people are. They just don't appreciate Southwestern art and Navajo rugs. Lots of 'em think they're for wiping your feet."

They shared a laugh, and I caught the young woman giving Bones the look-over. He was wearing a navy blue polo shirt and neatly pleated dock slacks with moccasins, Navajo of course. He'd bought them half an hour before entering the shop. By and large, Bones looked like a well-to-do, laid-back Californian. Certainly like someone you could trust and believe.

"I'll notify the owner you're here, sir."

I watched her disappear through a narrow hallway in the back. Bones gave me a slight nod to indicate everything was cool and in control. I continued the false browsing as the woman returned to her place behind the counter. She told Bones the owner would be with him in a minute. He thanked her and then engaged her in small talk. He wanted the owner, when he did appear, to see them in casual conversation. That always looked good. Silence bred mistrust and suspicion. Pleasant din eased the situation.

The owner was a strikingly handsome, chicly dressed woman in her late forties. Perhaps she was a bit too much for the casual laid-back "artsiness" of Santa Fe, but what remained to be seen was if she was too much for Bones. I didn't think so.

"Hello," she greeted him, with cold, businesslike warmth. She eyeballed him for a second, before her gaze dropped to the carpet still rolled up on the countertop. Bones immediately stepped toward it in a gesture suggesting he wanted to help her spread it on the floor. They did so as the salesgirl and I looked on, rather cryptically.

After the rug was completely spread, the woman cocked her head at Bones and asked, "How much do you want for it?"

Bones gave a small laugh, accompanied by a calculated embarrassed frown. "To tell you the truth," he said earnestly, "I really have no idea what the rug is worth. My wife bought it before we were married, and I don't know if Navajo rugs appreciate or depreciate with time."

The handsome woman regarded Bones without a hint of wariness. "That depends," she said. "The value of Navajo rugs tends to change more with the strength and weakness of the economy than with the passage of time." Without touching the rug she made her initial offer. "I think I can offer you fifteen hundred for it. Would that be suitable?"

To me that fifteen hundred sounded like nirvana. That was nearly half the amount the Ellis Travers Museum had been retailing it for. Hardly, if ever, did merchandise obtained illicitly command such a fair exchange.

But of course Bones would not accept it so quickly. And I knew it. It was that simple rule that real estate taught so well: Never accept the first offer. Robin had explained markups on Navajo rugs and how they fluctuated in the marketplace. She'd said our rug should fetch seventeen or eighteen hundred from an honest dealer. A dishonest one would pay less, of course, but in dealing on the sly there'd be less risk. We'd decided, cautiously, to first experiment with honest, reputable dealers. Besides, I wasn't familiar with any crooked ones. The only link I had in that direction was Martinez and his brother, and I really did not want to involve them on the selling end of the scam.

"I was hoping for something a little closer to two thousand," Bones said with minor disappointment, his face etched to show it.

Now the woman decided to bend down and feel the rug, though Bones and I knew this was for show, part of the song and dance that people looking to strike a bargain could never avoid. After a few strokes along the fabric and mild grunts of indecision, she straightened and said, "I can go as high as seventeen hundred."

Bones knew he could probably get another hundred out of her. But it was safer to finalize the deal quickly and get out of there with the cash. Once that money was in our hands, we knew there'd be more of it coming from the same well.

"Fair enough," he said, offering her his hand.

The woman shook it firmly. "Would you like cash or a check?"

"Since you mentioned cash first, I'll take that," Bones said with a smile, at which the woman smiled broadly for the first time. She went back through the hallway, probably to get the cash or make believe she was getting the cash. She could have already had it on her person, but it wouldn't have looked very discreet if she dived into her pocket and pulled out a wad of one hundred dollar bills. I heard her say something to someone in the back, maybe her husband or partner, or both. I couldn't make out the words, but there wasn't a trace of alarm or suspicion in her tone.

She returned promptly with the cash and handed it to Bones. They shook hands again, then he left the shop. The woman turned to the salesgirl and said as she pointed to the rug on the floor, "Ticket this as a Ganado eyedazzler for thirty-four hundred." She returned to the back. I left the store as the girl began writing up the ticket for their new rug. The shop's markup on it was only 100 percent.

Bones and I were in heaven. But we quickly landed back on earth to get to work. A new scam was born. It looked like it would be a beauty.

Bones stayed at our house for four weeks. Robin stayed on her job in the Ellis Travers souvenir shop for two. During that time no mention was made by the museum's staff about Mr. William Finch's credit card purchase. He'd probably not yet received his bill. When he did, the shit would hit the fan. Robin would be long gone.

I continued on as the night desk clerk at the Hopi Lodge for one reason: I still had a lot of work to do photocopying credit card imprints and choosing the ones we'd use for purchasing more Navajo rugs. I selected imprints from gold and platinum cards attached to room vouchers whose home addresses corresponded to wealthy towns and neighborhoods I recognized. Then I called museums all over New Mexico and Arizona that sold expensive Navajo rugs in their souvenir shops. I asked for general information on their stocks to give me an idea whether a trip to particular museums was warranted.

On my days off, Bones and I went on Navajo rug shopping expeditions. We mostly worked the major museums in Santa Fe and Albuquerque, and then crossed the border into Arizona. First I would go inside the museum's souvenir shop, scout out the target rug, then telephone the clerk working inside and give the same spiel about having been in the museum and regretting that I hadn't bought the Navajo when I had the chance. Even over the phone, salespeople were always thrilled to take down my credit card information. They had me hold while they verified it, and then would happily inform me that I had been approved for the over-the-telephone sale. Not once was I denied.

And there were many requests. I was "Avery Howard from Scottsdale," "Daniel Myerson from Colorado Springs" and "Sir Malcolm Duff from England," (international sales made the use of a courier even more credible: it's cheaper than shipping the rug to London). I became so adept at sounding affluent over the telephone that I began believing it myself.

Bones became the courier. And he added a new twist to that function. He wore a brown deliveryman's uniform that was nearly identical to the one worn by United Parcel Service drivers. Each time he entered a museum, the clerk in the souvenir shop was waiting for him. Sometimes the rug was already packed and ready to go. Bones would sign the receipt, then haul the heavy rug outside to the van we'd bought for transport. He was never inside a museum for more than a few minutes. On that end of the scam, there was no use for small talk and personality. Bones was just a courier. His job was to pick up the rug and get the hell out of the museum with it.

While he was inside, I waited in the van in the parking lot. I would survey the area and make sure no setups were in the works. Sometimes a sheriff's patrol would cruise the grounds and I'd feel a lump in my throat. But I'd just follow it with my eyes until it disappeared. If Bones ever sensed trouble inside, he could abort the fraudulent transaction and dash out of the museum and into the van. In that case we'd have a getaway plan, though we never used it.

Before long, my garage across the street from the Ellis Travers Museum became a veritable storage facility for Navajo rugs. We accumulated three dozen of the dazzling rugs before deciding to devote our time to selling them.

We sold the rugs in the same fashion. Bones would enter a shop or outlet dressed as a casual Navajo enthusiast with Santa Fe flair, while I waited in the van ready for an escape. He'd engage and charm the dealer as he negotiated a deal bringing us at least 50 percent of what the museum had been selling the rug for. We never tried selling them back to museums, figuring they had their own buyers who traveled the Navajo circuit looking to procure rugs. However, it wouldn't be surprising if some of them ended up with their former rugs back, given their buyers probably visited many of the places we sold to.

With time and increased confidence in the scam, we began using the credit card imprints to buy rugs for as much as $10,000. Near Sedona, Arizona, we found the biggest dealer of Navajo rugs in the Southwest. It was a large shop called Howfield's, owned by three brothers, whose interior had hundreds if not thousands of them on display, probably several million dollars' worth. Bones initially sold them the most expensive rug we'd obtained to date from a credit card. It had been on sale in a Tucson museum for $8,000. One of the Howfield brothers paid Bones $4,400 for it. Now we were getting better than half the retail price on all our stolen wares.

We went back to Howfield's a second and third time. They bought again and again without asking questions. Soon Bones struck up a friendship with all three brothers. On a morning before having coffee with them, he rushed over to the town library and crammed into his head as much knowledge about Native American and Southwestern art and culture as he could. He was not about to let himself slip up in a conversation with his new friends.

They even invited him to one of their homes for dinner. Bones gladly accepted. He dined and drank fine champagne while jovially talking the Navajo rug trade as if he'd been practicing it for decades. Bones had such a good time that he apologized for not having been able to bring me along. He recounted how they had dined poolside at a beautiful sprawling ranch house and that each brother owned one of the same. Bones had all three convinced he was a rich hobbyist trading in Navajo rugs for pleasure. By the time his dealings with them were over, they'd given us nearly a hundred grand for our heap of eyedazzlers and other Navajo beauties, including more than $10,000 for a select few.

By the time the Navajo rug credit card scam was over, we'd earned nearly a quarter of a million dollars. It was enough money for all of us to live on for two years. We finally packed it in because we knew the authorities would eventually put the whole scam together. They'd learn that each victim had one credit card detail in common: he'd used his card at the Hopi Lodge in Taos, New Mexico. They would also figure out I was the culprit, given my departure which would coincide with the end of the Navajo rug spree, and maybe even tie in Robin if they learned she'd been living with me while working at the Ellis Travers Museum.

In anticipation of all that plastic fallout, it was time to leave Taos and return to California. Greater credit scams were on the horizon, ones that would involve many millions of dollars and spread not only across the entire United States but to foreign lands as well. These, however, would be carried out with an ingenious new tool called "identity theft." No longer would using other people's credit card numbers suffice to commit perfect credit crimes. As I was one of the first to realize, it would be infinitely better to assume another person's identity (dead or living) and obtain real credit cards in their name, or even create new people from scratch and rake off millions from America's massive credit industry by posing as people who never really existed.

In the early morning of July 4, 1988, Robin, Bones and I, like parting spirits in the wind, drifted away from Taos in the predawn darkness. Robin and I gave no notice to our employers. We didn't advise our landlord, either. I figured it was better to sacrifice the security deposit and leave behind the furniture than to hang around Taos and wait for all the heat to come down.

A year later I called the Hopi Lodge and asked to speak with Martinez. He was still working security there, and when he came on the line he greeted me warmly but said absolutely nothing about the Ellis Travers Museum or anything else related to my scams in Taos. That was surprising. I didn't know if something had happened at the Hopi and Martinez was just wisely keeping quiet, or if the authorities had somehow not yet cracked the case. I didn't ask. I told Martinez to take care and that I'd stay in touch. Of course I never called or saw him again.

A research paper that's not at all academic

San Diego, California, 1990

IN EVERY BUSINESS, BOTH LEGAL AND ILLEGAL, SOME KIND OF inventory must be taken. At least periodically. Bottles, boxes and bricks have to be counted. Storage space has to be accounted for. In my business, all goods on hand fit snugly in a file cabinet's drawer, even though I had a thousand units in stock.

Those thousand units were credit cards, but not one was in my name. They were all frauds and fakes, though as real as any banker's puzzled frown upon realizing his bank had been had.

It's called "identity theft," and by that time I'd done a lot of it.

As my fingers lovingly caressed the smooth plastic of the credit cards and then ran along the upraised ridges of the sixteen numbers spanning their widths, my eyes admiring the inlaid photos and art designs of different epics in American history, I couldn't believe how fascinatingly simple it had been to obtain all of them. Each offered at least $2,500 in credit. Some had $5,000 credit lines, others $10,000, and, of course, there were those special platinum Visas and MasterCards with $20,000 limits.

As I went through them, I gazed upon the panoramas they presented: a Visa from the Citizens Bank of Massachusetts with its nocturnal depiction of the Boston Tea Party; a MasterCard from the First National Bank of

Missouri with the golden arch towering high above St. Louis. Everything from Wild West cattle drives to modern skyscraper skylines, all under bright blue skies and prettily hued rainbows. But their real collective beauty was that all this multicolored plastic would eventually turn into stark green cash—every penny of credit right up to each card's limit.

Before I show you how I got to that point, let's go back to the day the whole scam began, when I—not very innocently—walked into the University of San Diego library on a beautiful Southern California morning in May 1990. I had blown all the money from my share of the Navajo rug scam. Even sold the Ganado I had brought back from Taos and laid on the living room floor of my apartment—to Robin of all people! Now she had two eyedazzlers while I was faced with the grim prospect of having to unload my car.

I had entered the library with an idea hatching in my head. I knew nothing about computers, but my criminally enterprising brain more than made up for that lack of technical skills. I'd already guessed at the time that what nearly everyone still believes today about identity theft is false. The almost universal misconception is that one needs to be extremely computer literate to be able to assume someone else's identity. Not so. It wasn't true then and still isn't today. All you need is a little creative know-how and an ability to find your way around a library.

And I knew my way around this one. I passed through the lobby and approached the middle-aged lady sitting behind the information desk. She was perusing a magazine with librarian's glasses slid halfway down her nose. No one else had business there, so I interrupted her reading. I had learned early in life that when you want to know something, you should just ask. Don't be afraid to interrupt.

"Can you tell me where to find the *Marquis Who's Who* reference volumes, please?"

She looked up, but not at me. Her eyes went to her computer screen as her fingers rapidly pecked at the keyboard. For some reason, I sensed she was going to say the sixth floor. The USD library had nine floors. Why my imagination went two-thirds of the way up I didn't know, but she confirmed it. Sixth floor. One of my talents seemed to be the ability to sense things, and this was extremely important when you were sitting in a bank trying to finagle a multimillion-dollar mortgage in somebody else's name. You had to be able to sense when some square or snotty banker with a pointed nose was thinking you were full of shit. If not, you might end up in jail very quickly, facing a host of federal charges and impending disaster.

"Take the elevator up to the sixth floor," she said flatly. "Our entire reference section is located on the floor. The *Marquis* volumes you'll find in the PP and QQ shelves along the back wall, so just walk straight ahead when you exit the elevator."

I thanked her and went directly to the elevator. The adrenaline began pumping through my veins. In a matter of seconds I'd know whether my dream scheme was feasible.

I remembered flipping through a few *Who's Who* volumes at Berkeley when I was a student there back in the mid-seventies. I'd been doing a research paper on American cinematography and had consulted the *Marquis* tomes to ascertain key bio facts on famous film producers, directors and actors. I remembered the information given about stars' birth dates, birthplaces, parents' names, etc. I'd been shocked to learn how old some of these people had been and their real names. The memory of this had sparked the idea for the incredible credit scam. One the Federal Trade Commission could not even begin to imagine.

The doors slid open to reveal the sixth floor. I stepped out into an encompassing armada of bookshelves and walked straight ahead. Through tall bay windows at the rear, bright sunlight cascaded into the large rectangular room. The battalion of reference shelves created blotches and streaks along the pale Formica floor. Dictionaries and thesauruses began the reference section in sturdy formations stacked four levels high on the AA, BB and CC shelves. I turned right and walked alphabetically along the DD and EE shelves, reading the brown wooden plaques with large white numerals and lettering that indicated what was found there. At the end of the line I reached the LL and MM rows, then with increasing impatience snaked around the NN shelves, ignoring their voluminous historical chronicles containing everything from prehistoric man to both World Wars. Then I abruptly turned around to face the OO shelves, lined with several of the country's major newspaper indexes, before finally falling upon the sought-after PP and QQ sections.

Suddenly I was a kid in a candy store. With wide eyes and mouth agape, I stared upward at two full rows of what were now my adult goodies. Instead of chocolate bars and cherry-flavored licorice, my gaze fixed on beautifully tall, red and blue volumes whose gold lettering sewn proudly into the outer folds showed off *Marquis Who's Who* with an eminence matching the distinction of the people profiled inside them. There was *Who's Who in*

American Business, Who's Who in American Law. These volumes were red and two inches thick. And they were up to date, 1990. Then in blue was *Who's Who in Medicine* and *Who's Who in Real Estate,* just as thick and with the same gold stitching. My first thought was that the red and blue volumes, with their handsome gold lettering, reminded me of the imperial military pieces from the board game Stratego I'd enjoyed so thoroughly as a kid.

Past volumes going back twenty years for each category filled the shelves, though some of the older ones had lost their luster and were now of a fading version of their original colors. The categories were not only by profession. There were geographical distributions as well: *Who's Who in the West, Who's Who in the South* and, of course, the north and east, even Puerto Rico and Hawaii. In all, there were hundreds of volumes. Each contained secrets I hoped would make me rich.

I didn't know where to start. For several seconds I just stood there and gawked at them, as though mesmerized by some twentieth-century literary chimera. Then I had a notion and pulled the current 1990 edition of *Who's Who in Real Estate.* The book was heavy, and I thought of bringing it to a table where I'd be able to sit down. But I was too excited to move, so I rested it on my forearm and admired its exterior for several seconds. The hard vinyl binding was flawless, not a scratch. The same gold lettering graced the front cover. Finally I opened it and was pleasantly assailed by the scent of fresh print.

The "real estate" heading made me think of Donald Trump, so I thumbed carefully through toward the back of the book and the "T" pages. The volume was so stately and in such perfect condition that I had respect for it. I didn't want to inflict any damage on it, not even crease a page.

Of course Trump was listed there. There were no photographs in the *Marquis Who's Who* editions, but every quick fact you wanted to know about the self-promoting "Donald" was found precisely below some other important man named Trumm. Two concise paragraphs neatly summarized the famous real estate developer's life. The first gave his date and place of birth, his parents' full names, including his mother's maiden name (a crucial piece of information to be had in the identity theft business), his schooling, university degrees and other honorable mentions. The second was a summary of his real estate exploits right up until that day. It included mention of all boards and associations of which he was, or had been, a member.

Someone searching for the ingredients of identity theft, though, only needed the first paragraph. Professional histories would become important, but at a later stage when you began putting another person's identity to work for you.

My back began aching from the sheer weight of the volume pressing down on my forearm. I carried it over to a pale white rectangular table with three chairs on either side near the window. The table was empty, which suited me fine. My finger was still squeezed inside the closed book, on the Trump page, so as soon as I was seated I reopened it. I took a quick conspiratorial glance in front and around me—I don't know why—and then got back to my examination of the "T" page.

But it was no longer the paragraphs on Donald Trump that interested me. I knew at that early stage I couldn't impersonate someone whose face was known across America. I couldn't one day walk into Bloomingdale's with a credit card in Trump's name and buy a couple of $2,000 designer suits. Someone might just get suspicious, and I might very soon thereafter end up in a building with a lot fewer of life's luxuries than the golden Trump Tower on Manhattan's Fifth Avenue.

Instead my eyes jumped up to the top of the page, to the left column. The not-so-famous real estate developer's full name was Herbert Alan Trumm. He was forty-six years old, but that posed no problem since Bones, my yet unknowing partner in the identity theft business, was fifty. He'd be able to impersonate anyone in the forty to sixty range. I'd handle the impersonations for anyone under forty—if the scam proved feasible.

The first alluring aspect of the *Marquis Who's Who* was that everyone in its pages definitely had good credit and probably a wallet full of gold and platinum credit cards. After all, it was highly doubtful that America's leading businessmen and women—without exception prominent people— flouted their credit card bills. There was always the possibility some of them were degenerate gamblers, or practitioners of other vices that drained their finances and ability to pay debts, though I figured that percentage to be extremely low.

Good, solid credit. This was the key, my starting point that would one day lead to a gateway of riches. Why go through the pains of establishing credit under phony names when there were thousands of real people whose excellent credit was right at my fingertips? Why not just borrow some of that credit? These were my thoughts as I began studying my first candidate.

Herbert Alan Trumm was born to Rudolph Charles Trumm and Mary Harriet Fisher in Baltimore, Maryland, on January 3, 1944. A Second World

War baby, I sensed he might be the full-grown weapon I needed to launch my private war against the nation's credit and financial institutions. Several prerequisites had to first be fulfilled in order to steal Trumm's ID and then his credit history. A little time and a few well-placed phone calls would determine if I could.

Trumm was an Ivy Leaguer. He graduated from Cornell in '66, where he'd been editor of a campus newspaper and received a degree in business management. His grade point average was not given, nor did I care. Whether he'd made As, Bs, Cs or flunked would've had no effect on his credit rating. Only his personal wealth and whether he paid his bills on time reflected his creditworthiness.

After college, apparently choosing not to pursue a graduate degree, Trumm went to work for Harry Helmsley Enterprises in New York. Helmsley was a famous Manhattan real estate mogul, capable of buying and selling Donald Trump five times. His wife, Leona, was equally infamous. She'd gone to prison for income tax evasion and before that had garnered the moniker "The Queen of Mean," because she was perceived as nasty and rude to employees working at Harry's hotels. I imagined that old Harry surely had his own paragraphs in the *Marquis Who's Who in Real Estate*, though I hardly cared since he was too well known to be impersonated.

After Helmsley, in 1973 Trumm went to work for Olympia York, another huge Manhattan real estate conglomerate. He didn't give it the seven good years he gave Harry, but stayed on until 1977, when he went out on his own and became a shopping mall developer based in Baltimore. There was a listing of four business and real estate associations of which he was a member, two in New York, two in Maryland. Nothing more about his professional activities was mentioned. This meant that Herbert Trumm was either still developing shopping centers on his own or had simply retired. One thing was for sure: he sounded rich and probably had excellent credit.

He also had two children, at least two as of the publication date for the 1990 *Marquis Who's Who in Real Estate*. Even their names were given but were, of course, not useful to me unless they somehow wrecked their father's credit. The last bit of information provided was that in the early eighties Trumm had been mayor of a small village in Maryland. This was another plus as far as honesty and integrity were concerned. Further evidence that he honored whatever debts he and his wife, Sherry, amassed.

I was flabbergasted at all this information squeezed into two paragraphs. The only key detail needed to steal Trumm's identity not included was his

Social Security number—but that was no problem. A simple call to the 800-number for the United States Social Security Administration did the trick. In fact, it would do the trick a thousand times!

The *Who's Who* was certainly a Mecca of ID theft potential. Flipping through the real estate pages, I noticed how the quantity and quality of the information was the same for practically every tycoon, mogul, entrepreneur or whatever else you wanted to call them. Of course in some of the paragraphs a key piece of information was missing: a mother's maiden name or an exact date of birth, both of which nullified any chance of stealing those persons' identities. But there were hundreds of good ones, complete with the vital details. And this was just a single volume! If I lived to be a thousand years old, I'd have enough credit-stealing fodder to keep me living in style for that whole millennium.

But where would I start? And with whom? Whose ID and credit history would I try to steal first for the inauguration of my new business? Obviously I didn't want to choose someone recognizable to anyone who watched TV or scanned a newspaper. It had to be a person of impeccable standing but equally unknown to the public.

I thought that maybe I should discuss it with Bones, but then figured it was too early to involve him. I wouldn't tell my longtime criminal partner anything until I was sure it would work.

"Why not," I finally reasoned, "start with Mr. Herbert Alan Trumm from Baltimore"? He, just like everyone else in the *Who's Who*, was a name in a hat, albeit a very promising hat with a minimal number of credit deadbeats. I could also safely assume that his face was as vague to the population as mine.

I pushed away from the table, grabbed the volume and replaced it on its shelf. It was noon when I arrived at my one-bedroom Pacific Beach apartment, and three p.m. in Washington, D.C. The call I was about to make was crucial and could not be blown. Social Security numbers are paramount in the modern, industrialized United States. Everything pertaining to an individual's financial status—from his employment records to his bank records to his income taxes—is classified by his Social Security number. *Everything.* You couldn't take a piss in a bank or government agency without having your little rectangular SS card.

I had rehearsed my script like an anxious stage actor preparing his lines for a play. I was afraid of giving myself away as a fraud over the phone. If I didn't get it right, they wouldn't fall for my performance. I ran through it a dozen more times, and then finally dialed the number.

I received a small shock when a live female voice picked up on the first ring. Even from her first words of "Social Security Administration, Alicia Valdez speaking," I knew I was dealing with a lowly clerk in a mountainous hierarchy.

Alicia read off her employee number and let me know that the phone call might be monitored for her protection as well as mine—whatever that meant. Hearing it gave me a little chill, but I forged ahead as planned.

"Hello, ma'am," I began carefully, having already forgotten both her first and last name, completely out of nervousness. "I have a problem. Maybe you can help me." I made my voice sound brittle and unsteady, as though I were someone ill and weak. Playing the sympathy card, of course.

"Well, maybe I can," she said helpfully with only a slight trace of a Hispanic accent. "What exactly is it you need, sir?"

Now was the moment for my pitch. "You see, I haven't worked in a long time. I've been in and out of hospitals for the past five years…"

"I'm sorry to hear that," she said with seemingly genuine pity, which further pumped me up.

"Thank you," I said, almost believing that I merited her pity. "But now my doctor says I can finally go back to work," I went on. "I'm so happy. I can't wait to be able to get out of this dank apartment every day. Of course I have to take it easy at first, only part-time, but within a few months I should be ready to resume a normal workload."

"That's wonderful," she said, falling right in. She even asked what line of work I was in, to which I responded general factory work. No use telling her that the person I was planning on impersonating was a real estate magnate worth millions. Doubtful she had a *Marquis Who's Who* lying on her desk.

"What exactly is your problem, sir?"

"It's a little bit embarrassing," I said with premeditated hesitation, now into the crux of my script. "Sometimes I'm forgetful. I constantly misplace things, and now I lost my Social Security card. Without it, my new boss says he can't put me to work."

"No problem, sir. We can help you get a replacement card. Can you give me your Social Security number, please?"

Now the big hump. Make it or break it. If I could pull the reverse and get her to give me that vital piece of information, I would be able to move on to the next step in becoming Mr. Herbert Trumm. If not, my next trip to the library would be in search of a book treating clinical depression.

"I'm afraid not, ma'am," I said, letting my voice break up even more, trying to extract as much sympathy as possible through the receiver. My mentor Bones had taught me well. Getting innocent people on our side had been an integral part of many scams we'd done together in the past. "You see, because of my sickness I don't remember numbers too good anymore." Hopefully she might take me for someone in the early stages of Alzheimer's.

I detected a slight hesitation on her end, as if she knew she would be obliged to do something she didn't want to or wasn't supposed to, i.e., giving out a Social Security number over the phone. At length she said, "Let's see if we can find that for you, sir. What was your full name at birth?"

A wave of relief doused me. "Herbert Alan Trumm," I said clearly and in a slightly stronger voice so she'd get it on the first shot. The last thing I wanted was to create confusion and have to repeat myself. I spelled out T-R-U-M-M.

"And your birth date, Mr. Trumm?"

"January 3, 1944."

"Place of birth?"

"Baltimore, Maryland."

"Do you know your mother's maiden name, Mr. Trumm? I will need that information in order to give you your Social Security number."

Now I loved it. I felt like a batter getting that perfect pitch right down the pipe and swatting it. That invaluable piece of information used by the banking and credit world for verification of identity. If you lost your checkbook or credit card and sat across a banker's desk wanting to replace it, he would demand your mother's maiden name, which you had filled in on your original application. The ensuing comparison was solely to verify that you were who you said you were. No one falsely claiming to be you could know your mother's maiden name—so the banks and credit card companies thought. That was the whole basis of my scam.

"Yes, ma'am, that I *do* remember. She's dead now (more sympathy-pulling), but her maiden name was Mary Harriet Fisher. It always stuck in my head." I spelled out Fisher and pictured her pecking away at her keyboard. Just a few moments passed before she said, "Mr. Trumm, do you have a pencil and paper handy? I'm going to read you your Social Security number."

"Yes, ma'am, I do," I said courteously.

"Very well. It's one-two-eight-four-four-six-seven-three-seven."

"Bingo!" raced through my mind.

"Did you get that, sir? Do you want to read it back to me?"

"Sure thing," I said, and caught myself being a little too upbeat. I quickly toned it down and recited those magic numbers. She confirmed them and then had some advice for me, which she couldn't have known I already knew.

"Mr. Trumm, what you'll need to do is take your original birth certificate, or a certified copy, to the SSA office in Baltimore. The administrator there will issue you a temporary replacement card. The permanent one will arrive at your home address within four to six weeks."

"Thank you so much, ma'am," I said, re-weakening the voice for the final knockout sympathy punch. "Now, thanks to you, I'll be able to go back to work and put some food on the table."

"It's been a pleasure serving you, sir."

I hung up and breathed another sigh of relief. I realized I'd been sweating profusely during that conversation. Rivulets had broken out across my forehead. My underarms were soaked. I got up and washed myself in the bathroom, splashed some cold water on my face. In the kitchen, I poured a glass of juice and sat at the table.

I didn't have a copy of Trumm's birth certificate, but obtaining it was even easier than the phone call to the SSA. I didn't have to pass muster with live people. I simply telephoned directory assistance for Baltimore, Maryland, and got the number for the Baltimore Vital Statistics Bureau. I dialed it right up and asked the clerk on the other end what was required to obtain a certified copy of a birth certificate by mail. She told me I'd need to furnish in legible print my full name at birth, my father's full name and mother's maiden name, along with my birth date. Then a check or money order for $5 would complete the request and begin the process. She said I'd have the certificate within three to six weeks.

My first major decision for the scam was to never use my real address or phone number for *anything*. I went down to a local Mailboxes USA outlet and rented a small box. I gave the clerk my authentic California driver's license, but filled out the rental form with my last name misspelled. He didn't check the spelling nor did he note the driver's license number, so in effect the box rental was not traceable to me.

I instructed him to put Trumm's name on the box as an authorized receiver of mail. No ID for Trumm was necessary since he was not the renter of the box. I already knew that the SSA did not balk at sending Social

Security cards to postal boxes, but later on would learn that banks did not send credit cards to them for security reasons. That standard refusal would later lead to a host of rental homes befitting any *real* real estate developer.

As I'd both hoped and sensed, the birth certificate for Trumm arrived at the Mailboxes USA just ten days after I'd sent out the request. It was a certified copy on light green parchment with the official seal of the city of Baltimore neatly creased into its surface. The information on it matched exactly what I'd read in the *Who's Who*.

Bones would carry out the next step. He would go down to the San Diego—not Baltimore—SSA office posing as Herbert Trumm. He was four years older than Trumm, but no governmental clerk would take notice or care.

It was time to let Bones in on it. I called and told him to hightail his ass over to my apartment. When he arrived, I wasted no time laying out the scam.

Bones was ecstatic. "You're a fucking little genius!" he said with his sharp blue eyes alight in immediate praise and comprehension. "We could get rich off that."

We discussed in great detail how we would set up the operation, get hold of credit reports on prominent people and then use that knowledge to obtain additional credit in their names. But that was further off in the distance. For the moment, we needed only to work on the ID phase of the scam. The tiniest fuckup there could put us right out of business and into prison, before we ever saw a penny's profit from our labors.

We drove downtown to the San Diego SSA office in my beat up MG Midget that barely qualified as a sports car. I accompanied Bones inside the building, a modern three-story red-brick job with uniform windows running along its façade, not far from San Diego's public library and main post office. He tore his number from the little dispenser at the front of the large room. Ironically, and I hoped not fatefully, the little ticket said thirteen. I surely didn't want to believe that this random number assignment was an omen of things to come.

We sat in little school-like chairs, the kind with oval holes in the rear, and waited. There were two dozen people scattered in front of us. The red digital display on the wall behind the clerks said they were currently at number three.

Forty minutes later, the digital flicked to thirteen. Bones got up wordlessly and proceeded to the counter. I watched him a little nervously, albeit less than I had felt when telephoning the SSA office. As that phone call had gone smoothly, just like the receipt of the birth certificate, there was no reason to believe this step to obtain the actual Social Security card would not go as Ms. Valdez had told me over the telephone. After all, Bones was now equipped with Herbert Trumm's birth certificate and Social Security number, and he knew Trumm's mother's maiden name.

Bones was a master at his craft, a longtime grifter with rocklike credibility. I watched the back of his head and could tell by its jerking that he was smiling and laughing. I could also hear him chatting with the clerk. He had a very distinct yet pleasant and ingratiating voice. He was the consummate con man, and I knew that when the time came for him to walk into whatever situation as Herbert Trumm, he'd be up to the challenge.

His smile focused on me as he approached. "Let's go, my son," he said. He often referred to me that way, even though he was only sixteen years my senior.

"How'd it go?" I asked as soon as the elevator doors enclosed us alone for the trip down to the lobby.

"Without a hitch," he said. "We'll have the 'hard' Social Security card in four to six weeks."

"Maybe sooner," I said encouragingly.

It actually came to the Mailboxes USA in three weeks. As soon as it did, I gave it to Bones. Now he had a birth certificate and Social Security card in Trumm's name, two forms of unquestionable identification. With that he could go right down to the state's Motor Vehicles Office and get a driver's license in the stolen name with his own photograph on it.

I drove Bones to the California Division of Motor Vehicles office in La Mesa. It was a little out of the way and expected not to be crowded; neither of us liked waiting. This would be the first major test of our fraud concerning the state of California. Up until now we had only been fucking with the federal government. It would also be the first key step in *physically* becoming someone else, having your photo on your driver's license in the other person's name. Then once you had that, you could build up your portfolio of false identity documents to gradually solidify your existence as this person.

We knew from our own driver's licenses that California demanded the thumbprint on the application of everyone applying for the legal right to drive on its roads. This did not impede us. The procedure was only for file purposes. The thumbprint would be researched and compared with others only in a criminal investigation. The truth of the matter was that if fifty identical thumbprints were on fifty different applications submitted by fifty people with no physical likeness, the California DMV would never know it. Same held true for one person holding fifty different licenses with the identical thumbprint on each of his fifty applications. That, however, we'd learn later. And when we did, it was to our great and pleasant surprise.

Bones filled out the application for Herbert Trumm with an absolute precision matching his own appearance. For height he put down six feet, for weight 190. His hair was brown but graying, his eyes blue. Though the application didn't ask for it, his nose was long and sharp, his jaw cut solid and well-defined. Overall he was handsome, which didn't hurt when he was putting a super hype on an assortment of unsuspecting people. A good con artist always maximized his appearance, for he knew the importance of the first impression he made on his victims.

The Latina clerk punched in the application, with its physical description of Bones, into her computer. The application declared that Trumm had never before held a driver's license from any other state. While she was entering this info, Bones was chitchatting away about how his entire life he'd been an East Coast city-dweller and had now finally made the big move out west and needed to learn to drive. "It's about time!" he exclaimed. It was all a crock of shit designed to make the clerk buy the story about his never having had a license.

The charade wasn't necessary. The clerk asked no further questions. I, however, did ask Bones one: Couldn't the DMV find out through its computers that Trumm *did* previously hold a license? Bones reassured me that cross-reference checks within the states did not take place, unless it was part of a specific inquiry put forth by the DMV's Investigations Division.

Flipping through the DMV handbook, Bones brushed up his knowledge of California's driving and parking regulations. He scored forty-five out of the fifty multiple-choice questions on the written exam, a pass. Soon he'd be scoring perfect fifties all over the country. He would also set the record for most DMV tests taken, one that would never be broken.

Bones passed the road test with flying colors. The instructor gave him the paperwork, which he took back inside the building to complete his application and receive his license. There were no waiting periods as with Social Security cards and birth certificates. No temporary issues. The DMV took your thumbprint and photograph, and then issued your laminated driver's license. Bones placed his new one, inscribed with the name Herbert

Trumm and the address of my Mailboxes USA, snugly in his wallet.

The final step in the identity theft makeover was obtaining a valid United States passport in the victim's name. Who could ever question your identity when you had a perfect American passport to go along with a perfect driver's license from one of the fifty states?

The next morning, we drove up to the US Passport Office in Los Angeles. The clerks there were of the same semi-competent variety we'd found at the DMV, much to our liking. Once again Bones filled out the application for Trumm. Since Trumm was in reality a successful entrepreneur, it was safe to assume he'd already been issued a passport long before Bones showed up asking for a new one in the same name. To get around this potentially dangerous obstacle, Bones simply said he'd lost his current passport and was planning a trip to Europe. He was asked a few routine questions, and gave answers that satisfied the clerk. People lost or had their passports stolen regularly, especially when traveling abroad. Seldom did Passport Control become suspicious. Apparently the State Department was not too concerned about people securing federal documents under false pretenses and had not, as of that time, issued directives to passport offices to run checks on people's lost passport claims. Remember, this was 1990, a decade before the national hysteria over terrorism had gripped the nation. This type of finagling to obtain passports would have never worked post-9/11.

Bones was told to return at the end of the afternoon to pick up his passport. We went for lunch, took in the film *Dances With Wolves*, then returned to the passport office. Without incident, Bones was promptly given his freshly made navy blue American passport giving him the right to travel internationally as Herbert Trumm.

Before returning to San Diego, we took a ride out to Santa Monica Pier. We got there as the sun was fading. Watching it from the strand, we discussed the future.

"We're gonna get right on this," Bones said, squirting mustard on the hot dog he'd just bought at a refreshment stand. "I have a feeling the potential is endless. It's the perfect last hurrah for an old grifter like me."

I couldn't disagree. It wasn't a bad "hurrah" for a relatively young grifter either. I was tired of my small-time hustling. Since the Navajo rug scam I hadn't copped any scores to get out from under. My checking account was overdrawn. My MG badly needed a paint job. I'd even begun experiencing thoughts of going on the straight and narrow in search of a real job.

Of course that changed the day I walked into the USD library.

Bones downed the last mouthful of the hot dog. "Starting tomorrow you and I are going to be very busy. We're opening up our first real business together."

That sounded strange. "What about the Navajo rugs?" I asked. "Wasn't that a business?"

"No," Bones informed me. "It was an *operation*. What we're getting into now is really going to be a business, and I think a big one."

"What do you want to call it?" I asked kiddingly.

Bones set his gaze toward the vastness of the blue Pacific. For a moment he looked like an eighteenth-century artist deep in thought, perhaps waiting for the seascape to give him the inspiration that would name our business. I observed him for several seconds. Finally he turned to me and said with a crooked smile, "Identity Theft, Incorporated."

I burst out laughing. I immediately liked it, and why not? After all, there had already been a Murder, Incorporated. So then why not an Identity Theft, Incorporated? It had a great ring to it.

"Do you think we should check at the city clerk's office if another corporation is already using that name?" I asked laughingly.

Bones laughed, too. "Imagine seeing it on the *Fortune* 500 list of corporations," he said.

Little did I know at that moment, but soon our little identity theft business would be expanding at a mind-boggling rate, almost like a real *Fortune* 500 company. And if we never got busted, it might just become one.

Setting it up

San Diego, California, 1990

NOW THAT WE HAD SUCCESSFULLY MARRIED HERBERT ALAN Trumm's identity to Bones' physical appearance, it was time to make their fraudulent union pay dividends. Like Bones had said, we were launching a new "business."

But we had overlooked the most elementary of components: how to do it. How should we go about obtaining credit in Trumm's name? We couldn't just walk into a bank, pick up a Visa application and fill it out arbitrarily in the hope of getting it approved for a credit card. True, we had already envisioned plans of establishing the "paper" Trumm as a California resident, but how could we gain knowledge as to his existing credit portfolio? We would need that information to fill out applications. We had to know which credit cards he already had. We had to know of any car loans he may have taken. What about mortgages? We couldn't assume he didn't have one. We couldn't assume anything.

Bones and I were sitting in my apartment smoking a joint. Despite his being sixteen years my senior, Bones liked his pot even more than I did. He took a hit and passed it along. "I can't believe we didn't think of that," he said.

"It would be pretty stupid having Trumm apply for an American

Express card if he's already got one," I noted with a roll of my eyes.

"Right," Bones said, "but we wouldn't have to worry about that with Visas and MasterCards."

I exhaled my hit and gave him a puzzled look. "How's that?"

"Visa and MasterCard don't operate like American Express and Discover," he said. "In fact, Visa and MasterCard are not even credit card companies. They're just instruments of credit used by the banks." Bones went on to explain how American Express and Discover were actual credit card companies. People seeking their credit cards applied directly to them, not to a bank. Once an applicant was approved and a card issued, all transactions pertaining to it were managed internally by the company. Banks were involved no further than supplying the fiduciary instrument to pay the bills.

Visa and MasterCard, however, were bank credit instruments or simply bank credit cards. When you applied for either, you were applying directly to whichever bank furnished the application. The bank's credit department decided whether or not to issue the card. When a card was issued, the bank supervised and regulated its activity through a gigantic "credit card clearinghouse" comprised of a nationwide network of lending institutions, whereby Visa and MasterCard were the association.

The crucial point Bones made in clarifying the difference was that cardholders were able to obtain as many individual Visas or MasterCards as they fancied. Each particular bank extended or denied the credit. A person in good standing could have a Visa from Wells Fargo, another from Bank of America and a third from Citibank. He could also hold three or more MasterCards. But such was not the case with American Express cards. Since American Express was a credit card company and not a bank or lending institution, its cardholders could only maintain a single personal account.

Bones's explanation may have enlightened me to the internal workings of America's credit card system, but our problem of how to falsely obtain the first card remained unsolved. The one thing we did come to realize was that we needed direct access to TRW (now Experian), the giant credit-reporting agency. I was all too aware of its existence. Many times when notified that my rental application for an apartment had been denied, the leasing agent would mention something about my "TRW" not being up to par. Not having a job would of course come next.

Recalling those occasions, I said to Bones, "What we need is to get a job where employees have access to TRW. Someplace like a residential apartment complex or a real estate office."

Bones chuckled. I wasn't sure what he found funny, the prospect of my being a real estate agent or just my getting a job. "You haven't had gainful employment since the Hopi Lodge in Taos."

"You have to admit that that job was rather gainful."

We shared a laugh, then got back to thinking how we could solve the problem. If I lacked the résumé necessary for respectable employment, Bones lacked one for *any* employment. He *never* had a job. And he wasn't about to enter the job market as a middle-aged trainee.

At that dead-end, our conversation turned to how we could recruit someone to supply us with TRW information. But that was another roadblock. What honest working person would be susceptible to giving or selling TRW credit histories?

"What about Robin?" Bones suddenly asked.

"She's doing fine. She's still got the two rugs from Taos in her La Jolla apartment."

"Two rugs?" Bones had remembered that she and I had brought back one each from the land of enchantment. I told him how certain financial difficulties had forced me to sell her mine. Then I gave him the news that Robin and I had been on the outs, and that she'd been dating some sugar daddy up in La Jolla from whom she managed to siphon off enough cash to make a down payment on a small condo.

"The guy finally dumped her," I said.

"What's she doing now?"

"Last time we spoke she was working as a receptionist in some criminal lawyer's office."

Bones laughed and said that next time we needed a good one, Robin might be able to recommend somebody. Then he said seriously, "Unfortunately, lawyers don't usually have TRW access."

My mind was racing ahead of his. "Maybe she can find a new employer who does."

Bones looked at me askance. "You just said you two are on the outs. Is she really about to risk what she's got going to help you out?"

"No. But she'd do it if we cut her in." One thing I knew about my lovely ex, Robin, was that she'd do just about anything for the right price.

As far as I knew, Robin had never been connected to the Navajo rug scam. When we got back from Taos, she spent most of her time getting tan and blowing her money on designer clothes and jewelry. She went through her money as fast as I had. Then just as she went broke, she dumped me for the rich dude in La Jolla, who hooked her up with the law office job. Had there been heat on her from the Ellis Travers Museum, the law office would have gotten wind of it and canned her on the spot.

Now that her sugar daddy had tired of Robin's conning him out of cash, she might be amenable to participating in our scheme. I hadn't spoken to her in weeks, but now I couldn't dial her number fast enough. She wasn't home; I left a message. The next day, the three of us lunched at her condo.

"Nice kitchen," I said, admiring its peachy airiness and the row of high-quality cooking utensils pegged to the wall above the counter. "Looks like it must've cost a fortune."

"It did," she said. "It all went on my ex's credit card." She said this with a pained smile indicating her own credit card did not wield the buying power her ex's did.

We were eating pizza delivered by Domino's on Robin's shiny Tupperware plates. Not that she was averse to cooking us a meal with all those imposing pots and pans. It was just that she was in one of her lazy funks and hadn't been food shopping in a while.

"Just what we wanted to talk to you about," Bones said, lifting a slice from the pizza box.

Robin immediately looked at me with aroused curiosity.

"We need you to get a job somewhere that has TRW access."

"Like to get copies of people's credit reports?" Didn't take Robin long to catch on.

At first, Bones and I had wanted to treat Robin's involvement in our ID theft scam on a need-to-know basis. But we quickly wised up in the realization that she would immediately guess what we were up to. After all, she did play an integral role in the Taos scam. How long would it take her to figure out we were setting up credit in other people's names?

"What's in it for me?" she asked. Her tone was all business.

"Why don't we discuss that later," Bones suggested. "First we need to see if you can get a job with a link to TRW."

Robin nodded in deference to Bones. She didn't really like him but respected his experience in dishonest endeavors. "I guess the best would be to land a job in a real estate rental office."

"Exactly what I was thinking," I said.

Bones threw in a joke about how she'd be able to turn her head on my credit report and rent me an apartment.

"How are you gonna set this all up?" Robin asked.

"We don't know yet," I answered. "But without TRW access we can't do it."

Robin agreed to search the Help Wanted section of the *San Diego Union-Tribune*. Two weeks later she landed a new job, not working in a real estate office but rather for an automobile-leasing firm. This was just as good. Her firm had TRW access and thus a link to credit histories for every individual in the United States. Our idea was that she'd be able to feign prospective clients coming in to lease an automobile and run their credit reports. Naturally none of these people would be leasing cars.

The first of these phony prospective clients was, of course, Herbert Trumm. But Robin had to be extremely careful at the leasing company. Employers with TRW merchant memberships were ethically strict in matters concerning misuse by employees. They did not tolerate workers abusing the system to obtain sensitive information on people's financial histories. A common, if not harmful, abuse was when employees with access to TRW reports obtained them for personal reasons, perhaps to check out their own credit report or give a friend his or hers, saving them the time and money needed to mail a request to TRW's service center for the same report.

Oftentimes the abuse was malevolent. Unscrupulous agents sold reports to shady telemarketers willing to pay for credit information on individuals they might subsequently dupe by telephone. Knowing their accounts, they could estimate their spending habits and even what types of goods and services appealed to them.

And sometimes, albeit less often, unauthorized transmission of TRW reports was in furtherance of a major criminal conspiracy.

Robin informed us that a completed application was required in order for her to request a TRW credit report. Following my instructions, she brought an application to my apartment one night after work. It wasn't much different from a car-rental contract, except that personal income figures had to be provided. We filled it out in Trumm's name. The next day, Robin used the pretext that Trumm had come into her office when everybody else was out to lunch, inquiring about leasing an automobile. She quickly phoned in her request for Trumm's credit report mixed in with ones for a handful of legitimate clients. TRW promptly faxed her the reports. She made a copy of Trumm's and stuck it in her handbag.

That night, we marveled at the three pages of unblemished credit. I'd expected it, and Trumm did not disappoint. There were half a dozen credit card accounts: three Visas, two MasterCards, one American Express and another dozen major department store accounts. There were also first and second home mortgages, automobile loans, a boat loan and other satisfied loans whose origins we could not determine. Also in the report was a listing of banks with which Trumm had various financial accounts, though no balances or other particulars were furnished.

We didn't need any. All we had to know was that every rating in the report was AAA. Trumm was cream of the crop as far as his credit history was concerned.

The next morning, Bones and I drove through downtown San Diego. We stopped at the major banks and picked up applications for Visa and MasterCard.

Back at my apartment, we went to work on the applications. Bones, a stickler for neatness and perfection to the tiniest detail, meticulously typed the information onto each one. We decided there was no risk in applying for second, third and even fourth Visa and MasterCard accounts.

Credit card applications were more detailed in 1990 than today's quick online forms. The information required included your full name, date of birth, current address, current employer, salary, and home and business phone numbers. In addition, you had to furnish bank accounts and all your existing credit accounts as precisely as possible. They wanted to know about all your major credit cards, your department store charge cards and even your oil company cards. They wanted account names and account numbers for each and every creditor. In some instances, especially when applying for a gold card, they demanded detailed personal financial statements or copies of tax returns for a period dating back three years. Sometimes they insisted on both.

You also had to list previous addresses. Creditors wanted to know where you'd been living for at least a decade before applying to them. In all, it was a pretty thorough process.

Bones was in the middle of typing that first Visa application when he suddenly stopped. I was sitting on the sofa munching on potato chips.

"To what address are we going to have the credit cards sent?" he asked.

Of course we couldn't have them sent to either of our addresses. In case of discovery of the fraud, our asses would in turn quickly be discovered and then shipped off to prison. As well, we knew banks did not send credit cards to post office boxes, one of their strictest policies for safeguarding against fraud. Therefore, the only solution quickly popped into my head.

"I guess we're gonna have to rent an apartment or house under Trumm's name, just for an address to receive the cards."

Bones nodded his agreement. We would have to find Trumm a real residence with telephone service before sending out the applications. It would be costly, but it was the only way to receive the credit cards.

But for now, we had to concern ourselves with the bulk of information required by the banks. First and foremost was employment. We had duly anticipated this and our solution was to keep Trumm self-employed, giving the impression that the developer from Baltimore had relocated to California for the purpose of moving his operations to the West Coast. Among people with vast reserves of both cash and credit, this was an extremely common practice. For salary, we determined that $300,000 a year was a reasonable figure. We'd discussed higher earnings but didn't want to come off too lofty without first knowing more about the process. The real Trumm was probably a million-dollar-plus earner, but if we put that kind of income on the application, we might inspire unwanted interest in the applicant. Who knew?

In addition to finding Trumm his new residence, we would have to find the location for his business operations. For this, however, we would not need an actual physical address. Just the appearance of one would suffice. The key was to install a telephone number that banks' credit departments could call to verify the legitimacy of Trumm's business operations. This phone number had to be manned, but it also had to be independent of Trumm's residential address. Even though Trumm was to be self-employed, we didn't want to have him working out of his home. We felt that multiple phone numbers and addresses connected to Mr. Trumm lent more credibility to an important businessman.

To man that business telephone we would hire an answering service. A simple answering machine might lead one to believe that Trumm's operation was either small or unprofessional, neither of which was conducive to seducing creditors. The answering service personnel would be trained to properly answer the phones and to give the important verifications banks sought.

The section of the applications for listing Trumm's existing credit accounts posed no problem. We simply transposed the account names and numbers from his credit report. Those loans whose type we weren't sure of we included but did not classify.

From the TRW report we were able to supply Trumm's previous addresses. They would match those the bank came across when conducting their background check. The only details we had to fudge, for lack of exact knowledge, were the dates and lengths of time spent at each previous residence. But this was of lesser importance. Banks were not overly concerned about how long you lived where. However, it was imperative that we got the previous addresses right. A major alarm flag would pop up if an address on an application conflicted with that in a prospective creditor's database.

A more challenging aspect of the applications was the part pertaining to marital status. The problem we faced was that we had no pertinent knowledge on Trumm's wife. The information required for the spouse was nearly identical to that for the primary applicant, mainly date of birth, Social Security number and employment history. We did not have this information, nor could we get it. All we had on the wife was her full name, not enough to risk including her on the applications.

There were two alternatives. One was to simply omit it. If follow-up requests came from banks, we could then say that the wife had died and therefore Trumm saw no reason to include her on the application. The second option was to state he was single. As no joint accounts appeared on Trumm's TRW reports, it was a fairly safe assumption that reviewers would find no financial links to his wife. There was always the probability that information on the wife had been included on previous applications, but it was just as likely that banks considering the issuance of new credit to Mr. Trumm would never garner those applications. They would only be concerned with the data on his TRW reports.

We decided Trumm would apply as a single man. If banks found conflicting evidence, we could again say that the wife had passed away. The logic behind it was that a widower is the same as a bachelor. It would be unlikely that a credit issuer would delve into the actual death of a primary applicant's spouse. Another factor enhancing the charade was that single people, however they may have come to be that way, generally established credit on their own bankability and individual merit. As primary applicants, they did not need or want anyone else's creditworthiness attached to their applications.

A major decision with which we grappled was how much credit we should ask for. Trumm's TRW report did not give limits for his accounts. Neither did it contain any information about his annual income, which would have helped guide us in making this decision. The only way to ascertain his earning power was to obtain a copy of his tax returns, but at the time we didn't dare attempt that.

Again we had to be especially careful. Asking for too much credit might trigger alarms, partly because Trumm already had two Visa accounts. Asking for too little might also appear suspicious. After many hours of discussion, we finally opted to leave it blank. Let the banks make the decision for us. We figured they would extend credit either along the same lines of his existing accounts or greater. Later on, we would be delighted by the banks' generosity and willingness for risk-taking associated with Mr. Herbert Trumm's new credit accounts.

Everything that could be filled out on the applications thus far seemed in order. Now it was time to establish Trumm's residential and business addresses and phone numbers. Since Bones currently possessed all the ID documents needed to impersonate Trumm, we could pursue all avenues in search of locations. First we looked in the classified section of the *Union-Tribune* under "Apartments and Homes to Rent." We preferred dealing directly with owners since the scrutiny and requirements would be less in comparison to dealing with professional real estate agents.

We looked at a few apartments scattered around the city. Most were in large rental complexes run by corporate management companies. This type of "organized living" we tried to avoid. Knowing we would neither furnish nor inhabit any such apartment, we'd have to worry about potential security breaches set off by nosy neighbors or the property's management staff. Privacy, an element of supreme importance to any criminal enterprise, would be at a premium. Next-door neighbors might knock on Trumm's door to borrow milk or invite him to a tenant's barbecue. Maintenance people might have cause to enter the apartment, and then find it bare. That a tenant rarely occupied the premises was not in itself cause for suspicion, as it could always be his second residence. But upon learning that not a single piece of furniture was in the apartment, management's suspicions were sure to heighten.

We didn't need an ostentatious address, just a respectable one. Many powerful businessmen lived in middle or upper-middle-class neighborhoods. The key factors regarding the address were its location, as far as accessibility was concerned, and the security to the operation it provided. Needless to say, we wouldn't want Trumm's residence to be in a high-crime area or some place that drew unnecessary attention or surveillance from law enforcement.

Naturally we had to consider costs. Our combined bankroll at that embryonic stage of the scam was ten grand. Half came from Bones, the other half from Robin, who'd bitched and squawked but finally agreed to sell her Navajo rugs. A rental unit priced at $1,000 per month would require a minimum of $2,000 to move in, $3,000 when landlords demanded first and last month's rent to go with a $1,000 security deposit. This was a big expense to maintain an empty apartment whose only value was its mailbox.

After a week of fruitless apartment hunting, we shifted our focus toward houses and condominiums. Renting was more expensive than apartments, but worth the additional cost. Bones went to see a real estate agent named Stephanie. He made enough small talk to convince her that he was charming, financially stable enough to handle $1,200 a month in rent, and, of course, Mr. Herbert Trumm. She showed him several houses before Bones took a liking to a small two-bedroom in a middle-class neighborhood in Mission Valley. After walking through the house, Bones accompanied Stephanie back to her office. There he filled out the application, presenting his flawless California driver's license in the name of Herbert Trumm. Stephanie reviewed the application and picked up on an omission we'd hoped she'd miss.

"I'm going to need to contact your previous landlord. You didn't fill in his phone number."

Though we had discussed this eventuality, Bones was momentarily caught off guard. But he was as quick a thinker on his feet as they came. "Oh, I'm sorry," he said, "but I left his number at home." Then with a smile he added that he didn't know the landlord's number by heart because he rarely had occasion to telephone him. That explanation was meant to show signs of a good tenant, one with whom the landlord didn't need to communicate. The underlying tone was that the rent was always paid on time and there were never problems.

"It's no biggie," Stephanie said cheerfully. "However, I'll need you to phone me with his number. It's company policy to check with previous landlords and ask each prospective tenant for a local personal reference. Do you have someone here in San Diego who knows you?"

Well, Bones knew quite a few people as Bones but only two as Herbert Trumm. Thus Robin would be the personal reference and I'd be the landlord. The previous address Bones had put on the application was that of the Mailboxes USA where I'd rented the box under my misspelled name. It was highly improbable that the rental agent would check the address in addition to calling the landlord. In any case, we could not use any of our real addresses for Trumm's previous residence. If something went wrong, the feds would be able to trace the scam back to us using the agent as a starting point. Neither could we use our telephone numbers, as the scam could lead back to us the same way.

As soon as Bones returned from Stephanie's office, we picked up Robin and hurried to one of the voicemail answering services that at the time were expanding in the United States like cell phones are today. Robin and I rented phone numbers. When we got back to my apartment, Robin called her phone number, entered her code and then recorded her greeting. I followed suit with my mine.

The next morning, Bones called Stephanie at the real estate office and gave her the phone numbers for his "personal reference" and "previous landlord." An hour later, Robin and I called our voicemail numbers to check for messages. Stephanie had already left a message on both. From Robin, whose voice greeting identified her as Eileen Brenner (the name Bones wrote on Trumm's application for personal reference), she wanted to know how long she had known Mr. Trumm and if she considered him to be an upstanding person. Boy, did that make me laugh!

From Jack Taggart, the name my voice greeted callers with, she inquired if Mr. Trumm was what I would consider an "ideal tenant."

Robin returned her call first. When Stephanie came on the line asking questions, Robin answered, "I've known Mr. Trumm for twenty years. He was my neighbor in Baltimore for ten. In fact, I'm the one who suggested he move his business to San Diego."

Obviously the real estate woman was satisfied with that reference. Neither Bones nor I had expected Robin to go so far, but she raced through it in dazzling fashion.

When my turn came, I told Stephanie that Herbert Trumm was "one of the best tenants I've ever had." I added that his rent was either on time or in advance and assured her that he didn't have any dogs, not even a cat. Five minutes later, Stephanie called the voicemail number that Bones had already been maintaining in San Diego. She congratulated him for being accepted as the new tenant in the two-bedroom house occupying 413 Encino Lane, San Diego, California. She asked him to stop by later in the day to sign the lease and pick up the keys. A check for $3,600 payable to the agency would conclude the deal.

We realized we'd overlooked a major detail. In our exuberance to get the scam off the ground, we didn't think of opening a San Diego checking account in Trumm's name. We'd been too busy concerning ourselves with credit card accounts. This meant that Bones would have to pay the $3,600 to the real estate agency in cash, which might raise an eyebrow or two in the office. It was certainly uncommon for legitimate businessmen to pay rent and security deposits in cash. But we had no choice. Bones would give Stephanie the cash with an accompanying excuse for having misplaced his checkbook and credit cards, in case the agency suggested Visa or MasterCard for the payment.

It turned out to be insignificant. Stephanie told him that many clients stopped by her office and paid rent in cash. Bones then delivered a quick line of flattery, saying the probable reason for that was those clients' pretext to see her again. The fact that Stephanie was homely and overweight did not stop Bones from laying his line of shit. He was a firm believer of warming up to people whose confidence he needed to win over. He was terribly good at it.

As soon as we had the keys to the house, I called Pacific Bell and had them install a telephone line, instructing the representative to list Trumm's new address and telephone number with directory assistance. That would serve as more concrete evidence for banks that Trumm was a legitimate resident of San Diego. Sometimes unlisted numbers bred suspicion. But when a banker perused an application and was then able to dial up directory assistance and immediately have the applicant's address and phone number verified, he often smiled upon hanging up the phone. We would do everything necessary to have our "double" appear as genuine as the real Herbert Trumm in Baltimore.

With our first fictitious person living at a verifiable address, we set out to find the "location" for his business office. Since Trumm's credit applications were of a personal nature, all mail correspondence from banks would be directed to the house on Encino Lane. Therefore, we did not need an actual tangible address for Trumm's business, which we fittingly called Trumm Enterprises. All we had to do was secure yet another telephone line to receive inquiries coming from credit departments.

But for this we could not use voicemail numbers. The phones at Trumm Enterprises had to be answered by live "receptionists." The first of these receptionists turned out to be Barbara at ABC Answering Service. (Not joking, that was the name.) Bones filled out an application and showed the owner of ABC his driver's license identifying him as Herbert Trumm. Once he was assigned a telephone number, Bones instructed Barbara, ABC's chief operator, to answer incoming calls "Good day, thank you for calling Trumm Enterprises." Barbara passed the instructions to her employees. Anyone wishing to speak to Mr. Trumm would be told he was unavailable and asked if they'd like to leave a message. Anyone seeking information about the company or Mr. Trumm himself would be referred to Mr. Woodson, another fictitious person serving as the company's director of human resources. Then I would make the callback as Woodson and give whatever verifications the banks requested.

With Trumm's residence and business addresses established, we now had to set up his bank accounts. We decided to open two personal checking accounts in different banks.

There was one pronounced danger facing Bones when he entered a Bank of America branch posing as Trumm to open the first checking account. Even at the time, federal and state banks operated a highly efficient computer network that stored oceans of detailed banking data on virtually everyone in the United States who'd ever had an account. The system worked much like the FBI's National Crime Information Center. By punching in your name, bankers would have instantaneous access to every tidbit of information concerning your banking history, in addition to personal details such as your Social Security number, date and place of birth, and last known addresses. They could pry into your fiscal behavioral history as easily as credit bureaus viewed your credit files. They would know if you'd ever written a bad check, if your account had ever been overdrawn, if you'd abused any bank services such as overdraft protection and, of course, if you had ever been linked to any type of bank fraud or questionable banking activities.

This procedure was not to be taken lightly. Had Bones marched into the bank and sat across the desk from the new-accounts officer, who then came up with some bad dope on Trumm in his computer, a serious problem could arise. However unlikely that might be, there was also the chance that something else on Trumm would pop up in the system about which we'd been totally ignorant. Perhaps some minor detail that, despite seeming trivial, might spark the fuse to blow up our whole operation.

It was also vital that we never overlooked the fact that the FBI automatically involved itself in bank mishaps. Therefore, if any lowly banker had even the slightest suspicion about the man claiming to be Herbert Trumm, we would have to assume the FBI would be alerted. Although we knew the feds would eventually learn of our scam, we certainly had no intention of letting that happen before it got off the ground.

Bones's never-ending smoothness under pressure breezed him

through the procedure at Bank of America. He was required to fill out forms and present two pieces of photo identification. The Encino house's address and telephone number satisfied the requirements for personal information. Trumm's California driver's license and United States passport did the same for proof of identification. The new accounts clerk made a photocopy of each.

We stopped at a coffee shop, then Bones went into the San Diego National Bank and opened Trumm's second checking account. Again there were no complications. He was given his temporary checkbook, told the permanent one would arrive within ten business days, and of course didn't miss the opportunity to complain about the blandness of the counter checks he was issued. He let me know that the design he chose for his new checks at both banks were colorful and of the nautical variety, which he attested went great with San Diego's image.

We were finally ready to send out the applications. But in spite of having worked so diligently to arrive at that juncture, we were faced with the most important and problematic decision to date: how many applications to send out at one time. Being novices in the dual business of identity theft and credit card fraud, we had absolutely no idea as to the extent of interbank communication and how it in turn coincided with TRW's database. In other words, how many applications could be sent out simultaneously before word got out that somebody was flooding Credit Card, USA, with a torrent of counterfeit paper?

We exhausted hours on this topic. When twisting it optimistically, I would say, "Maybe we could get fifty Visas and MasterCards and use them all up before the banking networks catch on." Perhaps it took thirty days for TRW to compile all that information and enter it into its database. If that were true then any prospective creditor considering Trumm's application wouldn't know about the deluge until that time-period expired.

But that rationale collided head-on with the reality of TRW's term "excessive inquiries," used to indicate an inordinate number of computer-based inquiries being made into someone's credit history. Once a person's name was branded by excessive inquiries, TRW automatically alerted the banking network that a possible fraud was in the works. Upon receiving that warning, banks systematically denied any further credit requests in that person's name.

Before I became privy to that policy, I was still sensible enough not to believe we could carelessly toss bundles of credit applications into a mailbox and then be invited to do so even more. Bones, on the other hand, was more aggressive in his thinking. He believed that since the *Marquis* volumes gave us access to literally thousands of upstanding identities we could steal to obtain credit, we shouldn't worry so much about overloading on the very first of them.

"Not to worry," he said, administering his favorite vote of confidence. "We hit 'em hard now and concern ourselves later." He suggested applying to a dozen different banks for Visa and MasterCard.

"Are you serious?" I exclaimed. We were sitting at my kitchen table, a heap of filled-out applications lodged between our coffee cups. "That's insane! We might as well change Trumm's name on the applications to Freddie Fraud."

Bones didn't think that too funny. "What's so insane about it? Have you forgotten the Navajo rug scam? If we were able to fleece fifty museums in two states out of a half-million bucks in rugs without showing a single credit card, don't you think we could fool a dozen banks for thirty days?"

He did have a point there, but I was still reluctant to try for so much right out of the box. By nature I was more conservative than Bones. In previous scams we'd pulled together, I often took a less drastic approach while he went straight for the jugular. But this scam was by far the biggest either of us had ever envisioned. We both knew that, long before it became the biggest identity theft-credit card fraud operation in American history.

We finally settled on applying to six major financial institutions serving California among other western states. This was to be our first "wave." Then after evaluating the banks' reactions to these credit requests, we would determine how many more cards should be applied for in Trumm's name. That second wave would include department store charge cards, which we considered second-tier credit instruments and figured would be easier to obtain. If the overall results turned out negative, we would trash Trumm altogether and get on with the next case of stolen identity. Having to do so would be a bitter disappointment and a waste of three months' hard work, but also a learning experience.

On a rare stormy night in San Diego, two weeks after we'd begun filling out the applications, Bones and I left my apartment on foot and headed to the mailbox down the street. We carried no umbrella, though Bones had the applications safely sealed in a plastic bag. At the box, he flipped open the slot but did not immediately drop the bundle through. Instead he looked at me while holding the slot with one hand, the applications in the other. Then he looked up at the pouring rain and said in a grand voice, "Kid, you're a genius! Let this be the beginning of a most profitable venture." With that he kissed the bundle of credit card applications and let them drop.

What neither of us knew at that moment was that we had embarked on a trail leading to a multifaceted, multimillion-dollar business enviable to anyone anywhere who ever dreamed of using a credit card for any illegal or corrupt purpose.

It's raining credit cards!
San Diego, California, 1990-1991

THAT COMPLIMENT BONES BESTOWED UPON ME MADE ME FEEL good. In fact, I was really beginning to wonder if I was not some kind of criminal genius. When I'd thought up the Navajo rug scam, I crossed over a demarcation line making me a real criminal, although still not an exceptional one. But with the inception of the world's first major identity theft scam, perhaps the term "mastermind" was justifiably applicable to me. I really hadn't believed I was so deviously smart, but considering Bones's evaluation of my abilities I had to take that possibility to heart.

We got back to my apartment sopping wet but were totally oblivious to it. In lieu of drying off, we uncorked a bottle of champagne and toasted the incipient operation. We were in such good spirits that I called Robin and invited her to join us. She was half asleep and reminded me that she had to go to work in the morning, but before hanging up let me know that she was expecting her fair share of "the cash you guys make."

Bones and I ended up getting pretty sauced, downing champagne and recounting old war stories. He finally passed out on the sofa. The next morning we had a breakfast fit for kings: croissants, assorted Danish pastries and fresh juices I whipped up in the juicer. Then we left together in my MG and ran a few errands for Trumm's house on Encino Lane.

We had two sets of keys made, one for me, the other to be hidden on the property. We bought a few lamps and time clocks. We'd decided that the house should emit some light at night to give the appearance someone was home. We also bought a clock radio. While one of us was there waiting for the mail, he should have the luxury of listening to the radio and knowing what time it was. One good thing about the house was its mail slot built into the front door. Nobody from the outside would see unsightly accumulations of mail, and we wouldn't be subscribing to home-delivery newspapers.

We stopped off at San Diego Gas and Electric. Bones filled out an application for service, showed his ID as Trumm, and paid a hundred dollar security deposit. Then we picked up some blinds and shades for the windows, a few more odds and ends, and called it a day.

Now there was nothing to do but wait. We estimated it would take approximately two weeks until we began hearing from the banks. For me, the interval was interminable. Every day seemed like a century. After the first week, I couldn't take it anymore. I started going over to Trumm's house at eleven o'clock in the morning to wait out the postman's arrival. I made good use of the clock radio and even convinced Bones to splurge for a small television I could watch while sitting on the floor.

The second day of my vigil, Bones showed up with a telephone and answering machine he plugged into the jack. "Looks like you're waiting for Godot," he cracked.

"I know he's coming."

"We should call the answering service on a steady basis," Bones said. "Not only to check up that they're answering the phones correctly, but also to give them some calls so they don't get the idea they're working for a business that never does any business."

"Why bother?" I asked. "We can just tell them that we use their service only when no one's in the office, at which time we call-forward our calls to them."

"No, that's not good enough," Bones argued. "It's better to give them some action. Believe me, the less you have these people thinking, the better off you are."

I didn't argue.

Bones smiled and dialed up ABC. When Barbara answered with the correct greeting, Bones assumed a comical Hindu accent and asked to speak with Mr. Trumm. When he was told he wasn't in the office, he asked when Trumm would be back. Barbara said she didn't know but would be glad to take a message. Bones didn't leave one. When he hung up, he nodded his approval at Barbara's performance. An hour later he called again, this time using an American voice with a southern drawl. The guy was quite talented. I would soon get to see just how talented he really was.

Before leaving, Bones began referring to Trumm's residence as the "scam house." It was contagious. After all, it made sense to call a house used to perpetrate scams a scam house. Naturally we would come to call all our illicit dwellings scam houses. Like the FBI and CIA have their "safe houses," we criminals have our scam houses. Whereas a safe house is used by government agencies to hide and protect certain key people, usually important witnesses and foreign turncoats, a scam house is used to hide and protect scams from those same government agencies.

The premise of a safe scam house is that of its ability to blend unobtrusively into its surroundings. The choice location of a scam house is commensurate to the type of scams operating inside its walls. For instance, a crack house more often than not would be found hidden among a row of similar dwellings in a low-income urban area. A house dealing in the receiving and selling of stolen merchandise would be secreted away somewhere that facilitated pickup and delivery.

Our scam houses needed to be in affluent neighborhoods or have addresses that sounded affluent, as was the case with Encino Lane. We certainly wouldn't want to apply for a gold credit card and have El Segundo Boulevard as the address. Not only would a card never show up in the mail, but a letter of general sympathy might arrive in its place.

Each day I spied the postman's mail truck as it stopped on Encino Lane. On the third day he came up the walk leading to the mail slot in the front door. I got all excited and waited anxiously on the other side. I listened to the metal crank when the postman opened it and dropped the mail through. My heart raced but then sunk when I saw it was nothing but junk mail. The next day he showed up again on the front porch, but this time it was just a confirmation notice from the electric company telling us the power was on, and some more junk mail.

Two days later, seeing white envelopes in his hand that I sensed were the coveted goods, I swung open the door with a blush of excitement that made me look truly stupid, and was perhaps even a faux pax. There was no reason to let the postman have a look at me.

 He handed me the mail and quipped, "Must be your answer from military school."

I forced a laugh and took the mail. I slipped right back into the house with the envelopes. There were four. The first was again from San Diego Gas and Electric, a leaflet advertising their different services. The second was a notice from Pacific Bell confirming the telephone service.

The third was from Union Bank.

The fourth was from First Interstate Bank.

Like an eager child I edged my forefinger and thumb around the Union Bank envelope, feeling for the plastic credit card that had to be there. Not encountering it, I didn't become immediately discouraged. I convinced myself that the card was securely fastened to the stiff folded paper inside. I didn't feel it because the card's issuer wanted to protect against potential thievery by making the contents of the envelope undetectable.

But then I noticed the words "Do Not Forward" were nowhere on the envelope. I thought Bones had once mentioned that when credit cards were sent through the mail, their envelopes were always marked with that directive for obvious security reasons.

I still held out that the card was inside. How could it not be? I began frantically squeezing random spots on the envelope, expecting my pinch to reveal the card within. But there seemed to be nothing. Only the feel of paper. I became anxious and finally ripped open the envelope.

Nothing but a letter. It read:

Dear Mr. Trumm:
Thank you for your recent application for a Union Bank Visa card.
However, at this time, we are unable to issue one to you.

It hit like a thunderbolt. Suddenly I felt unsteady, as though I might pass out. It was like receiving a bad medical diagnosis. I could only be saved by the next envelope.

But that did not have the words "Do Not Forward" on it, either. I tore it open right down the middle. Then I split each half. The First Interstate Bank card had to be there.

The letter that had been inside was now a crumpled, torn mess. But I didn't have to put it back together to read its contents: another denial.

Another fucking denial!

What was going on? How was this possible? I couldn't believe it. Couldn't accept it. Going two for two on the downside was not possible. Bones had said we'd be good for at least 50 percent on the first drop. That would be three credit cards. He'd said the second drop would yield a rate of return half as successful, 25 percent. But with this terrible start, I swallowed the possibility there might not be a second drop.

A million thoughts streaked through my head, but the dominant one was that the whole scam was a misfire and there'd never be any credit cards.

But why? We had set up everything immaculately. Down to the tiniest detail we had checked and double-checked. We'd established residence, business address, phone numbers for each, personal references, previous address, bank accounts and a comprehensive credit history for Herbert Trumm.

My brain jangled with possible reasons for this failure. I sorted them out the best I could. Nothing could have gone errant with the scam house on Encino Lane or the business using the answering service's address and phone number. It was inconceivable that both denying banks had checked out Trumm's and Trumm Enterprises' addresses and discovered they were façades. Impossible. Therefore, the problem had to have a connection to the financial information we'd put on the applications. Either the new bank accounts caused the problem or there was something amiss with the information we listed for Trumm's current credit accounts. Perhaps the denials were linked to the few omissions we'd made due to the lack of certain details on the TRW report.

Finally I called Bones and gave him the bad news. That I'd been expecting him to react with shock and disbelief turned into the second major surprise of the day.

"You're overreacting, kid."

I certainly overreacted my response to that.

"Relax, it's just two denials."

"But it's the *first* two denials. Without having received any cards."

"Doesn't matter."

"Of course it matters!" I was getting angry with him. How could he make that statement when two denials arrived having nothing to do with "excessive inquiries?"

Bones remained calm. "Listen, kid, you're jumping to conclusions. The fact that two banks denied us does not mean the other four will do the same. In fact, I guarantee you at least two of the remaining four will come through with the cards."

Bones turned out to be wrong. We did not receive two cards out of the remaining four banks; we received all four! Naturally I was in seventh heaven, though Bones took it as though he'd expected the windfall.

It was he who'd gone to the scam house to find the first envelope containing a credit card lying on the foyer's floor. He telephoned that night on the pretext that he needed me to help him hang some blinds and shades on the rear windows. I had stopped waiting for the postman because I'd begun losing faith in the scam.

When I entered the house through the back door, as had become customary to avoid curious glances from nosy neighbors, Bones was sitting on a sofa watching TV. There was also a glass coffee table fronting it.

"A little surprise," he said, indicating the furniture.

"What for?" I asked. "I don't get the feeling we're gonna be here that long."

"Here's another surprise for you," Bones said, and suddenly held up an envelope he'd kept hidden under his butt. He playfully waved it in front of my eyes. I understood it was our first credit card. Within a second I felt an emotional lift take hold of me.

In a thespian voice Bones said, "Would you like to guess how much the limit is, my son?"

"Fifteen hundred," I said, purposely understating what I thought the amount might be. I did not want to be deflated by a disappointing credit line.

"I'll say five thousand," he said in lofty tones.

He ripped open the envelope as I waited like an eager trick-or-treater.

It was ten! Ten grand of credit extended by the Bank of America to Mr. Herbert Trumm, newly of San Diego.

I nearly hit the roof with joy. "How did you know?" I asked Bones. "How the hell did you know we were gonna get the credit cards?"

Bones shrugged. "I didn't."

"You were just trying to buoy my confidence. Is that it?"

"So to speak."

I felt like cracking him but just hi-fived him instead. Then he got off the sofa, and we embraced.

"Do you want to frame it?" he asked.

"What do you mean, frame it?"

"You know, like they do in bars and diners. Haven't you ever seen dollar bills framed on the walls? It's the first bill they ever took in, so they memorialize it."

"And you want to memorialize our first credit card?"

"Why not? We can always get a duplicate card to use while this one hangs on the wall."

"You're fucking crazy, you know that? How 'bout we burn it up first, then after we have the cash you can put it on the wall?"

"Good idea," he said as though it was, and we laughed.

Out came the bottle of champagne he'd brought with him. We didn't have glasses, so we just swigged on the bottle. Passing it back and forth, shaking it up and down, it became so agitated that I started spraying Bones the way Formula One drivers winning the Grand Prix do on the podium. After half the bottle was emptied, I suggested we invite Robin over to join the festivities.

Suddenly Bones got serious. "No," he snapped. "Robin never has to see this scam house." He then gave me a lecture about how Robin, being my ex and probable next girlfriend notwithstanding, was still a woman, and women were not to be made privy to anything outside the realm of necessity.

I reminded him how cool she had been during the Taos scam.

"We have to protect our asses," he said as though she were a danger. "You never know when a woman can turn on you, and when she does, you end up in prison for a long time."

I took note that Bones did not say, "*If* she does..." I protested that Robin would never turn me in, no matter how much or for what she got pissed at me, but Bones didn't want to hear it. He insisted that the last thing a guy on the scam wants to do is over-involve his girlfriend. I finally relented. Deep down I knew Bones was right. Robin's function was solely to provide us with TRW reports. She would indeed participate in the spoils, but her stepping foot inside the scam house, which was becoming the center of our criminal operations, was uncalled for.

The next day our second credit card arrived. It was a Visa from Washington Mutual with a $5,000 credit line. Then came our first MasterCard from City National Bank, another $10,000 line. The last Visa from the California Bank and Trust was good for $5,000 more in credit. In light of the initial denials, this deluge of credit seemed that much more fantastic. I wondered why those first two banks declined our applications. What had they seen that the four accepting banks had not? I engaged Bones's opinion, but he said it was useless trying to figure it out. It could have resulted from human judgment as much as from a computer glitch.

In any case, we were thrilled. All of the sudden we had obtained $30,000 in unsecured credit in Herbert Trumm's name. The operation, which had been looking bleak, had now taken on a gilded forecast. A pot of gold was within reach over the rainbow.

But the first battle of what Bones referred to as "our war against the banks" had hardly begun. While the next platoon of applications in Trumm's names would be prepared, we had to search out methods to turn our current batch of plastic credit into cold cash.

The first thing to do was conduct a test purchase with each card to activate the account. A small purchase was all it took to determine if everything was cool. If anything were wrong, we'd know it immediately. There was always the chance, however small, that something negative popped up in a bank computer after the card had been mailed. In that case, the card would most likely be confiscated by the merchant on orders from the credit card clearinghouse. At the very least, the card would be denied at the register.

What better time to make the initial purchases than during the July Fourth weekend? The malls were packed with holiday shoppers taking advantage of sales. Clerks at the registers would be swamped with customers. If a problem did arise, we'd be able to quickly get out of stores without detection by security personnel.

We drove up to the La Jolla Village Square Mall, a fashionable collection of shops near the heart of the upscale coastal community. Bones carried the tools of the trade in his wallet: a valid driver's license in Herbert Trumm's name and four credit cards with matching spurious endorsements. The department stores were so crowded that we decided to forego them and make the first purchase in one of the small boutiques lining the corridors. Bones picked out a pair of $50 sunglasses and gave them to the lady clerk along with the first of our Visas. She punched the account number into the machine (card-swiping devices were not yet universal) and got immediate approval. Bones signed the voucher; the clerk bagged his glasses and thanked him for the purchase without asking for ID. We'd anticipated that merchants might demand ID for the initial transaction on credit cards, as they were in fact supposed to do. But this one did not even bother checking the back of the card to see if the cardholder signed it. Once an account was activated, rarely did retail people demand ID for credit card transactions.

We strolled through the mall, making small purchases with each card.

They all went smooth as silk, and not one merchant demanded identification for the transaction.

By noon we were hungry. We drove into the ritzy town of La Jolla. We took a table for two in a chic outdoor café overlooking the rocky beach and Pacific Ocean. We dined like a king and his prince, celebrated those first credit card purchases with a bottle of fine wine and ran up a hefty tab of 150 bucks. The waiter took our Washington Mutual Visa, ran it through and smiled at the $30 tip Bones wrote in on the voucher before scribbling "Herbert Trumm" at the bottom. Another strength of the operation, if ever questioned, was that Bones's signature as Trumm matched up perfectly with his signature on each credit application sent to the banks.

Over cheesecake and cappuccino we began discussing the next phase of the operation. "This afternoon we go for the cash," Bones announced.

My eyebrows arched as if to say, "So soon!" but Bones said there was no reason to wait.

"All the cards are good," he declared, rolling his eyes over the wine and delicacies that we had just paid for. "We have more than thirty grand in cash waiting for us. Now we have to go out and get it."

We had several ideas of how to go about that. The first was obvious: take the cards to the ATMs, punch in the PINs and withdraw the cash. But the problem with this was the $200 (at the time) maximum daily withdrawal limit from ATMs. Which meant that to suck out the entire $10,000 limit of a card in that fashion, we'd have to hit the ATMs fifty times. This was not possible for the most basic of reasons concerning security for a continuous criminal operation: avoiding getting caught. How would it look to bank officials, who very closely monitored credit card activity, when they saw a spanking new account was being used on a daily basis to exhaust its limit by means of cash withdrawals from ATMs? Certainly not normal. In fact, they'd have to think that the collective intelligence of the perpetrators amounted to less than that of an ATM.

No, ATM withdrawals would be okay once or twice per card, but not more. We tossed around the idea of buying travelers checks off credit cards and then cashing them. But that would take too much exposure, and then having them repeatedly cashed out by individuals rather than merchants would breed further suspicion.

We had to come up with a faster, safer means of turning the cards into cash. If not, we'd be constrained to buying merchandise and then selling it, like we'd done with the Navajo rugs. Not only was that extremely time-consuming, but it would also drain away half the cash return on the cards. And that was before taking into consideration the possibility, or even probability, that the banks would cancel out the accounts before we had a chance to deplete the cards' limits. We knew very well that sooner or later the real Mr. Herbert Trumm, back in Baltimore, would get wind that someone was trafficking his credit, especially when he was denied a loan or advised by his personal banker that he all of sudden had *too much* credit.

The next day we hit four different ATMs with the two Visas and two MasterCards. To disguise himself, Bones wore a ball cap and the sunglasses he'd purchased the day before. The cameras embedded in the machines would never recognize him. Each machine obligingly spit out $200 in cash. Although this was very encouraging, we decided not to press onward with the ATMs.

A few days later I had an idea. Bones and I were at his apartment watching a Padres-Dodgers baseball game on TV. During a commercial, I said excitedly to Bones, "Casinos!"

"You know how negative I am about gambling," he retorted with a frown.

"No, not that. I'm talking about cash advances at the casino cages. Through Comchek."

Bones's eyes flickered with delight at what he perceived as a brilliant idea.

Comchek was basically a clearinghouse for cash advances on credit cards. These cash-fueling machines were invariably found wherever legalized gambling took place: casinos, cardrooms, racetracks, Jai Alai frontons. They were also found in the lobbies of large hotels, not necessarily limited to gambling areas like Las Vegas. Comchek worked similarly to ATMs, except that you had to deal with a live person when receiving the cash, which availed cash advances right up to the credit limit on the card. There was no daily or one-time limit that ATMs imposed.

The major difference with Comchek was its telephone connection to a central operator on the line twenty-four hours a day. For large withdrawals or repeat transactions in a short time-period, the machine might very well send the cardholder the message: "Pick up telephone." When that happened, you had to speak with the live Comchek operator or the transaction was cancelled out.

This posed no problem for us, and we were prepared for it. The operator could only verify the information listed on the original credit card application: current address, Social Security number, date of birth, etc. Then when approval was obtained, the clerk giving you the money asked no additional questions, for Comchek was ultimately responsible, not the institution that forked over the cash. The process was identical to picking up a money transfer from Western Union. Comchek, like the banks, took 3 percent for its trouble, but what did we care?

We flew to Vegas. We figured gambling casinos were the ideal place to attack Comchek machines since large cash advances were extremely commonplace amongst losing gamblers looking to reload. In fact, a safe bet was that cash advances happened in casinos with more regularity than in any other environment dealing with money.

Inside Caesars Palace, I went to the main casino cashier cage to confirm the feasibility of my idea. Affixed to the wall at the end of the long counter, behind which sat casino cashiers like a row of tellers in a bank, was the cash-advance apparatus with an attached telephone line to Comchek. The machine was very inviting with Art Deco-designed credit cards splashed across its façade.

In the casino's keno lounge, I reminded Bones not to withdraw funds up to the cards' limits because the 3 percent Comchek fee had to be taken into account. The maximum withdrawal allowed was $5,000, which meant that separate withdrawals of $5,000 and $4,500 on the $10,000 cards would avoid our going over the cards' limits with the inclusion of the fees. On $5,000 cards we could safely withdraw $4,500.

After this discussion, Bones took his first trip to the Comchek machine. He inserted the Visa card with the $10,000 limit. After the opening purchases and ATM withdrawal we'd made with it in San Diego, there remained approximately $9,700 of credit available on the card. The greeting on the screen was: "Welcome to Comchek, Mr. Trumm. Please enter the amount of your withdrawal." How nice it was to be greeted personally like that.

Bones punched in $5,000, the maximum. He waited by as the machine's screen told him the transaction was in progress. Next he hoped to see the message "Go to cashier," which meant approval. I stood and watched from a bank of blipping slot machines ten yards away. Though ostensibly I was posted there as security to watch over him, we hardly expected any problems from Caesars Palace personnel.

After two minutes of waiting, it became obvious the transaction was not to be approved electronically. We were prepared for that eventuality. Bones read the message "Pick up telephone" from the machine's screen. He was going to be cross-examined by a live Comchek operator.

As he put the receiver against his ear, he flashed me a reassuring smile. I didn't worry. Bones was an old pro. He'd dealt with dozens of delicate situations like this before. I remembered how coolly he'd handled a particularly daunting Navajo rug dealer in Santa Fe. Whatever affronted him on the phone here at Caesars Palace, he'd handle it just the same.

The live Comchek operator proved to be a security agent for the cash-advance services company. Comchek, which made its money solely through commissions charged to Visa and MasterCard for processing these transactions, worked like ordinary bank clearinghouses. Its computers were linked to the national credit-data files that banks and credit card companies used to monitor accounts. When Comchek received a request for a cash advance on a Visa or MasterCard, it simply passed it along to the card's issuing bank through the computer networking system. If more information was needed, or if a security identification or verification had to be made, the Comchek agent on the phone would have instant access to the issuing bank's computer files regarding the cardholder. Thus it was a near certainty that whoever questioned Bones had on his screen the Visa application and transaction records for the account pertaining to a certain Herbert Trumm. The phone conversation between Bones and the Comchek security agent went like this:

Agent: Are you Mr. Herbert Trumm?
Bones: Yes, I am.
Agent: Are you currently requesting a cash advance of five thousand
* dollars against your Visa card?*
Bones: Yes, I am.
Agent: I'll need to verify a few personal details for security reasons.
Bones: I understand that.
Agent: What is your middle name?
Bones: Alan.
Agent: Your date of birth?
Bones: January 3, 1944.
Agent: Place of birth?
Bones: Baltimore, Maryland.
Agent: Social Security number?
Bones: One-two-eight-four-four-six-seven-three-seven.
Agent: Can you state your mother's maiden name, please?

Bones: (with a slight smile in my direction) Mary Harriet Fisher.
Agent: Thank you, Mr. Trumm. You may proceed to the casino cashier
cage. Your request has been approved.

When Bones told me he'd been asked to cite Trumm's mother's maiden name, an enormous wave of fulfillment rolled over me. It was at that moment that I knew we had a super scam, one that could earn us millions.

The teller already had the computer printout authorizing the transaction. She asked Bones for two pieces of photo ID, in accordance with the instructions she'd received from Comchek. Bones obliged with his California driver's license and United States passport, two pieces of picture-perfect identification. She noted the numbers, then had him sign a voucher, gave him the yellow copy and finally counted out fifty hundred-dollar bills. She slid them across the counter and said it was a pleasure serving him.

The pleasure was all ours. Five thousand dollars' worth!

An hour later we sat in the keno lounge of the Las Vegas Hilton, another classy casino with loads of gaming tables and a Comchek machine by the cage. I couldn't believe we were about to do what we were about to do.

"Are you sure this isn't too risky?" I asked Bones.

"It will go down exactly the same way," he asserted.

I had been concerned that Herbert Trumm's requesting another large cash advance through Comchek so soon after the first one would trigger enough alarms to short circuit the entire system. Bones reassured me with a touch of French. "*Au contraire*," he said. "Nothing matters as long as the info I give their operators on the phone jives with what they have in their database. They don't give two hoots about my depleting the available credit on the cards." He reminded me again that we were in Vegas, the gaming capital where people were known to blow fortunes in a single weekend.

He was right. Not only did a second Comchek operator approve his second $5,000 cash advance, a third and fourth for $4,500 a piece followed suit at Bally's and the Mirage. The last operator sneaked in a quick security check by asking how many withdrawals Trumm had already made. Bones answered three, and added he was having a terrible run of luck at the crap tables.

It really was amazing. I just couldn't believe that Comchek would authorize four credit card-depleting cash advances within two hours from the same man. But as Bones kept drilling into my head, they just didn't care as long as procedure was adhered to and proper verifications made. He had to remind me to keep faith in the operation.

"Kid, you're the one who thought this whole thing up. Don't quit on me now. Believe me, we're gonna get filthy rich off this. Richer than in your wildest dreams."

I was starting to believe him. Our first cash-turning day had already grossed nineteen grand, and the expenses with air tickets and meals were less than five hundred. With that kind of "markup," the only thing we could get was rich.

The day was not over. We still had $9,000 to extract from Comchek, the $4,500 that remained on each of the $10,000 limit cards.

"You're gonna go back and do it again at Caesars Palace?" I asked Bones in mild shock.

"Of course," he replied, as though he were just returning to the corner deli to buy another carton of milk. "They won't think anything of it. I'm just another reckless, steaming gambler hitting Comchek in a frenzy. As long as they get their commission, everyone's happy."

At Caesars, Bones pushed the withdrawal button for $4,500. He was again directed to pick up the Comchek telephone. The security operator actually asked him why he was taking such another large cash advance so quickly. Bones told him that "the crap tables are running real bad." On his second visit to the casino cage at the Hilton, the teller remembered him. After he lamented his losing streak, she wished Bones better luck as she counted out the money.

Before leaving town, we stopped at an ATM to cash out the remnants of credit remaining on the cards. Bones at first cussed himself out because he'd forgotten to bring the slip of paper on which he'd written the PIN numbers. But then, true to himself, he jogged them from his memory and got them right the first time he punched each into the ATM. Both first requests for $200 were denied. But when he dropped to $100, the ATM spit out successive hundred dollar bills. This meant that all we had left on the credit cards were "scraps," the term Bones used to indicate trifling amounts of credit.

We flew back to San Diego like a pair of happy campers with the best beds in the bunk. Those Comchek transactions were the easiest cash rip-offs I had ever seen. Even in movies, I couldn't recall having seen something so easy.

We drove directly to my apartment from the airport. I phoned Robin and told her to come over. Coming in the door, she had that expectant gleam in her eyes. I'd told her we'd been planning to hit Vegas on the cash run. Now she was anxious for her payday. The agreed-upon deal was that she would receive 20 percent of the profits. Bones and I had felt that her end was a bit high, but the fact remained that without her TRW access we couldn't confidently apply for the first credit card. And as far as giving her a fair shake, it was unthinkable not to. There had always been honor among thieves between the three of us. Nothing would change that. It was the one rock upon which we stood.

After the exchange of cheek-kissing, Robin asked, "How much did you guys pull in?" Spoken like a real gangster's moll.

Bones unfurled a sheet of paper. All the day's transactions and expenses were detailed on it. It was the first inkling of what would become his meticulous record-keeping system, to which he would faithfully adhere until IDT, Inc. dissolved.

"We grossed twenty-eight thousand," he said clearly. "The plane tickets cost two hundred forty, cabs were sixty, food and beverage another hundred fifteen. That makes a total of four hundred fifteen in expenses. The net profit is twenty-seven thousand five hundred eighty-five. Twenty percent of that is five thousand five hundred seventeen dollars."

I hadn't seen Bones using a calculator and wondered if he'd done the math in his head. He passed me an envelope that I gave to Robin. Her cut was stashed inside it.

"Is this after the expenses of the house you guys rented and everything?" she asked.

"No," Bones said. "We'll take that into account at the end of the month. It comes off the top before the first distribution of the following month."

That sounded like a proper way of doing things, so everybody agreed. Later on, when I reminded Bones that we forgot to include in the tally the $200 we'd taken from the ATM before leaving Vegas, Bones wrote out an IOU from him to Robin for $40. She would get that in the next cash distribution. Whatever Bones wasn't, he was certainly honest with us.

That night Robin stayed over and we made love. It had been months and finally feeling her naked body against mine did me a world of good. Afterward, she turned on her elbow and stared at me as though studying my thoughts. Her sun-darkened skin glistened in the moonlight streaming through the window.

"Do you realize what we're getting into?" she said softly, stroking my arm above the sheets.

I laughed and sighed at the same time. "No, I don't think I do. And I don't think either one of us should try to realize it, whatever that means."

She nodded. "When are you going to find your next guy?"

"I have to wait for the information from my connection." This was a lie. In accordance with Bones's need-to-know treatment of Robin, she had no knowledge how I was getting hold of the people whose ID and credit we would steal. I had told her a guy I used to do business with before we'd met was the supplier. I even tagged it at $500 per identity. She had no reason to doubt this, nor did I have a reason to tell her the truth.

"We're not done with Trumm," I informed her. "Since he's got a month to pay his credit balances, his overall credit standing remains good until the bills go unpaid. Therefore, we can apply for more cards. We're also gonna apply for department store cards and even oil company cards."

"Those you can't turn into cash, right?"

"Well, certainly not directly."

"So what are you going to do with them?"

"Start by going on a shopping spree. Wanna come along?"

Robin jumped up like a gymnast and sat squarely on the bed. "Can I! Please!" She was being theatrical, but I loved it. "I could use a new wardrobe, and lots of shoes, too. Hey, did you guys ever think of making minimum payments on the cards? You know, to prolong their lives."

Bones and I had discussed that option but quickly discounted the idea. There was no reason to prolong the life of fallacious credit accounts with hundreds if not thousands of future accounts awaiting us in the pages of the *Marquis* volumes.

When Robin settled back on the bed, she turned serious again. "Look, baby," she said, "I don't know exactly how you guys are pulling this off, but it seems awfully big. Just be careful. Sometimes Bones scares me. Sometimes I think he wants to get caught. Like he has some kind of death wish or something. I don't want him to take you… us… down with him."

Hearing that from her was eerie. I had the same feeling. Often Bones acted with reckless abandon. He was capable of downright stupid behavior. But he was immensely talented despite his tendency to get carried away.

I would have to be very careful. Maybe I was getting into something over my head. The Navajo rug scam had been easy pickings. Plus we didn't have to manufacture all that identity. But now we were fucking with the state and federal governments. Before falling asleep, I had thoughts that perhaps I should back out of the scam. But they were quickly displaced when I thought of the twenty-eight grand that spilled out the Comchek machines.

The next day Bones and I sat in the living room of the scam house waiting for the phone to ring. We knew who'd be calling.

It rang at two o'clock sharp.

"Mr. Herbert Trumm, please," said an officious masculine voice into Bones's ear.

"Speaking," Bones said into the receiver as he gave me a quick double-nod, indicating it was indeed the expected call.

"My name is Lawrence Mathews," the man said. "I'm with security for the Bank of America in California."

"I see," Bones said with the same equanimity of voice one might have upon hearing from the next-door neighbor. "What can I do for you, Mr. Mathews?"

"It's about your Visa account with our bank, sir. Yesterday you took two cash advances against your card for a total of nine thousand five hundred dollars."

"I certainly did," Bones said aggressively, almost interrupting. Strength of voice was part of his playact to deter suspicion.

"That's practically the limit on your account."

"Yes, I'm aware of that, Mr. Mathews. How might that concern your security department?" Bones was so smooth I couldn't help but admire him.

"Well, you see, Mr. Trumm, that kind of activity on a new account is very unusual, thus we have to verify that it was indeed you who took the cash advances."

"It was indeed me," Bones said.

"Just one thing, sir. Can you state your mother's maiden name?"

"Certainly," and as soon as Bones smiled at me, I knew the question he'd been asked. "Mary Harriet Fisher."

"Thank you, sir, and forgive us for the intrusion."

"You need not ask for forgiveness," Bones said with almost literary intonation. Then he dropped it a notch and said evenly, "I'm glad to see your competent security department is doing its job."

Bones hung up and we hi-fived. As we'd anticipated, the bank's security department checked up on us—and it gave us the green light to continue.

Three more identical calls followed, from the three other banks whose cards Trumm maxed out at the Comchek machines. Each security person asked the same questions of Bones, who verified that he was indeed Herbert Trumm and had by his own volition taken cash advances in Las Vegas. In a comical moment, one of the callers said, "Thank you very much, Mr. Trumm, we just wanted to make sure it wasn't a possible thief or impostor who signed for the cash advance."

It's time to get the cash

California and Las Vegas, 1990-1992

WE MOVED OUR BUSINESS OFFICE TO BONES'S APARTMENT. This seemed natural since he was adamant about keeping all the records and doing the books, for which he had my blessing. Another thing Bones insisted on was preparing all the applications himself. He was a stickler for neatness, and my penmanship did not pass muster with his standards. So my participation in filling out applications was limited to checking Bones's work. It was essential to verify each detail in order to avoid costly mistakes. Account numbers had to be checked against TRW reports. Birth dates and Social Security numbers had to be checked and double-checked. The slightest error, even a simple transposition of numbers, could lead to a denial and, even worse, suspicion and ensuing investigation.

We had gathered the applications for the next plastic wave we hoped would hit Encino Lane. A credit card application from every California banking institution sat on the large mahogany desk in Bones's study. In a separate pile were department store applications we'd picked up from the city's shopping malls. We had applications for all the high-end stores serving the West Coast, including Saks Fifth Avenue, Neiman Marcus and Nordstrom. We chose a bunch of middle-of-the-road stores including the Broadway, May Company and Robinson's, and didn't neglect lower-tier stores such as Sears, JC Penney and Montgomery Ward.

Along the way we had also picked up applications for oil company credit cards, which we called gas cards. At first we had decided to do without credit from the oil companies but then reconsidered under a closer examination of their worth. Obtaining gas was their obvious face value, but there were also automotive items and repairs that could be charged on the card. Since we'd now be spending lots of time on the road, a Mobile or Exxon charge card could come in quite handy. An expensive mechanical repair could cost hundreds, even thousands of dollars.

But we had to be careful with gas cards. Each time you paid for gas with any credit card, the attendant was required to note your license plate number on the payment slip. Even at self-service stations where you normally went inside the shop to pay, cameras at the pumps filmed you and your car. Our first idea was to steal license plates from parked vehicles and then screw them onto ours each time we filled up with gas or needed a repair. But that would prove too burdensome and just as risky. Then we thought of registering a car under Herbert Trumm's name. At first it seemed like a plausible idea, as Trumm was already a licensed driver in the state of California who'd only be doing what millions of other residents did by registering his car there. But once we burned out his credit cards and the heat came down, we couldn't be caught driving a car in the victim's name. The cops would have such vehicles on their "hot sheets."

It's funny how you overlook the most obvious of solutions when your mind is swamped by the complexities of a multifaceted operation, be it legal or illegal. Since we'd been renting everything else in Trumm's name—scam house, phone service, utilities, answering service, voice mailbox—wasn't the next logical step to rent a car in his name and dispose of it once Trumm's credit cards were all burned up?

Of course it was, but blind oversight had us discussing other alternatives before settling on the obvious. With a rental car we could charge up all our gas in addition to any automobile parts and supplies we needed for our own cars. We could take care of Robin's car as well. The car-rental fee for a month would be more than offset by the advantages of being able to charge everything we could on gas cards.

Upon checking department store applications Bones had filled out, I noticed their inquiries into personal and financial histories were less stringent than banks'. They did not require detailed information about your existing credit accounts. Some asked which major credit cards you held but not their account numbers. Others simply had you check boxes indicating the types of credit cards you held, such as bank, department store and oil company cards. Few asked about your income and none asked for tax returns or how much credit was desired. Either they had a standard initial credit-issue or they made that determination based on the applicants' TRWs.

On the personal information part, store credit departments did not care about your previous address if you'd been living at your current one for at least a year. Most did require a personal reference but not the name and address of a "relative not living with you."

The applications for oil company charge cards made even fewer forays into your personal and financial histories. They asked only for current data about where you lived and what types of credit cards you held. We assumed that approval would be automatic for Herbert Trumm.

While we waited for the next batch of credit cards, I returned to my favorite library at USD to select the next businessmen whose identity and credit we would hijack. The *Marquis* volumes up on the sixth floor still stood as handsomely as ever on the shelves. They looked so undisturbed that I wondered if anyone had touched a single volume since I'd last been there.

I removed the *Who's Who in American Real Estate* volume, skimmed through it and landed on the page containing Herbert Alan Trumm and Donald Trump. I continued thumbing the pages looking for ripe real estate men. We'd decided to set up three men in the same age group as Trumm, men in their mid-forties. They were plentiful on the pages, dozens and dozens of them.

Suddenly I had an impulse. I replaced the real estate volume and pulled out the *Who's Who in American Manufacturing, Who's Who in American Law* and *Who's Who in American Medicine*. I carried the tomes to my favorite table, near a window. The sun streaming through the blinds was again creating streaks across the white-tiled floor. Again I was mesmerized as the sheer numbers of prospective ID theft victims took hold of me. Who would I choose? Which three would I draft for my ID theft victims team? It was like going through the phone book of a major city and randomly selecting three names. Each person on the pages was most likely a millionaire with excellent credit. Each had about the same chance of my picking them as they did winning the lottery.

After much painless searching through the volumes, I chose two men from each volume, one as a primary candidate, the other for a backup in case the primary had less than excellent credit or some other problem his TRW report alerted us to. Selecting two doctors and lawyers, I enjoyed a private laugh about how doctors and lawyers were always screwing everyone and that now one of each was going to be screwed himself.

The primary doctor's name was Leonard Bloom. He was a prominent dermatologist from Philadelphia. Naturally he was board certified and a member of the American Dermatology Association. I read that he'd been a pioneer in the latest hair-transplant techniques, had a thriving practice going and spoke at numerous dermatology symposiums. Bones's hairline had been drifting back over the years, so I wouldn't miss the chance to needle him about going to see Dr. Bloom for a couple of "plugs" once we were done with his credit.

The primary lawyer was a certain Dominick Morra from New York. His practice had once been criminal law but he'd since become a highly successful "ambulance chaser" who'd won several seven and even eight-figure judgments for his clients. Despite his high-standing in the *Marquis* volume, with a name like Morra I couldn't help thinking he was or had been a mob lawyer. Before I wrote down his details, I made sure he had never become a judge. Something told me not to fuck around with judges in any way.

The first of two men I selected from the manufacturing volume owned a large plastics company in Chicago. His name was Arthur Carlson and he'd patented several rubber and plastic products developed by his company, Carlson Manufacturing. He was a big shot in several industry associations. His wife was also influential in big business. I had a fleeting thought of Robin assuming the identity of the wife, but for the time being we were not seeking female victims for the scam. I doubted anyway that Robin would have the nerve to pull off an identity theft. Besides, we needed her where she was at the leasing company.

Bones and I met in his apartment to discuss the prospective identities. He liked my selections as much as any football coach could like his team's first-round draft picks. He approved the three backups as well, with the comment, "We can use them right after these three."

Funny I had never thought of that, but it surely was a viable alternative.

I made two calls to the Social Security Administration to get the SS numbers for Bloom and Morra. I acted out the same just-got-out-of-the-hospital routine I had done when calling to obtain Trumm's. Then Bones called to get Carlson's. His "been ill" act was even better than mine. The result was that we obtained all three SS numbers from operators who then advised us to go to the nearest SSA office to obtain the replacement cards.

We did that on the same run we mailed out the requests for their birth certificates. On the way, I met Robin during her lunch hour and gave her the information she needed to run TRW reports on all three. She said it would take a few days, as she had to be careful avoiding the eyes of fellow employees. That was fine; we weren't in a rush.

We sat idle for a few days until more credit cards in Trumm's name came in. They didn't just come in; they poured in! Especially the department store charge cards. Not one in twenty applications had been denied. Whatever amount of inquiries department store credit managers considered excessive, they obviously relished the idea of doing business with Herbert Trumm.

The first store card I touched came from Neiman Marcus. It was gold with black print and came with a magnificent charge limit of $10,000. Images of spending that ten grand flashed across my mind. I pictured myself at the jewelry counter selecting from a handsome assortment of gold watches. Then I saw myself trying on a beautiful designer suit in the men's department. Since store charge cards were not readily turned into cash, it appeared at that time their utility would be limited to personal wardrobes and household items. But "appeared" would later be overcome.

We received $5,000 charge cards from Saks Fifth Avenue, Bullocks, Dillard's, Nordstrom and, surprisingly, Sears. Bones was ecstatic about the generous charge limit from Sears. He envisioned shopping there for all the hard goods we needed. He'd been talking about buying new televisions and stereo equipment for all of us. Neither Robin nor I disagreed, though Robin was much more eager to prance around Neiman Marcus and Saks than she was about accompanying us to Sears.

The mid-level department stores, as expected, granted medium levels of credit. The Broadway led the pack with $3,000, followed by Robinson's, May Company and Macy's, all of which extended $2,500. Montgomery Ward, which we considered a lower-tier department store, also came back with a $2,500 credit line. The rest of the low-end stores returned cards with limits of $1,500, with the exception of Mervyn's, whose card was the runt of the litter at $500.

Payment on store cards worked basically the same way it did with bank cards. You were billed for purchases made and given thirty days to either pay in full or make a minimum payment. If you chose to make the minimum payment, you were charged interest for the remaining balance financed by the department store. In our case, we would "bust out" the store cards in the same fashion we did the bank cards. The charge limit on each card would be exhausted as quickly as possible, preferably during the initial entry into the store. Just like with banks, we had to worry that our abuse of department store credit would eventually trigger an alarm within TRW. Since we assumed that every issuance of credit made in the United States ended up in TRW's computers, we had to in turn assume that the credit bureau would notify any creditor of such abuse; therefore, it was always in our interest to deplete each credit account at the first available opportunity.

One timesaving advantage we had with store cards was that no "account-activating" charge had to be made. Since each card was only valid in one particular chain of stores, you were always activating your card on their turf while making the initial purchase, thus you could activate it right up to the limit.

Five more bank cards came in with the haul. One matched the previous high credit line of $10,000, the prestigious Visa from Citibank. Wells Fargo came through with a $5,000 MasterCard, as did First Pacific Trust and Southwest Community Bank. But Imperial Capital Bank got chintzy and only issued $2,500 worth of credit on Trumm's Visa.

There were six denials, which we chalked up to excessive inquiries. Bones had predicted that the success rate would drop off for the second wave. But we were still pleasantly surprised to receive five bank cards out of the last twelve applications. We'd been expecting no more than three or four. There were still two applications outstanding.

Now in possession of five more major credit cards in Trumm's name, it was again time for the cash hunt. We caught a morning flight to Vegas with $27,500 in "uncashed" plastic. The first thing we did was walk along the strip going in and out of souvenir shops. We made minor purchases with each card to activate the accounts. Bones bought a few T-shirts and sweatshirts; I opted for some inexpensive Native American jewelry and a little golden Buddha, both of which I would present to Robin as a gift. The Buddha was really cute and cost sixty bucks. Bones kiddingly scolded me for going over the spending limit.

We entered the Desert Inn, a really classy-looking casino I remembered from the '70s private-eye show "Vegas." I was really nervous. How many times could Bones, or should I say Trumm, hit the Comchek machines for cash advances right up to the limit of brand new credit cards? Surely this whole thing had to blow up in our faces. I recalled what Robin had said in bed that night: Did I really know what I was getting involved in? How long would it be until the FBI and Secret Service lay in wait and swarmed us at a Comchek machine?

Bones approached the machine and securely inserted his $5,000 Wells Fargo MasterCard so that its magnetic strip could be easily read. He pressed the black button for $4,500. The machine directed him to the cashier, where he was promptly paid.

We continued on to Bally's. Bones inserted the $10,000 Citibank Visa, pressed the button for $5,000. The machine hit us with a hammer blow when "Transaction denied" appeared on the screen.

Bones and I exchanged a very confused glance. We had been batting a thousand and now this.

Then the words "Try lower amount" appeared on the screen.

Bones took the machine's advice, pressing $4,500. Again he was advised to wait while the transaction was in process.

Then: "Transaction denied."

"Something's wrong," I said in the voice of doom.

"We just used the card an hour ago at that gift shop," Bones recalled. "It couldn't have gone bad so fast."

"Well, maybe it did." I retorted. "Maybe Citibank cancelled out the account."

Bones examined the card in his hand as though he might actually see the problem on it.

The machine spoke up. Again it was "Try lower amount."

We stared at those words as if they held our fate.

"Let's try for a thousand," Bones suggested. "If that doesn't work we might be up shit creek."

Again the transaction was denied. It looked as if our $10,000 Citibank Visa had turned into a worthless strip of plastic.

Naturally we assumed that Comchek had gotten on to us from Herbert Trumm's previous $28,000 cash-raking trip to Vegas. It was certainly no wonder. I never really believed the scam could go on much longer. There was only one way to know for sure: call Citibank.

Bones always carried banks' 800-numbers with him. We exited Bally's and crossed the strip to a pay phone. Not that we expected danger inside the casino, but until we identified the problem it was better to get out of there.

I watched Bones's facial expressions while he listened to a Citibank customer service rep. When his lips curled into a smile, I realized that we were still in business.

"You're not going to believe this," he said, replacing the receiver. "Citibank's maximum allowable cash advance for one billing period is three hundred ten dollars. That's why Comchek denied us."

"You're kidding me! On a ten thousand dollar card you can only take three hundred ten bucks in one cash advance?"

"Not one cash advance, the entire billing period. That means if we take the three-ten today, we can't take another advance on the card for a month."

"So how're we gonna get the cash?"

"We'll figure something out," Bones said confidently. "But for now, let's cash out the rest of these cards."

We made the rounds of casinos without encountering additional problems. At the Aladdin, we took $4,500 off the First Pacific Trust MasterCard. At the Sahara, we collected another $4,500 from the Southwest Community Bank card. Inside the Flamingo Hilton, we siphoned two grand off the lowly Imperial Capital Bank Visa with its $2,500 limit. The total cash payoff for Comchek was $16,000. We rushed to the airport to make the flight back to San Diego.

We found my MG in the long-term parking lot at the San Diego airport. Before heading back to Bones's apartment, we drove up the hill to downtown San Diego and stopped at an ATM outside a First Interstate Bank.

After taking three $200 cash advances, including one off the Citibank Visa to confirm the card was still valid, Bones slipped in the Wells Fargo card and asked for the same $200. He got it. Then a funny thing happened. He inadvertently inserted the same Wells Fargo card after having just pulled it out. He hit the key for $200 and received it again. As the cash came out, he realized his "mistake."

"Hey!" Bones cried out. "That's weird. I know we didn't have $400 of credit left on this card." He pulled out a neatly folded slip of paper. He had all the transactions and credit card balances on it. He shook his head. "No, something's wrong here."

"Maybe you mean something's right," I offered.

Bones gave a "hmmm" and reinserted the card a third time. "Guess we got nothing to lose if the machine eats it now."

The last thing on the machine's mind was eating the card. That's because it coughed up another $200. Then another. And another. Eight times in all.

Finally, after $1,600, the machine finally ate the card. We'd received a $1,400 bonus along with a very valuable lesson about ATMs.

This occurrence definitely was a fluke, but now we knew that the machines were not foolproof. Every great while, a "bug" infiltrated their system. We came to the conclusion that this serendipitous happening would be most probable just after midnight when the system's inner clock changed. Following that belief, we adopted the strategy of hitting ATMs one minute after midnight. It actually paid off, and once more we were the beneficiaries of an ATM gone bonkers, spilling its green guts out.

We cashed out all the scraps over the next three days. At the end of that week, the two outstanding bank card applications came back denied. Bones entered them on his "major credit card" spreadsheet and put them in his files. The final success rate for major cards was nine out of eighteen applications, 50 percent. Those nine cards turned $50,000 in cash. All in all, it was a propitious beginning to our identity theft operation. Bones and I were quite satisfied, though like any other businessmen new to their field, we would search out ways to improve that rate of return.

One decision we made at that point was to send off all future credit applications for one individual simultaneously. There would be no more "waves." We figured that going for the kill right off the bat would ultimately have the highest rate of success.

But for now, it was time to turn our attention to department store charge cards. We had a bunch of them, and everyone was in the mood for a good old-fashioned shopping spree.

"I think we need new wardrobes"

California, Arizona and Mexico, 1990-1992

IT'S HARD TO DESCRIBE EXACTLY HOW I FELT THAT SATURDAY morning when we walked into Neiman Marcus for the first time using a bogus charge card. To use the phrase "like a kid in a candy store" is the epitome of cliché, but for lack of a better, or more appropriate, expression it must be excused here. The fact that I had already been part of the $50,000 Comchek scam did in no way mitigate my excitement over marching into the world's classiest department store armed with its gold $10,000 charge card. I felt an indescribable exuberance upon entering an opulent atmosphere of expensive clothiers and bejeweled glass cases with the power to steal. It surpassed taking cash out of cold steel machines in unattractive places. I don't know if Bones experienced the same sublime feeling as I, but I'm sure Robin did. In fact, she was the first one through the doors.

We had parked our new rental vehicle, a stylish Lincoln Town Car, in the lot on the other side of Fashion Valley Mall. In case we had to make a speedy escape, we couldn't hang around waiting for the valet to fetch the car.

We'd decided beforehand that Bones and Robin would be together; I'd be the lone shopper. The couple would stroll through the departments buying up merchandise while I watched them as well as the clerks who'd handled their transactions. My job was to make sure each transaction was "clean."

The main concern was that department stores had their own security forces to patrol their floors. When withdrawing cash from an ATM or a Comchek machine, we didn't have to contend with any onsite security or surveillance people. Even in the Las Vegas casinos, security departments were not on the lookout for people using illegal means to obtain cash advances. Casinos were not at risk to financial loss from any of our illicit transactions.

But a department store suffered the loss when attacked by credit thieves carrying its charge cards. Therefore, its security staff was alerted immediately when a customer was suspected of any wrongdoing pertaining to a charge card. That customer would be placed under surveillance and subject to arrest.

I followed Bones and Robin to the men's shoe department. Bones wanted to test the charge card by making a relatively small purchase. He tried on an assortment of Bally dress shoes before settling on a pair that fit. Robin accompanied him to the register, where a smiling clerk checked the shoebox to make sure it contained a shoehorn, and then put the box in a Neiman Marcus bag. After Bones signed the voucher, the clerk, still smiling, politely asked for a piece of identification. We'd suspected it was department store policy to verify customer ID for the initial purchase on new accounts.

Bones complied with a smile of his own, handing the clerk the California driver's license with a signature that matched Herbert Trumm's on the back of the charge card. The clerk thanked Bones for his business and bade the couple a pleasant day.

Bones slung the bag over his shoulder and leisurely strolled hand in hand with the woman who appeared to be his younger wife or girlfriend. They looked great together, though Robin had earlier professed some aversion to playing the role. But Bones had insisted. Part of the scam was to embellish the roles of its participants. The older man out on the town lavishing his young female companion with gifts was very chic in high-class stores like Neiman Marcus.

She was about to get the first in the series of gifts. Over coffee that morning in a trendy La Jolla café, Robin had cut herself a very attractive deal. She was getting 20 percent of the cash off the credit cards but felt she was entitled to a bigger chunk of department store spoils. Who could argue that? After all, she was a woman.

I had expected Bones to yield to an even third, but when he said Robin could have "half the spoils from the malls," even I was taken aback. There was never any question about Bones's fairness and generosity, but I felt he'd gone overboard. Out of respect, however, I did not object.

The pair walked into the fine jewelry department housed off the main floor in a separate sunken salon with silky beige carpeting and dangling chandeliers. Holding hands, Bones and Robin stepped into it and were greeted by a classy saleswoman in her forties who looked delighted by the site of a lovely couple ready to spend. Bones wore a sharp leather jacket. Robin had on an elegant summer outfit her ex had bought for her, probably in that very store. Together they reeked of cash.

The woman led them to the case containing the shop's finest jewelry, apart from whatever pieces might be stowed in the safe. When Robin said: "I'd like to see some of your ladies' diamond bracelets," it seemed as though the woman heard the words before she said it. She opened the glass case and gingerly removed a velvet tray containing six beautiful gold bracelets studded with diamonds. From where I stood at the fringe of the men's department, not far away from an Armani blazer I'd been eyeing, I couldn't see the jewelry they were looking at. But as I found out later, the cheapest piece on the tray was $16,000, the most expensive $200,000.

I observed the saleswoman replace the tray and remove another one from the case. This one contained an assortment of ladies' gold watches. Robin genuinely fell in love with a sleek 24-karat Piaget watch with a diamond bezel. The price tag was $13,000. Unfortunately, that number was three grand more than the limit on Trumm's Neiman Marcus charge card.

The saleswoman noticed Robin going into a sulk when her sugar daddy admitted that his charge card only had a $10,000 limit and he'd left his credit cards in his other wallet. She gave them a good once-over, and quickly came to the distressed damsel's rescue.

She delicately stepped between them and said to Bones, "Mr. Trumm, are you aware of our revolving credit policy?"

Either Bones didn't know or he made believe. "No, I'm not. Would you be so kind as to explain it to me?"

The woman flashed her best smile. "Of course. We can instantly extend you a credit increase up to double the amount of your charge limit." She gave a slight but practiced gesture of mild embarrassment. "I couldn't help but overhear. Your charge limit is ten thousand dollars, therefore, if you qualify, we'd be able to extend that limit to pay for the watch, provided, of course, that the amount open on your account is at least three thousand."

Like a true stage actress, Robin purred, "Honey, you haven't used your Neiman card on anyone else, have you?"

The saleswoman laughed, but not until Bones did first.

Bones followed the ad-lib like a natural. "Now, sweetheart, would I ever do a thing like that? In fact, I just opened the account, and if my memory serves me correctly, today is the first occasion I've had to use the card."

Bones was really waxing the bullshit. I had moved within earshot and heard the whole exchange. Watching them together, it was hard to believe he wasn't her sugar daddy.

"Let me make an inquiry of the credit department," the saleswoman said. "It'll just take a minute."

She went behind the counter and slipped through an open door that she closed behind her. While she was gone, Bones and Robin turned around and spotted me. They both smiled, and Bones made a subtle gesture of lightly rubbing his chin to reassure me he had everything under control.

I, on the other hand, was apprehensive. Here's a guy in the jewelry department of Neiman Marcus trying to get his credit line doubled the first day he used the card. If that weren't ridiculous, what was? But then I remembered how ridiculously easy the cash advances had gone through Comchek. That was fifty grand. So in light of that swindle it was not difficult to believe that Neiman Marcus would jack up the credit line by $3,500.

When the woman came back into the salon smiling, she didn't say the charge limit had been increased by $3,500. She said, "Mr. Trumm, the credit department has authorized you to charge up to twenty thousand dollars on your card."

Twenty fucking grand! On a department store card! What was the world coming to?

"That's so nice of you," Bones said exuberantly.

Robin gushed. "Thank you so much."

The woman eased the watch onto Robin's wrist and fastened the clasp. Before they left the salon, Bones had a watch on his wrist, too. It was a $3,000 Cartier tank watch. The second Cartier he bought was in its case in his jacket pocket. With the three watches and Bally shoes, Trumm's Neiman Marcus card carried $19,300 in charges. Before exiting the store, Bones marched into the men's department and bought me the Armani blazer. With the tax, the total charge was $689. Bones had now spent $19,989 on Trumm's card. There remained $11 worth of credit on the card.

Well, there wasn't much you could buy in Neiman Marcus for eleven bucks.

Over lunch in one of the mall's fancy Italian eateries, Bones laid the Cartier he'd had in his pocket on the table. "That's for you, my son," he said sincerely. "You deserve it. You really are a criminal genius."

I was touched by the way he said it. I opened the case and put the watch on my wrist. It was a beauty. While I admired it, Bones decided to give us a history lesson on Cartier tank watches.

"Do you know why they're called tank watches?" His question addressed us both.

"Couldn't have anything to do with real tanks," Robin finally said.

"*Au contraire*," Bones said in the French he liked so much. "Not only with tanks, but strictly French tanks. You see, during World War One, allied tank commanders in France had an affinity for wearing wristwatches with that face." He pointed at the Cartier on my wrist. "So when the Cartiers got wind of that, they decided to call it the tank watch."

Bones amused himself dishing out history tidbits like that, and I was certainly impressed by how well read he was.

We charged the meal on Trumm's Visa, and then headed to the Nordstrom on the other side of the mall. Trumm's Nordstrom charge card was good for $5,000. This time we all went in together. It was my turn to lead things off in the men's shoe department. I bought myself a nice pair of Italian loafers for $200. Then Robin, who couldn't wait to pounce on the women's department, conducted her own fashion show in the store. Like some elegant runway model, she paraded through departments admiring herself in mirrors to the applause of not only us but also to other customers who couldn't help but notice the foxy lady in so many different outfits.

She walked up to complete strangers to ask how she looked in this dress or that pantsuit. She really was having herself a ball. Bones and I got off on it, too. By the time she finished her little series of spectacles, Robin had loaded up on enough designer clothing to give her fall and winter wardrobes a good start. She bought blouses, skirts, shoes, a leather biker jacket and a business suit she would try out at the leasing company. Bones and I had planned to pick up a thing or two at Nordstrom, but Robin burned up the card in just under an hour.

Next it was on to a new mall, new store and new charge card. Saks Fifth Avenue was nearly as classy as Neiman Marcus. Its goods were certainly in the same league. Bones and I entered the store while Robin went "window shopping" in the boutiques lining the mall. Since we'd agreed that the Saks card would be spent in the men's department, there wasn't much reason for Robin to tag along. When she left saying she was going window shopping, we couldn't help but laugh. I would've bet my last dollar that whatever appealed to Robin in the windows would soon be on our shopping list.

My fall and winter wardrobes were in much worse shape than Robin's had been. I had virtually nothing. All the articles of heavy clothing in my closet were remnants from Taos. Since then I hadn't seen any snow, nor had I been anywhere else I needed lining in my coats.

But this winter I planned on making a few ski trips. In the men's department, I found a nice assortment of Columbia Sports Wear ski apparel. I bought two down vests, two down jackets with matching ski pants, and a warm-up suit. For après-ski I opted for a heavy suede jacket and a black leather coat with a detachable fur vest. Bones chose a suede number similar to the one I'd picked.

In the Ralph Lauren section, we each purchased lightweight Polo jackets and a few long-sleeved casual shirts. We moved from designer to designer, selecting a sweater here, a pair of trousers there. Standing at the register by the Tommy Hilfiger collection, dress shirts in hand, we were mildly embarrassed to learn we'd already run out of credit on the card. Bones immediately asked for an on-the-spot increase as he'd received at Neiman Marcus, but the salesman advised him that it was store policy to issue revolving credit only in the jewelry department. Bones shrugged it off and we left.

We hit Bullocks next, burned up that card, then the Broadway, Robinson's and Dillard's, where we finally ran out of time. Yes, the store closed on us and we were forced to leave before using up all the credit on the charge card.

The trunk was packed to the gills by the time we headed home. So was the inside of the car. Robin sat on one side of the back seat. The other side was crammed with bags and boxes from every high-end department store serving California. Looking over my shoulder and seeing that mess, it was apparent that we'd be in need of a van. Herbert Trumm would have to trade in the Town Car for a vehicle with a heck of a lot more storage capacity.

We dropped Robin off at her apartment, helped her inside with her bags and boxes, then headed over to Bones's so he could do the books. He maintained a separate ledger for store charge cards in the new file cabinet he'd charged at Montgomery Ward and installed in his study. Working from the sales receipts, he made entries for each of the day's transactions, remaining balances on accounts, and the breakdown on how much dollar-value of merchandise went to each person. Bones insisted on keeping accurate records of everything.

We realized that in the future shopping would become hard work. We still had in excess of $20,000 in available store credit that had to be used up. Down the road we'd experience an influx of store charge cards obtained in the names of each new identity we assumed. We'd accumulate literally tons of merchandise. Where would we store it all? What would we do with the excess? I mean, how much clothing and hard goods could three human beings need?

Of course these were great problems to have, but they were still problems. We would have to find a way to dispose of bulk merchandise, somehow turn it into cash.

On Sunday, Robin and I took a ride into Mexico. We drove my MG and put the top down. She was wearing a peach-colored Liz Claiborne outfit we'd purchased at Bullocks; I wore a Ralph Lauren T-shirt and jeans that had come out of Dillard's. We both sported our expensive new watches— though hers certainly outshone mine.

We cruised along the coast to Ensenada. The open-air breeze caressing our faces felt delightful. We pulled over at a sea shack restaurant that served great lobster with a panoramic view of the orange sun dipping over the horizon. We gorged on two-pound monsters, drinking Chablis while gazing at the Baja California sunset. When the sun finally fell into the darkening waters, I paid the check with one of Trumm's Visas that Bones had given me. Signing the voucher marked the first time I used a fraudulent signature in the scam. It would be far from the last.

We left the car parked at the restaurant and walked across the highway to a motel. We'd planned to go back to San Diego that night, but we were both feeling too good and buoyed by the wine to even think of it. We checked out early the next morning and drove up to Tijuana. While walking along *Avenida Revolución*, the main drag, we stumbled upon a Ralph Lauren outlet store. I was curious about the prices, so we walked in.

The merchandise looked legit but the prices were awfully cheap. The Polo shirts were priced at less than 50 percent of American retail, lower than could be found at Ralph Lauren wholesale outlets in the States. Naturally I wondered. My Spanish wasn't all that bad, so I decided to have a little chat with the slick young guy working there.

"*Buenos dias,*" I said. I asked him in Spanish, "Are all the clothes in here genuine?"

"What do you mean, *señor*?" He replied in English.

"I mean, is anything in the store counterfeit goods?"

"Of course not, sir."

"Then how do you sell it so cheap?"

The guy chuckled as if about to let me in on a big secret. "It's all in the buying of the merchandise, sir. We buy very cheap, and we have very little markup because we do much business with all the gringos like you, sir."

We shared a laugh.

"Do you mind telling me how much you pay for goods?"

"Yes, sir, I mind. But I'll tell you anyway." This guy had a sense of humor, and he was certainly likeable. "We pay thirty percent of retail and sell for forty-five percent of retail. You don't have to be a genius to figure out that our profit margin is fifteen percent of retail."

"No, you don't," I agreed.

He told me his name was Alberto. When he said "*Adiós,*" I told him that I thought we might be seeing each other again.

Outside the shop, Robin asked, "What do you mean, 'You might be seeing him again?'"

I suddenly grabbed her and kissed her squarely on the lips. "I think I just found a way to get us into the merchandising business."

Merchandising the old-fashioned way—signing, then selling

California and Mexico, 1992

I DROPPED ROBIN OFF DIRECTLY AT WORK BECAUSE SHE WAS already late. Then I hightailed it over to Bones's. He was in a sour mood. Chewing me out was the first order of business.

"I told you to be here at nine o'clock sharp," he snapped.

"I had to drop Robin off at work."

"What's the matter with her car?"

"Nothing. We spent the night in Ensenada, that's all. We just got back."

"Glenn, this is a serious business we're running here. And Robin is part of it. I don't know if it's such a good idea you rekindle a relationship with her."

This was strange. He'd never come off that way about it before.

"Did you ever hear that too much philandering weakens the legs?" He smirked at me.

"Who the fuck are you, Vince Lombardi? I didn't know you were running a football team here."

He softened. "Did you guys have a good time?"

"You bet. We had some delicious lobster at this place overlooking the Pacific. But I got something better to tell you. Don't think that just because I spent the night screwing Robin's ass off, I forgot about business."

Bones seemed curious.

"You ever hear of Tijuana?" I said.

"What's that supposed to mean?"

"I think I may have the solution for turning merchandise into cash. That is if you trust Mexicans."

"If it's selling them stolen merchandise, I trust 'em."

I told Bones about my encounter with Alberto at the Ralph Lauren outlet. When I finished, he took a few moments to digest it.

"What makes you think he wants to do business?" Bones asked at length.

"It was the way he was so candid about how much he pays for his merchandise."

"You mean how much his boss pays."

"Yeah, so, whatever. If Alberto was putting out feelers, then his boss is ready to do business."

Bones nodded. "He told you they pay thirty percent of retail for Ralph Lauren goods?" I nodded. "So maybe we could work out something where they pay twenty-five."

I figured Bones was shaving it a little close, but then again if Alberto was coming on to me to do business, he was probably full of shit about paying 30 percent. He was probably paying a few points higher, even if his selling price was only 45 percent of retail.

"Then you think it's worth going back down there to see him?"

We were on the road half an hour later. Alberto did not seem surprised to see me back so soon.

"Who's the other gringo?" he asked.

"The other gringo wants to talk business."

Alberto motioned to a young girl working in the store. I'd noticed her there that morning. I concluded that either she didn't speak English or Alberto didn't care what she overheard, which meant she could be trusted. He told her in Spanish to take care of any customers.

It took but five minutes to solidify the fact Alberto wanted to do business. We were not the least bit wary because, after all, this was Mexico. When Bones asked who his boss was, Alberto said, "I am my boss." Whether or not that was true didn't matter. The message was that we would only deal with him, and on his terms.

"I can buy any designer clothing you bring me," he said with a smile. "It doesn't have to be Ralph Lauren."

Bones and I understood that Alberto was running a major swag operation. Bones asked if he dealt in hard goods. Only clothing, Alberto informed us. He said he was willing to pay 15 percent of retail on all brands, "*no mas.*"

Bones's response was: "*Mucho mas.*"

We bickered over the price. Alberto refused to budge from 20 percent; Bones was adamant for 25 percent. Finally when Bones relented and offered 22.5 percent, Alberto got stubborn and kept repeating "twenty-two" as if married to it. Bones finally agreed.

"I can receive any quantity you have," Alberto said after the round of handshakes. "When and what and how large will your first shipment be?"

"I don't have anything now. I don't know when I will have it. I don't know how large it will be." Bones sounded hilarious running that off, and I don't think he intended to. I started laughing, then Alberto cracked up as well. I had to admit that he was about the funniest Mexican I'd ever met. I just hoped our business dealings would be as serious as his personality was funny.

Bones asked Alberto how we should contact him for a deal. We expected Alberto to instruct us to call a pager and leave a number where he could reach us. But he said to call his shop. He gave us a business card with the Ralph Lauren name and insignia on it. Driving back and discussing it, I wondered aloud if Ralph Lauren even knew about the existence of the Tijuana outlet bearing his name.

The remainder of that week we spent burning up the rest of Trumm's store charge cards. Before doing so, we rented a van with the last of his MasterCards. Robin didn't join the fun but she did give us a list of more clothing to buy. Since most of the upper-end store cards had already been depleted, we couldn't completely satisfy her wishes. We finished off the Dillard's card filling her order, then the $2,500 card from May Company buying an assortment of Ralph Lauren clothing. With the lower-tier store cards we hadn't broken in yet, we bought an assortment of hard goods.

In Montgomery Ward, which Bones loved to call "Monkey Ward," we invaded the electrical appliances department where Bones purchased three Sony Trinitron TVs for each of our apartments. The largest, a twenty-seven incher, he planned to put in the living room of his apartment. He loved to watch old movies from the fifties, and I imagined that his new TV set would bring him vast amounts of enjoyment. The nineteen-incher would replace the Zenith I had in my bedroom, and the little ten-inch portable would fit snugly in Robin's kitchen, or in her bathroom. I didn't ask her lest she'd tell me it was none of my business.

Bones had also spied a refrigerator much to his liking, but unfortunately the card could support no more than the three TVs plus a few scraps. Those scraps took shape as various cleaning supplies all of us could use at one time or another.

At Sears, we loaded up on hi-fi equipment. Walking through their sporting goods department, I hoped to find ski equipment for sale. But they didn't carry it. Bones told me not to worry; either we'd get a charge card for the Big 5 Sporting Goods chain or we'd use one of the new major credit cards when they came in.

Bones found his refrigerator among the white walls of appliances. In fact, he liked this one better than the one he'd seen at Monkey Ward. It was on sale for $595. The only problem was transporting it. Of course Sears offered to deliver it, but we couldn't risk having his true home address appear anywhere in their records. Furthermore, the thing was too damn big to fit in our van. So with that same dying Trumm MasterCard, we rented a U-Haul truck for the day and picked up the fridge. Talk about squeezing the plastic out of a credit card!

Lugging the monster up to Bones's apartment was a real pain in the ass, but he was happier than a bee in honey when he looked at it sitting in his kitchen.

To wipe out the Sears card, Bones made what I thought was a peculiar purchase: an electric garage-door opener. "What the hell are you buying that for?" I asked him. "You don't live in a house."

"No, but Herbert Trumm does."

On our visits to the scam house, we'd been parking our cars in the driveway. There was a two-car garage built into the house, though we hadn't bothered using it. We would just leave the cars in front of it and walk to the rear of the house to gain entry. Naturally we wanted to keep our comings and goings as inconspicuous as possible, for the unwanted prying of nosy neighbors was always a concern. Therefore, Bones's idea to purchase the garage-door opener was a good one. It would facilitate our slipping in and out of the scam house.

It took a solid week to drain all the cards. During that span we learned a lot about the inner workings of department store charge cards. We developed our own system of internal security to protect this phase of our scam. Before going out on shopping sprees, we checked the status of charge cards we would use. We called each store's credit department to find out how much credit was available on the card. The operator would ask certain ID questions to verify it was the cardholder on the line. Once satisfied, the amount of available credit would be divulged. The universal term used by department stores for this figure was "open to buy" (OTB).

When credit departments informed us of any dollar amount of OTB, we knew everything was kosher. If, however, they came up with anything else, such as "I'm sorry, sir, but you'll have to come into the credit office at the store" or "I'm sorry, sir, the computer doesn't reflect your account balance," then we knew we had a problem and could not go back in that store with a charge card in that person's name.

In certain cases, credit departments had legitimate reasons for not being able to tell us the OTB. If their computers were down, we continued calling until they went back online. Sometimes they couldn't find your account at all. This was not a ploy, just a problem similar to an airline not being able to find your reservation.

When they requested a phone number to call back, we'd give them the number of the scam house, which, of course, was reflected on Trumm's applications. By using the phone's call-forward feature, we never had to be at the scam house to receive these calls. They could conveniently and in untraceable fashion be forwarded right to our apartments.

During the course of our fraudulent buying sprees, problems with some of our accounts periodically arose. But fortunately, department store policy was to notify a cardholder when something was amiss with his account. In the case of Herbert Trumm, we discovered two weeks after the initial shopping binge that we had never maxed out his Macy's charge card, and then couldn't find the card. In dealing with so many credit and charge cards, these things happened. Bones had probably lost the card. When I called Macy's credit department to obtain the OTB on the account, I was informed, "I'm sorry, Mr. Trumm, but your account has been cancelled. Your card has been returned to the department. My records show that we tried to contact you, without success."

That was about as direct and truthful as the Macy's employee could be. We'd been so busy that we must have missed the message about the card turning up. In any event, we never experienced an instance of a credit department trying to set us up via providing disinformation over the telephone.

After five days of shopping, Bones and I drove to Tijuana. We'd called

Alberto at his Ralph Lauren shop the day before to set up a meet. He'd asked Bones how much in merchandise we had to sell. Bones told him $3,000 retail value of designer "goodies." He offered to bring Alberto the receipts. The wily Mexican told him it wasn't necessary. He knew the retail prices of all Ralph Lauren's goodies on sight. He also suggested that it was better to wait until we had accumulated more merchandise before driving down to do a deal. Bones disagreed. He wanted to see immediately if the Mexican was for real, and if he was, he wanted to solidify the connection.

Alberto and the younger girl were inside the shop when we arrived. Each of us carried three large Dillard's and May Company shopping bags filled with articles of Ralph Lauren Polo and Chaps clothing. I expected Alberto to summarily get rid of the girl, whom we finally learned was his cousin, but he just said, "Open the bags and put it all on the counter."

We dumped the bags, forming a heap of Ralph Lauren clothing. The girl, Nina, hardly gave it a second look. Perhaps this was how her cousin received all his merchandise.

Alberto came over to give the pile of shirts, jeans, jackets and sweaters a look-over, and then chose a few items to examine with more care. From his back pocket he removed a small calculator. He went through all the items, punching in a figure as he tossed each one on the floor behind the counter. The whole process took twenty minutes. When he was done, he said, "Six hundred sixty dollars."

That was exactly 22 percent of $3,000. There would be no negotiating the price. We had agreed on 22 percent, delivered the merchandise, and Alberto kept his part of the bargain.

He delved into his front pocket and pulled out a thick wad of cash. Most of it was greenbacks but there were peso bank notes mixed in. He peeled off six hundred dollar bills and three twenties, and gave me the cash. I briefly wondered why he handed it to me instead of Bones. Probably had something to do with a gesture of kinship because we were about the same age.

"Put the tickets on the clothing," Alberto ordered Nina with a nod of his head at the merchandise on the floor behind him. Nina nodded back and gathered up the merchandise. It would be for sale in the shop's cubbyholes within the hour.

We all shook hands. At the door, Bones assured Alberto we'd be back with a much larger load in a few weeks.

The Mexican connection would be a key ingredient to the success of our merchandising operation. Although we didn't know it then, Alberto would in the future turn us on to some very big players in the Mexican underworld with whom we'd be doing business.

Back in San Diego with our cash marauding and shopping sprees on hold, we mulled over the problem of how to cash out the Citibank Visa card. We racked our brains. We needed a commodity we could buy and then sell without getting raped in the process. Remembering how we'd received 50 percent of retail on the Navajo rugs, we considered the idea of returning to New Mexico and Arizona to buy them with the Visa. But it was too risky. Our rug scam might still remain in the memories of traders, and perhaps someone might recognize Bones.

Almost ready to concede the Citibank card to goods and services, a childhood memory surfaced with the answer. As a kid I had a fascination for rare coins, especially gold coins. I'd had a few American ten dollar Eagles in my collection. I mentioned it to Bones.

"That's it!" he cried, nearly jumping off his desk chair in his study. "Krugerrands! We can buy 'em and sell 'em. Almost like getting the cash."

He was right. The South African Krugerrand was the premier investment quality gold-issue coin in the world. It was also the precious metal closest to negotiable currency. It revolved around its own fluctuating buy-and-sell market. Unlike diamonds, where an anxious seller could be manipulated by a buyer taking advantage of his plight, and would seldom realize what his stones were worth, he could go directly to a bullion dealer who would take Krugerrands off his hands with no dickering or bullshit.

We got right on it. At the time, one-ounce Krugerrands sold for $410 apiece. Dealers paid around $390, thus a buy-sell transaction resulted in a cash loss of only $20. However, we soon found out that our "Krugie" operation would not go as smooth as the edge of the coin itself. The problem was finding dealers who accepted credit cards for the purchase of gold coins. The majority of bullion dealers and coin shops were willing to do so for rare silver coins and paper money, but when it came to gold it was strictly cash or certified check.

Eventually we found a dealer in Chula Vista who accepted plastic for gold in accordance with a 5 percent surcharge. He had three "Krugies" in stock, which we bought for $1,300. Then before you could say the full name of the coin, we shot over to a Deak International currency exchange and sold them for $1,170. We only lost 10 percent in value.

Krugerrands would become the cash-turning operation for all Citibank cards until that institution changed its restrictive cash-advance policy. We managed to find other dealers in Southern California who accepted the credit card with a surcharge. We depleted Trumm's Citibank balance with Krugerrand purchases, but the last two coins we didn't sell. In a gesture commemorating our partnership, Bones suggested we each wear a Krugie on a gold chain around our necks. I felt it was a wonderful idea. We went into a jewelry store and had the necklaces made without damaging the coins. I still wear mine to this day.

While awaiting results from the applications we'd sent out for the three new identities, Bones grew restless from lack of action. I had observed how much he loved the shopping sprees. He really was like an actor on stage winning over the salespeople, getting credit extensions inside the stores and being serviced like a prince. There was no question that the stores turned him on more than the banks or casinos, in spite of the large sums of cash that came from ATMs and Comchek machines.

One morning after breakfasting with him in his apartment, in front of the big Sony in the living room, Bones abruptly picked up the telephone. I had no idea whom he was calling, though I suspected it had something to do with department stores.

"Good morning," he said into the receiver, "my name is Herbert Trumm and I recently did some shopping in your store. Let me say that I always enjoy shopping at Mervyn's; I think it's a wonderful store. However, I must inform you that the credit line I was given by your department is quite embarrassing…"

So that was it. He was calling the credit department at Mervyn's in an attempt to get Trumm's credit line jacked up.

He read the account number off the card in his hand. Then: "You know, a five hundred dollar credit line is what you give to an eighteen-year-old kid graduating high school and applying for his first charge card. You don't give that belittling amount to someone of my stature. I have long-term, excellent-standing credit, thus I am entitled to a much higher credit line than that. Your credit department has obviously made a terrible mistake. Can you please do something to correct this?"

I was awed by this display of self-confidence and authority. The woman on the line told Bones that she sympathized with him and that, yes, a mistake must have been made in the determination of his credit line. She said she was powerless to change it, but if he'd like, she would have a supervisor call him back within the hour. Bones thanked her and said he'd be waiting for the supervisor's call. When he hung up, he said to me, "See, that's how you do it. That's the way to get our buying power increased."

Forty minutes later the phone rang. It was the Mervyn's supervisor, who had dialed the number of the scam house, which was call-forwarded to Bones sitting on his sofa. Bones afforded me the pleasure of putting the call on speaker.

"Yes, this is Mr. Trumm," he said into the phone lying on the coffee table.

"Mr. Trumm, my name is Dan Walters. I'm the chief credit officer with Mervyn's department store. I understand you're not happy with your charge limit, sir."

"That's right, Mr. Walters." Bones made a point to courteously repeat the man's surname. He rehashed for Mr. Walters how insulted he felt by receiving a sophomoric credit line. Walters explained that it was Mervyn's policy to open new charge accounts with a maximum credit line of five hundred dollars. Bones protested that such a policy was "ridiculous." He wouldn't be able to buy half of what he needed from Mervyn's with such a "minuscule line of credit." He finished off his tirade with: "Mr. Walters, if Mervyn's does not want to do business with me, I guess I'll have to do my shopping at Sears and JC Penney." He carefully made reference to those stores that were in the same low-level category as Mervyn's. He added, "Sears gave my son a seven hundred fifty dollar credit line." Of course Bones had no son.

That last statement might have been a bit too much for the Mervyn's credit man to stomach. He told Bones to hold the wire while he checked to see if there was something he could do. When he came back on the line five minutes later, he apologized for the delay and asked Bones how much more in charge privileges he'd like.

"At least twenty-five hundred," Bones said, which almost knocked me off the couch.

Mr. Walters' voice suggested he'd also been thrown for a loop when he said, "Sir, no one has ever opened a charge account here with that kind of limit!"

Bones did not let up, and I wondered how far he'd push it. "There's a first time for everything, Mr. Walters. If you value me as a faithful customer in your store, then surely you can extend me a line of credit worthy of my patronage."

Say what you want about Bones, but the guy really knew how to toss around the bullshit.

Poor old Mr. Walters asked, "Would two thousand suffice, Mr. Trumm?"

Bones's reply of "Absolutely not" surprised me not in the least.

The Mervyn's credit manager once more asked Bones to hold on. However, this pause was much shorter. When he came back on the line, he apologized again and informed Bones that his charge limit was being increased to $2,500.

"Effective as of when?" Bones asked boldly.

"As of now."

I thought I'd detected a slight hesitation in Walters' voice.

Exactly twenty-nine minutes later we were at the Mervyn's store next to the San Diego Sports Arena. We would have liked to have breezed in and out of there, but it was difficult spending $2,500 in Mervyn's. After buying two dozen pairs of Levi's jeans, there wasn't much else in clothing that interested us, and Robin would surely scoff at anything on the racks we might suggest for her. We thought of Alberto in Tijuana, but no wares from any top designers were to be found there. Furthermore, Mervyn's carried little in hard goods.

We had $1,800 left in credit, which gave us a choice: either we load up on linens, bathrobes, towels and tons of other miscellaneous crap, or we grab any nondescript shopper in the store and announce to him or her, "This is your lucky day! Pick out what you want up to eighteen hundred dollars and I'll put it on my charge card."

We decided on both. At the register unloading three wagons filled with just about everything we could think of that came in handy for our dwellings, Bones turned to a little old lady behind him. "Ma'am, this is your lucky day!" he announced. "Whatever amount is left on my charge card, you're free to spend it all on yourself."

She took him for a crackpot, but two hours later as we helped her pack $882 worth of goods into her car, she broke into tears and said it was the happiest moment in her life.

Who said identity thieves have no heart?

Discovering a grifting way of life

California and Florida, 1965-1985

I DID NOT MEET BONES IN CALIFORNIA. NOR DID I MEET HIM anywhere in the west. That historical occasion took place in Florida, where I was deeply engaged in my first criminal enterprise.

Before that, however, I was the product of a relatively privileged and conservative upbringing that I constantly rebelled against. In grade school they told me I had a learning disability that later fell under the term "attention deficit disorder." I remember weekly visits to the school psychologist, who had me draw images depicting my life at home and in school among my classmates. I was horrible at drawing. That one day I would become a master forger was not in anyone's tarot cards.

What troubled the psychologist most was that when I read passages from a book, my retention of the contents was practically nothing. I could hardly remember more than two characters' names. He would have me read it again and again, but my retention level did not increase notably.

I also had a speech impediment. My mother told me that I didn't begin speaking until a tardy age. At first my parents suspected I was deaf, but hearing tests quickly dispelled that theory. Whether or not my speech defect was connected to my developmental delay, I don't know. But the result was that I couldn't separate the pronunciation of "th" sounds from "s" sounds.

IDENTITY THEFT, INC.

At home in Sausalito, I had a privileged, if unloving, childhood. I was an only child, but in spite of that my father was not a hands-on dad. He spent more time at his church and its various organizations than he did at my Little League games. I got periodic love from my mother but it always seemed distant. I don't have many memories of being hugged and cuddled. Sometimes I felt that the reason I had no brothers and sisters was because of me.

In school, I started off as a problem student, though not a bad one. I was not a disciplinary case, nor did I engage in fights with my peers. I was just academically straggling. By the time I entered high school, it appeared that I was well on my way to lasting academic failure. But then a funny thing happened in the middle of my freshman year.

Although blessed with a good head for mathematics, inasmuch as I was able to multiply and divide quicker than most, I was miserably failing my algebra class. The teacher, Mr. Wilson, was a numbers-crunching drone who instilled in me nothing more than an escalating disinterest in triangles and parabolas. In danger of getting an F for the semester, I sought private lessons from a tutor to make a last ditch effort to pass the course. The academics office told me that a certain Mr. Dowmay, another algebra teacher who taught the same courses as Mr. Wilson, offered private lessons.

Mr. Dowmay would become the first person in life whom I truly had respect for. He was a cherubic character in his sixties with wispy gray hair scattered across his crown. It was evident to him after fifteen minutes that I was perfectly capable of grasping even complicated algebra problems.

"Your problem isn't with your algebra, son," he said sympathetically. "It's with your teacher."

I was shocked hearing one teacher speaking derogatorily of another, but Mr. Dowmay's tenure at the school was such that he could say what he wanted about whom he wanted without backlash. He let me know that in his opinion Mr. Wilson was more akin to a bookkeeper than a high school mathematics teacher. We shared a nice laugh together then got down to business.

Mr. Dowmay actually got me interested in right angles and the Pythagorean Theorem. With pedagogic ease he prepped me for the final exam. We went through the entire semester's work in three weeks, after which he gave me the same exam he planned for his own students at the end of the course. I did well enough for him to guarantee that with continued hard work and studying I would fare just the same on my test in Wilson's class.

I did. I got a B on the final exam and a C-minus for the course. When I came in to give Mr. Dowmay the good news, he floored me with his suggestion that I request a transfer to his class for the spring semester. I had often thought how I'd like to be in his class, but figured I was stuck in Wilson's for the entire school year. Mr. Dowmay promised that he'd put in the good word for me with the principal.

My transfer into his class was approved, and I fit right in. One thing Mr. Dowmay did that was peculiar among high school teachers was to post student rankings for his classes on the bulletin board in front of the classroom. The way college football and basketball teams were ranked by sportswriters, math students were ranked by Mr. Dowmay. He did this as a way of motivating his students, and it worked.

His math course consisted of two weekly quizzes, two tests and a final exam. The way he arrived at a final grade was through a weighted process encompassing the three forms. A test was worth three quizzes. The final exam was worth three tests. After each quiz, and test, Mr. Dowmay posted the class rankings. Then after the final exam, he posted the final rankings.

The first four weeks of the semester, I made two Bs and an A on the quizzes and a B on the test. By that time, I was ranked seventh out of twenty-five. At mid-semester, I had climbed to third place. After the final exam, which I aced, I ranked second in Mr. Dowmay's class and received my first ever A for a school course.

He congratulated me and said it was a pleasure having me in his class. I grew very fond of him. I secretly wished he were my father. He certainly seemed more interested in my life than my real father did. He was curious about my activities outside of class and often asked which sports I liked and which TV shows I watched. He encouraged me to play varsity sports. I made the football team but later quit after a dispute with the coach, who, in a move of blatant nepotism, ousted me as quarterback to install his son as leader of the team.

I was very upset about that and was only rebuked by my father, who said that's the way life was and you couldn't rebel. Dowmay, on the other hand, commiserated with my situation and said if I wasn't comfortable with being benched in favor of a much weaker player, then I should feel free to quit.

Academically, I underwent a complete metamorphosis during my sophomore year. Not only did I receive an A and become ranked number one in Dowmay's class, I aced all my other classes as well. On my way up I bypassed the student honor roll and found myself listed on the high honor roll, a mark of distinction attained by just fourteen of three hundred in my undergraduate class. I even received special awards in math and history.

I really felt great about my sudden academic achievements. The booster was occupying the top rank in Dowmay's class. If my life had been errant and out of control, now it had purpose.

In my junior year of high school, I continued to excel. I again headed Dowmay's class and made the high honor roll. That summer, I got a part-time job delivering newspapers. My parents were of course proud of my turnaround, but my father still seemed more intent on spending time in church groups and attending municipal meetings than on taking an interest in me.

But by then I had grown used to my father's lack of interest and my mother's lack of being interesting. I looked upon Mr. Dowmay as a father figure. As long as he remained interested in my life's progress, I was happy. The relationship I maintained with my mother had gravitated to obligatory respect on my part. She was a faithful wife and a good mother. She cooked meals five nights a week and went willingly to church with my father. I tagged along, but with great reluctance. I had passion for sports, not religion.

Tragedy struck the first day of my senior year. I learned that Mr. Dowmay had been killed in a boating accident on Labor Day. I was devastated. The first immediate effect of his death was that it alienated me more from my father. However, I didn't tell my parents about his death. I kept it to myself. In fact, my parents never knew of the adoration I had for my math teacher.

The long-term effects Mr. Dowmay's death would have on me manifested just a few weeks into the semester. Previously, my experience with drugs had been limited to smoking a few joints at parties with friends. I had never gotten into the teenage reefer culture. But as I saw myself grow increasingly depressed and restless, I began getting high on a regular basis.

My grades got lower as I got higher. At the end of my first senior semester, I fell off the honor roll. In the spring semester, my grades dropped so severely that I had to resort to cheating and plagiarism to qualify for graduation. The plagiarism backfired on me. The term paper I handed in to my history professor was taken almost verbatim from an encyclopedia. He caught me. In spite of my admission of guilt, the guy was a real prick and did everything in his power to prevent me from graduating. He told the principal that in his twenty-five years of teaching, he had never seen such a flagrant case. The principal turned out to be a decent guy. He allowed me to repeat the history course during the summer session at a neighboring high school. I ended up graduating by the skin of my teeth. It was my total cumulative grade point average along with high SAT scores that got me into Berkeley.

By the time I got there, my head was screwed back on well enough to easily handle my curriculum. My grade point average the first semester was 3.5, but I had trouble staying interested in the classes. The only aspect of college life that kept me at Berkeley was the partying and sex. I felt myself turning more and more away from the conformist environment in which I'd been raised. While I still overachieved in classes, eventually earning a degree in business administration, my heart was never in it. I couldn't see myself working in the corporate world as an accountant or in any traditional job in the closed-down environment of an office. The pot smoking that had started in high school led to a few experiments with harder stuff at Berkeley. Though I had means and opportunity, I never did get hooked on any dangerous substances.

Boredom and the lure of excitement put the idea for the first scam in my head. I had some friends at Berkeley who came from New York and often went to Florida during winter and spring breaks. Some returned with stories of getting "bumped" off airline flights for which they had legitimate reservations. In many cases, vacations got fouled up. On the other end, people missed work on their way back home.

Airlines routinely overbooked their flights. Then when more people showed up at the gate to board the plane than there were seats for, they bumped the excess passengers. Popular routes were much more susceptible to this unfortunate occurrence at peak seasonal times.

The most common were those including the New York and southern Florida airports as either points of departure or destination. The times of year this happened were Christmas and Easter breaks. Airlines routinely overbooked these flights by as much as 25 percent to make sure none of their planes took off with empty seats. The result of this at departure gates was to send hordes of ordinarily civilized people into frenzies of violent agitation when they realized their planes were leaving without them. The chaos intensified when stranded passengers further realized that they might be stuck hours or even days at the airport because hotels were also overbooking with the same holiday spirit.

To deal with the hysteria, airlines adopted the practice of enticing volunteers to forfeit their seats and leave on a later flight. To make that inconvenience attractive, they offered a free round-trip ticket between any domestic cities their airlines serviced that was valid for a year. When I heard about this compensation for people bumped off flights, I figured I'd drop out of college to become a professional "bumpee."

Well, I didn't really have to drop out. All I needed to do was sacrifice California girls and beaches during those vacations and head east and south, or south and east. In the back of my mind were images of even better vacations I might take with those bumpee free round-trip tickets. Domestic cities serviced by American carriers, I soon learned, included those in Puerto Rico and Hawaii.

A major difference in how airlines booked reservations and sold tickets back then was that you didn't have to guarantee a reservation with a credit card for the airline to hold it for you. All you had to do was make it. By calling any airline's 800-number, you could give the agent the days, times and places you wanted to go. If they were available, the agent booked the trip and gave you the confirmation number. You wouldn't have to pay for the ticket until checking in at the airport.

On Christmas Day of my sophomore year at Berkeley, I flew from San Francisco to Miami. I had a thousand bucks in cash I'd made scalping tickets for Oakland Raiders football games. I'd decided that more bumping would happen in Florida's airports with the New Year's rush to get back to New York than in New York's airports during the pre-Christmas mass departure. I had no trouble getting a seat on a Christmas Day flight, as it's historically the calm in turbulent late-December air travel. The only setback was that the New Year's rush back to New York would not commence until January 2. I would have to kill a week at my expense. If my little venture failed to produce, I'd be out the thousand bucks and maybe not even have enough cash to get back to Berkeley.

I found the cheapest room in the cheapest fleabag hotel in Fort Lauderdale. All I needed was a bed and a phone. During the day, I hung out at the beach. At night, I hit the bars along the strip. The first two days there, I made a hundred phone calls from my room. They were all to airlines' 800-numbers. I had a hundred reservations in a hundred different names to confirm. They were all neatly printed on two sheets of paper from my college economics notebook. I had made those reservations in August, just before the fall semester, and repeatedly confirmed them so they wouldn't be wiped out of the system. Each reservation was for a flight that departed from either Miami or Fort Lauderdale. Each flight landed at JFK, LaGuardia or Newark.

A Wild Ride with the World's #1 Identity Thief

The days of departure were the second, third and fourth of January.

At eight o'clock in the morning on January 2, I arrived at the Miami airport. I proceeded directly to the gate. At that time, anyone could pass freely through the metal detector at the checkpoint and head to the gates. No boarding pass had to be shown. My first reservation of the day was an Eastern Airlines flight leaving for Newark at eight thirty. There was a throng of people gathered in the lounge, but I saw immediately that this flight was not overbooked. The first boarding call had been made and nobody among the crowd seemed upset.

At ten o'clock, I sat in the waiting lounge of a National Airlines flight bound for LaGuardia. The plane was leaving at a quarter after ten, and there'd been no boarding call. This was a good sign. People were restless and uneasy, pacing around and bickering amongst themselves. It was already apparent there would be trouble. By ten twenty, the lounge bore the sights and sounds of utter confusion. Everyone from spring-breakers to retirees engaged in pushing and shoving matches in their desperation to get to the counter and demand to know from the personnel what was going on with the flight. Obscenities hurtled through the air, and in some ugly moments physical altercations broke out.

Finally, after a spate of announcements that only further confused the situation, an airline official blurted out over the mike that the flight was overbooked and there weren't enough seats to go around. There was a thunderous roar of discontent during which every curse word imaginable was uttered against National Airlines. The man's voice (a woman's might not have been able to raise itself above the pandemonium) pleaded with the mass of malcontents to remain orderly. Then he made the announcement I was waiting to hear: Anyone willing to accept a later flight would be awarded a free round-trip air coupon that was valid for one year and could be used between any cities National serviced in the United States and its territories.

Jump-starting toward the counter, I wasn't thinking about a vacation in the Virgin Islands but rather the person who would take it in my place. When I got to the representative, she asked for my name.

"Harvey Connelly," I said.

"Can I have your ticket?"

"I didn't get a chance to purchase it. The line was too long. But I do have a confirmed reservation."

She showed a tinge of annoyance as she pecked her keyboard. It disappeared when Mr. Connelly's reservation flashed on her screen. "Yes,

Mr. Connelly, I have it. There's a flight leaving this evening at nine thirty. But it's to JFK. Would that be satisfactory?"

"Not really," I said with feigned irritation. "But I guess I have no choice."

Without comment she issued my ticket. Then she slipped the bonus coupon inside the packet. She thanked me and smiled.

I smiled, too, but it was more an expression of relief. The one flaw in my plan, not having ID in Connelly's name, was overlooked simply because airline representatives, harried by all this unpleasantness, did not have the time to ask for it. People behind me were pressing to get their flight coupons.

In a sense, I had committed an identity theft, but not really, as I had invented the name Harvey Connelly. In spite of that, maybe it was an omen of what would come later in my life.

By eleven thirty, at gate A-14, I was in a Northeast Airlines lounge looking through the glass at the airplane attached to the accordion end of a jetway ramp. That one was leaving at five past twelve for JFK. I got bumped and picked up another free round-trip coupon and a ticket for a later flight to JFK. I had a thought of trying to sell the ticket for the JFK flight, which of course I would not be on, but that was too dangerous. Instead, I moved along the concourse two gates down to A-16. I picked up my third coupon for the day, got a quick bite to eat at a Wendy's, and continued on.

That afternoon brought the day's total coupons to eight. I had been booked on twenty-three flights leaving Miami that day, but there was no way I could make all the gates on time. After another fast-food dinner, I found myself at an Eastern gate so crowded that the lines of disgruntled passengers spilled into the concourse. The flight looked like it might be delayed two hours before the officials got it straightened out. Taking that into account, I made my first business decision. It was better to let that one go and scoot over to a Delta flight on the other end of the concourse but still in the same terminal. It proved to be a good decision, as the flight was just overbooked by a few seats and took off nearly on time. I got my coupon and then hooked two more from Northeast before calling it a night. I taxied back to the fleabag with eleven round-trip coupons.

The next day, January 3, I hit the Fort Lauderdale Airport. The morning went as smooth as the previous day. I waited for the announcements at the gates, got bumped and picked up my coupons. As I progressed, I became more and more enamored by the scam. It was proving to be a huge success. Not one time was I asked for ID. Not one time was I regarded with suspicion.

The airline reps at the counters were just too busy and under constant pressure to assuage angry passengers.

That night in Miami, however, my feathers got ruffled. I was standing at the counter of an overbooked Eastern flight when the agent printing out my coupon suddenly stopped and said, "Didn't I see you getting bumped from this same flight yesterday?"

The bump in my throat must have been the size of a frog. I had indeed been bumped off the same flight the night before, but it had not departed from the same gate, therefore, I didn't make the connection. The only one my brain had to make now was to come up with a suitable answer. A bunch of replies in bits and pieces flashed through my mind. Finally I said, "I got bumped again." I couldn't come up with anything else.

The guy had a bemused expression on his face. I read it well. The thought in his head was that the occurrence of a person being bumped from consecutive flights was rare. The airlines must have had some sort of boarding procedure preferential to passengers who'd been bumped from one flight to make sure they weren't bumped again. Naturally they didn't want to deal with double-bumpees who might be prone to strangle them.

My only way out was through comedy, so I said to the guy, "It just hasn't been my day. I also got bumped off my hotel room."

He cracked up and then apologized. But I was the least sorry person in the world. I got my coupon and promised him I'd do my best not to get bumped again. But I did so three more times before the night was over.

The next morning back at the Fort Lauderdale Airport, something weird occurred. While sitting in the Delta Lounge waiting to get bumped, my eyes fell upon a man I thought I'd recognized from another lounge in the same airport. He was seated across from me and had no hand-carry items in front of him. He dressed like Joe Tourist. I suspected he was undercover security and had gotten on to me. He may have been following me from gate to gate. My next gate, I thought grimly, might be made of solid steel bars.

We made eye contact a few times, which only increased my anxiety. Who was this guy? Then I heard my assumed name announced over the mike. They were ready to book me on a later flight and issue my flight coupon.

Should I go for it? Or should I get the hell out of there and quit while ahead?

It was my nature to go for it, so I did. I approached the counter uneasily. Just before I got there, I turned sharply around to see if the guy was watching me. I caught his head snapping back as if he didn't want me to know he'd been watching. I had another second thought about going through with it, but I couldn't refuse the free voucher. I reassured myself that if caught I'd be a first-time offender and get off easy.

I received my voucher and left the gate. When I passed by the guy, he was reading a newspaper. When I turned around sharply before disappearing from his sight, he was still ostensibly immersed in the paper. Unless there were others surveying me, I was not being followed.

I still had several reservations left in the Lauderdale airport. But I also had a dozen that afternoon in Miami. I decided to make the hour trip south and arrived at the Miami terminal by two in the afternoon. I had picked up three more flight vouchers by the time I was seated at the gate of a Northeast flight to LaGuardia. The plane was leaving in a half hour at 5:30.

My world got rocked when I looked at the person taking the seat beside me. It was him! The same guy who'd been seated across from me at the gate at the Fort Lauderdale airport. Now three hours later he's sitting next to me at a gate in the Miami airport. Either this guy was some kind of Houdini or he'd followed me.

On second thought, he followed me. He'd *been* following me. The guy was an undercover cop. I guessed that meant it was time to display my wrists so he could lock the cuffs on me. I just hoped I'd get out of jail before I was due to graduate from Berkeley.

Suddenly he spoke. His words confused the fuck out of me. "Guess you and I are doing the same thing," he said.

What registered was that he meant we were both frequent flyers. "How's that?" I wondered aloud.

"Well, I saw you collect five round-trip flight coupons in three hours."

"So?"

"Congratulations, pal. That's one more than me."

It finally hit home. "I thought you were a goddamn undercover cop."

He laughed. "I've been doing this for years. First time I've run into competition."

So the guy was a real professional bumpee.

"You ever try it on the other end?" he asked.

"What do you mean?"

"The New York airports. They're good on the flights down here. Not *as* good, but good."

"To be honest with you, this is my first time doing this." I wasn't sure why I was being honest with him.

"I'll tell you what," he said. "I've got a few more coupons to get. Why don't we meet later and have a drink?"

For some reason I was drawn to this guy. I didn't know him from Adam, but if he was running around airports scamming free tickets, then he had to be my type of guy. "Where?"

"Where are you staying?"

"I'm at a fleabag in Lauderdale called the Beachcomber."

He laughed.

"Don't tell me that's where you're staying."

"Hardly, but I know the joint. I've been coming down here long enough."

"You're from New York." It wasn't a question. His brogue was as New York as my rebelliousness was Berkeley.

He extended his hand, and we shook firmly. "My name is Ike," he said. "But my friends call me Bones."

I didn't ask it then, and never would. "Okay, Bones, let's go have a drink."

So that's how I met Bones. We shot pool that night at a dive called the Elbow Room. Bones bought all the beers. He told me with absolute frankness that he was a lifelong hustler now in need of a partner. When he heard I was a student at Berkeley, he laughed and asked if I had any weed. It so happened that I'd copped some from a guy on the beach. We ended up taking a stroll down the beach behind the Elbow Room, Bones imparting a heck of a lot about himself to a complete stranger.

It turned out that he was once a stockbroker and even had his own consulting business. But he always had side action as a thief. By the time he hit thirty, he said, he cashed out his business and hit the road as a full-time thief. He didn't go into details on what kind of thief he was, but I sensed it was not the violent type, which appealed to me. He said he'd tell me more the next time we met up. Then, in the same breath, he proposed that this next time be at Newark Airport at the start of Easter Vacation, when the airports were hopping with action. I gave him my phone number at Berkeley. I told him I would fly to Newark.

"You make a hundred reservations," he said. "I'll make a hundred reservations. Then together we'll kick some ass."

I got back to Berkeley with twenty-seven round-trip air coupons courtesy of four major airlines. Before registering for the spring semester, I took out a classified ad in the "travel" column of San Francisco's and Oakland's largest-circulating newspapers. It read, simply: "Round trip tickets, anywhere in US and territories, valid one year, $300."

Two factors concerning domestic US air travel that no longer exist today made the selling of my air coupons for $300 practical. The first was that I had amassed those coupons before the government's 1978 deregulation of commercial airlines. Airfares were at an all-time high, and discounted round-trip tickets were in extremely high demand, especially those with unrestricted destinations.

The second, even more crucial factor, was that in the mid-seventies, airline counter agents never asked for proof of ID to board domestic flights. This meant that passengers could fly not only under assumed names but also with someone else's ticket. Airlines strictly forbade transferring of airline tickets, but doing so without demanding proof of ID was like asking people to honestly report income with immunity from IRS audits. I priced round-trip airfares on common routes and found that, even with substantial advance-purchase time, the average was more than $500. I concluded that my twenty-seven round-trip coupons to everywhere should sell like hotcakes.

They did. The ad came out the following Sunday in both papers. By nightfall the next Sunday, all twenty-seven tickets were gone and $8,100 was in my pocket. That's not bad for a nineteen-year-old pothead from Berkeley.

Bones called me a week later. He grudgingly admitted that he'd returned to New York with fewer coupons than I had to California, but he swore that his turned in to $11,000 in cash.

"How'd you manage that?" I asked him.

"You sold yours too cheap. You could've have gotten four hundred each. Piece of cake."

"Sure, but I'm not in New York. It's not the same market."

"With air tickets it is," Bones insisted. "They're like blue-chip stocks. Everyone buys them."

That was the first of many financial lessons I learned from Bones. After we met up in Newark and said goodbye in Miami, *I* proved him right. I arrived back at Berkeley with sixty-four tickets! I put the same ad in the newspapers but asked $400. Only a few people tried to bargain. I ended up with $23,000. That's practically $360 per voucher.

Spring break at the airports had been as hectic as Fort Lauderdale's streets teeming with drunk and disorderly college kids. Bones and I had worked together like well-oiled machinery. He taught me how to watch departure screens and catch certain flight-status movements that indicated which flights were more prone to be overbooked. Then we selected the right ones and split up departure gates so we would not overlap, and get the most flights in the least time possible. Since we both had reservations on nearly all the same flights, we had optimum flexibility in how we wanted to work them.

We did the airline scam every winter and spring break until deregulation hampered us in 1978. At about the same time, the airlines themselves became more stringent with their reservation requirements. They still were not checking IDs, but what hindered us was that they started to only guarantee reservations if you prepaid. Unless you were willing to give your credit card number over the phone, or pay cash at an authorized airline ticket counter or travel agent, you could no longer book a reservation. Thus the airline scam, which had proved to be a fast and safe way to steal money, met its demise.

With a Bachelor of Science degree in business administration in hand, I was recruited not by a *Fortune* 500 company, but rather by a suave hustler from New York named Bones. I have often heard it said that a large percentage of college graduates go on to professions for which their degrees are meaningless. In my case, the maxim couldn't be truer. Here I was, a graduate from a famous, if not a 100 percent reputable American institution, and my first job was stealing merchandise out of one department store and then refunding it back to other stores in the same chain.

That was how I made my living for two years. Bones and I traveled throughout California and the Southwest, entering department stores in broad daylight, carrying racks of clothing and other assorted merchandise out the door, loading it into a van, and disappearing as though we'd never been there. This was all possible because Bones had lots of experience in the field. He taught me what I needed to know about lifting merchandise and whatever else was necessary to a successful professional shoplifting operation. The beauty of it was that when we refunded the goods with phony receipts, not only were we reimbursed the full ticket price for each item, but we also reclaimed the sales tax!

Our next daredevil exploits were performed inside the country's chicest jewelry shops. Posing as a rich kid with money to burn, I would enter these shops in affluent locales such as Rodeo Drive in Beverly Hills. Preying upon the greed of jewelers eyeing hefty profits through sales of excessively marked-up merchandise, I would entice them to put the gems in my hand and then simply run out the door. Our trick was to hire prostitutes dressed up as fashionable ladies to appear outside the shops at the moment of truth. The jewelers, secure in the security of their locked doors, did not hesitate to display their highest quality diamonds and emeralds at arm's length. But then the woman would show up and ring the buzzer. Once the jeweler pressed the button to unlock the door for her, I grabbed the stones and fled the store, trotting a few blocks to where Bones waited in our getaway car.

We did that a dozen times. We had a couple of close shaves, one actual police chase through the streets of San Francisco, but came away unscathed. It was after that spree through the jewelry stores that Bones and I cooled it for a few years. We both settled in San Diego, where I soon met Robin. Had it not been for Robin's whimsical desire to migrate to Taos, New Mexico, I might have eventually become an accountant instead of an identity thief.

Expansion

California and Mexico, 1992-1993

IF HERBERT TRUMM HAD BEEN A GOOD LEADOFF HITTER FOR our identity theft team, then Leonard Bloom, Dominick Morra and Arthur Carlson would soon prove to be excellent second, third and cleanup hitters for our lineup. At least it appeared that way when judging by the responses to their first batch of credit applications.

Robin had run TRW credit reports on all three. As expected, each had stellar credit. We had applied to the same fifteen banks for Visa and MasterCards in each of their names, then to the same fifteen department stores for charge cards. The only significant change made to the applications was the increase of the applicants' salaries to $500,000.

But before those applications had gone out, Bones and I had done massive amounts of work, constantly scrambling, innovating and double and triple checking to make it all possible. We were now working with three new identities at once. The difficulties in managing that were not simply three times greater; they were exponential. Tremendous care was needed to coordinate them. Things got overlooked; things got confused and mixed up; things sometimes got out of hand. We had to do lots of patchwork in order to avoid having the whole thing explode in our faces.

The first problem to tackle was establishing residences for the three men. We would have liked to move them all into the scam house on Encino Lane, where they would undoubtedly get along just swell with each other and their roommate Herbert Trumm, but this was not possible. We could not have four people with the same address applying to the same fifteen banks and department stores at the same time. That would be tantamount to holding up Fort Knox with a squirt gun.

We tossed around several ideas and theories on how to avoid renting three different houses. None were feasible. We were forced to endure the time and expense of starting up and maintaining three new scam houses in the San Diego area. We were loath to do so, but it had to be that way in order to have the credit cards delivered. If only banks delivered them to post office boxes, we would have saved a fortune.

Two of the three new scam houses we rented directly from the owners. Bones met with one as Leonard Bloom, the other as Dominick Morra. We had obtained their ID documents through the same channels we'd navigated with Trumm. Bones visited two San Diego County California DMV offices, took the written test, passed the road test and had his thumbprint and photo taken, the latter of which was laminated on the licenses in Bloom's and Morra's names. A trip was taken to the Los Angeles passport office, where Bones obtained his US passport in Bloom's name. The office was too small to attempt getting one in Morra's name as well. We had to stagger securing the passports with successive trips to Los Angeles, and make sure Bones did not run into the same clerk who'd previously handled his application in another name. This delay in obtaining passports was not a serious matter, as we'd learned the banks accepted Social Security cards as the second piece of ID required for opening new accounts.

The first scam house was in Point Loma, not far from Mission Bay. We rented it from an elderly Hawaiian couple who'd moved to San Diego to be near their grandson who was stationed at the Point Loma Naval Station. Bones told me the elderly gentleman was so nice it seemed he hardly cared about any of the details pertaining to the lease. He only wanted to talk about the old TV series *Hawaii Five-O*, which Bones assured him he'd never missed. Had it not been for the man's wife, Bones said, we might have had that house rent-free.

The second scam house, which we rented in Hillcrest, a trendy San Diego quarter not far from downtown, was actually an apartment. We'd decided that apartments could serve as scam houses as long as we didn't draw unnecessary attention to ourselves. To furnish them we bought up junk furniture at garage sales and flea markets, which cost next to nothing. For a few hundred bucks we could decorate an entire scam apartment.

Hillcrest happened to be home to the city's gay community. This had no bearing on our business, for gay neighbors were no nosier than straight ones, but I did kid Bones that a lot of young hunks in the area might find him attractive—no matter what identity he used. The owner of the house was a woman and apparently not gay. She was the first landlord who asked Bones to pay the rent directly into her bank account. The others had simply directed him to mail them a check. She gave Bones a booklet of deposit slips and let him know that the Bank of America branch at which she banked was right around the corner. Bones made sure to let her know that he banked at Bank of America as well.

The scam house for Arthur Carlson, whose photo ID was manufactured at yet another San Diego County DMV, was situated in a middle-class area called Clairemont, to the east of Interstate 5 between downtown and La Jolla. It was brokered by a no-nonsense real estate agent named Clay Thome who Bones felt had been a little suspicious. In the course of conversation, Thome had asked Bones if he was married. Bones said he wasn't, but later suffered a mental lapse in mentioning that "my wife is a big part of my business." Thome caught on and didn't let it go. He reminded Bones that he'd said he was unmarried. Bones laughed it off and covered it up by saying he was referring to his ex-wife. The real estate guy didn't seem to buy it. Bones told me that he'd considered dropping the whole deal, but it had proved tough enough procuring scam houses, and applications, which couldn't be completed without a home address, were waiting to go out. Ultimately, Arthur Carlson's credit rating would have to quell any further investigation on Thome's part. It was AAA, and the bottom line for Thome or any other real estate agent was always commissions earned.

We now had four scam houses. Each was close enough to the next so we could pass by all four within an hour. Our personal apartments were to the north but not more than twenty-five miles from any scam house. This was ideal. Each day I made the circuitous run to check the mail. Two of the houses didn't have mail slots built into the door, but this was no longer of importance. Since we made a strict routine of consistently checking the mail at each house, there was never the chance of mail accumulating beyond the confines of the boxes.

For business names we decided to be a bit more creative than we'd been with "Trumm Enterprises." The fact that Leonard Bloom was a dermatologist made us implement a change right away. We felt it unwise to establish him in San Diego as a dermatologist. The main problem would be when bank credit departments began calling for verifications. Doctors' offices had a certain aura about them when you telephoned. Certain words were said, certain attitudes conveyed. We weren't sure if Barbara and her crew at ABC could convincingly front a dermatologist's office. And then, who would call back the bank to give that reference? With businesses there was always Mr. So-and-So who handled those affairs. But for a doctor? Suppose the banks wanted to speak with Dr. Bloom's accountant? It could get rather sticky and invited the opportunity for fuckups.

Another concern was the potential for problems with medical and dermatological associations. The boards of these associations might go looking for our renowned dermatologist to address a skin-cancer symposium. Or some other ADA gig somewhere in San Diego might want Bloom to speak about his latest hair-transplant technology. Thinking about such mishaps threatened to make my own hair fall out!

Our decision was to make Leonard Bloom the president of "Bloom Associates." His business would be as far from dermatology as you could get: a TV production company making documentaries. That's only if anyone asked. Neither Bloom nor his associates would ever have a camera.

In choosing a fictitious business and its name, it was important to choose one that did not draw too much "foot traffic." We didn't want the answering service to get swamped with callers asking about the new business. For example, had we assigned Bloom's company the name "Bloom's Travel Services," we might have hundreds of people calling every day to book vacations. Or if we used "Bloom's Restaurant Supplies," legitimate San Diego restaurateurs might begin making inquiries as to whether we could supply broilers and ovens cheaper than their current suppliers. The idea was to select a name that sounded as generic and meaningless as possible. Only the answering service had to be satisfied with the information on the companies. Bones and I would call several times a day, disguising our voices to give the people answering the impression a legitimate business was behind it.

Another touchy issue was the use of that answering service itself. ABC was already handling the phones for Trumm Enterprises. Mr. Trumm was, of course, none other than Bones. Since each potential client had to present identification in order to be accepted, Bones could not return to ABC as Mr.

Bloom or Mr. Morra. But then how could we get ABC to answer the phones for both those gentlemen's businesses?

We pondered moving on and hiring new answering services for each concern. But before doing that I suggested to Bones that we try a little trick. Why not call ABC and tell the owner that "I am going to be relocating my business to San Diego next month, but I want to establish phone communication there immediately. I'll send you a money order for three months of service, and upon my arrival in town I will give you my ID documents, which you can photocopy for your files?" If it didn't work, we'd raise the bar to an advance payment for six months of service, whatever it took to hook them. The service for each line only cost thirty bucks a month. What did we care?

ABC didn't care either. Its owner gladly agreed to our terms, and we sent out postal money orders in payment for the future lines. Soon ABC would be handling phone communications for four of our entities. When all four operations were over, we would cease using ABC, for the heat from our bogus enterprises would eventually lead back there.

Our attorney, Dominick Morra, was also going to make a midlife career change. We didn't want any criminal defendants calling upon Morra for his legal services, which, if they went wrong, might lead to two brand new criminal defendants in a much bigger case, namely Bones and myself. Nor did we want any dealings with the California Bar Association and other legal entities that might make inquiries into Morra's practice. We basically saw Morra's legal background as problematic as Bloom's medical one.

We made Morra a professional sports agent, a great choice because that real business was controlled by a select group of major agents. Clients came to them by word of mouth from athlete to athlete or by general reputation. People would not be calling the answering service out of the blue looking for representation to the San Diego Chargers football team.

Arthur Carlson was a big mover and shaker in the Midwest manufacturing trade. Instead of removing him from his line of business, we would reduce the size of his operation. Carlson Manufacturing would become the AC Manufacturing Company. This would look good to banks since AC obviously stood for Arthur Carlson. Credit department reviewers would surmise that the businessman new to California wanted his West Coast branch's name to differ from his mainstay Chicago operation, but not by that much. Plus "AC" had a catchy ring to it, like when people used those letters to refer to Atlantic City.

Everything was properly set up to move forward with the three-man scam. We now only had to wait for the results of the applications we'd sent out. We were anxious but more than cautiously optimistic. As the Trumm phase of the operation was so successful, there was no reason to think this second phase wouldn't be even more so. We had been better organized and more knowledgeable in its preparation.

It soon showed. The three-man wave of credit and store cards to hit the new scam houses was a certifiable tsunami! Whereas Trumm's initial credit card bullion melted down into nearly $60,000 in cash, each of our three new identities promised future cash rewards greater than that. The true cleanup hitter of the trio was Arthur Carlson, our manufacturer. The Banks flooded his mailbox with nine Visas and five MasterCards totaling $95,000 in credit. None of them had a limit less than $5,000. Had the lone bank denial been a credit card, Carlson's major bank card total would have reached a hundred grand.

All fifteen department stores came through with charge cards. Again Neiman Marcus topped the credit list with $10,000. Saks Fifth Avenue joined them, another ten grand. Carlson was also a hit with the oil companies, especially with Exxon whose credit department gave him $3,500. That very day we purchased new tires from an Exxon station for all our personal cars. Robin's tires were fairly new, so we just stored her future set in the garage of Trumm's scam house.

If Carlson was the tectonic plate that set off the credit tsunami, Bloom and Morra were certainly the swirling force that drove it inland. Bloom connected on twelve bank cards with three denials for $75,000 of credit, while Morra was good for eleven cards with four denials totaling $70,000. Each went a perfect fifteen for fifteen in the department stores.

The similar success rates for all three showed us how accurate our forecasting had been. The blue and red volumes of *Marquis Who's Who* were truly an elixir to the business. At that early stage, with just four men selected from its pages, we were able to ascertain that the overall creditworthiness of the tens of thousands of names in the volumes was close to 100 percent! What that meant, and it was mind-boggling when we stopped to think about it, was that every person on those pages was worth somewhere between $75,000 and $100,000 in cash, and at least that much in retail value of assorted merchandise. This was an infinite gold mine with enough reserves to keep us stewing in stolen credit for a millennium, notwithstanding the new fat cats with spotless credit added to the tomes each year.

The revelations aside, it was time to go to work and turn the cash—wheelbarrows of it. We went back to the Comchek machines, but not just in Vegas. This time we launched a full-scale assault that would carry over into the next hundred identities we stole. We visited California's racetracks, where machines were adjacent to the betting windows on every floor. Del Mar, just north of San Diego, was first on the list. On the ground floor, Bones pulled out his wallet and removed a $5,000 Visa in Carlson's name. He entered the card, spoke with the live operator, then went to the cashier and collected $4,500 cash. In the mezzanine, he repeated the process with one of Bloom's cards, disguising his voice on the phone with the operator. Not that it was likely the same operator who would be on the line. Bones just played it safe.

The next level up, Bones got Comchek for another $4,500. This time the card used belonged to Dominick Morra. I thought we were done, but then we paid five bucks each to gain entry to the clubhouse. That additional $10 expenditure brought dividends of $4,500 more, as Bones cashed out through Comchek a fourth time. The operator commented on Carlson's second $4,500 withdrawal. Bones told her he couldn't pick a winner if his life depended on it.

We drove up the freeway to Los Angeles. None of its thoroughbred tracks were open, but the Los Alamitos harness track in Cypress offered the same bank of Comchek machines. We made it in time for the first race. By post-time for the second, we were gone with the cash.

We fought horrendous freeway traffic and finally arrived at the giant Bicycle Club cardroom in Bell Gardens. It was eight o'clock and the cash run was still young. The vast public cardrooms around Los Angeles had Comchek machines next to its cashier cages, just like the casinos in Vegas.

If Bones had reached the highest hurdle of audacity at the racetracks, he cleared the next bar at the Bicycle Club. There were two cashiers: one in the main cardroom, the other in the Asian games room populated by throngs of Chinese playing Pai Gow. I figured Bones would make two withdrawals, one at each cage as Bloom and Carlson. But when he'd finished those, he returned to the Comchek machine near the main cage and went through the process again, as Morra. When he got the okay to go to the cage, I freaked.

"Are you nuts?" I asked him. "You just went to that cage as Leonard Bloom! Not fifteen minutes ago."

"Not to worry," Bones replied coolly. "Just busy the teller I dealt with on Bloom's withdrawal while I go to the other end of the cage to get the cash for Morra."

"The other end of the cage is only twenty feet!" I protested.

Bones looked at it, actually gauging its width with his eyes. "No, it's wider than that, but what does it matter? Just take out the teller. Keep her occupied for three minutes and it will all be over."

"Three minutes? What do you want me to do? Go up there with a hundred one dollar bills and ask her for a hundred dollar bill?" I said this quite sarcastically.

Bones pursed his lips and tilted his head. "Not a bad idea. Stay here, I'll be right back."

He walked off in the direction of the Asian games room. When he came back a few minutes later, he showed me a wrapped packet of one dollar bills, a hundred of them. He tore off the money wrapper and laid the bills in my palm.

"There you go, kid," he said. Then he looked at the main cage, surveyed it for a few seconds. He indicated the woman who'd cashed him out as Bloom. "Okay, get on her line. Keep your eye on me. I'll be on the line at the opposite end of the cage. When you see I've reached the teller, you get the one hundred dollar bill. Spill your ones sloppily on the counter, so she has to take her time gathering them up and counting them. If you get there too soon and see that I'm still on line, just let the person behind you cut in front."

I had to let two people cut in front of me, but it was no skin off my nose. When Bones reached the teller at the other end, I dumped my loosened packet of one dollar bills and said, "Would you be so kind as to give me a one hundred dollar bill?" My voice was charged by the swift, ingratiating tone I'd learned from Bones.

The woman was overtly annoyed. I guessed that maybe one person a year hit their cages looking to exchange a hundred singles for one "Ben Franklin." She gave me a look suggesting I was a mental case, but then got down to the business of scooping up and counting the bills. She didn't count them twice but did tally them slowly and thoroughly. She slipped a new Bicycle Club wrapper on the ones, tossed them in her cash drawer and slapped a hundred dollar bill on the counter. She did not thank me for the transaction.

Backing away, I glanced at the other end of the cage where Bones had been standing. He was gone. I turned my head toward the cardroom. Bones was leaning against a railing overlooking a cluster of poker tables. He had a big smile on his face: mission accomplished.

"You see," he said. "The old college takeout never fails." He was referring to the not very collegiate practice of busying one person in order to put something over on the other. "Now let's go back to the cashier in the Asian room."

I followed him there, and we pulled the $100-exchange trick again. When we walked out the door of the Bicycle Club, we had four more $4,500 cash advances under our belts.

We drove to the other major cardrooms surrounding Los Angeles. In Commerce, we hit the Commerce casino. Next was Hollywood Park casino, another huge poker room adjacent to the racetrack of the same name and the Los Angeles Forum, at the time home to the Lakers basketball team. We made additional cash-mongering rounds through card clubs in Gardenia. We pushed them all to the limit with our three credit card holders. Not once did we take heat, not even a tinge. Bones just kept going to the cages, signing withdrawal slips and collecting the cash.

By night's end we had taken twenty-four cash advances for a total of $108,000. We took a room at a Best Western and hit the sack. We were exhausted. Cash runs like that were not easy work, though we didn't complain. The next morning we had breakfast at an IHOP. The pancakes never tasted so good! And of course Mr. Carlson paid for the $12 check. So were the gas and oil we put into the van his credit card had rented. Anything and everything was paid by the credit cards, no matter how cheap.

We made the rounds through the same card clubs. The tellers Bones had dealt with the night before were not working, so there was no danger of his being recognized as Mr. Bloom while posing as Mr. Morra or Carlson. The day's take was $78,000, giving us $186,000 for twenty-four hours of work. The rest of the cash available on the battalion of credit cards we'd garner from ATMs.

On the way back to San Diego, I was in a subdued state of shock. Cash coming in at such a frightening pace twists reality into a surrealistic state. Staring out the van's window, I wondered about the euphoria people felt upon winning millions of dollars in lotteries. Was it similar to the euphoria I felt now? Granted, I was not the same as the average megabucks winner who, after a lifetime of middle-class income suddenly becomes superrich, but in spite of that, what I'd seen the past month was incredible. In my dreamiest moments I could never fathom nearly $200,000 in such easy pickings over a twenty-four hour period.

But that was not the scary part. What truly threatened my equilibrium and risked cutting me off from reality was the thought that this might go on forever. I was not a greedy person. Although entertaining thoughts about the luxury condominium I would soon buy on the beach and the new Porsche I'd be tooling around in, I was not excessively turned on by money. It was more the seemingly boundless frontiers of the crime that kept me so aloft that I found myself smoking less marijuana than at any time since I'd toked my first joint.

That high is what kept me on track. Each time I felt gripped by fears of getting caught and going to prison, my mind sucked up the soothing belief that I was a master criminal genius who had come up with the best credit fraud ever. My ego had always been in need of nourishment. I really did suck it up when Bones called me a genius. Now I was in the criminal major leagues.

Halfway home, I said to Bones, "What about buying personal stuff with some of this cash?" I was in unfamiliar territory. The money I'd made off the Navajo rugs was only enough to live normally and pay the bills. But now I really wanted to enjoy the fruits of my labor.

"We've got to be careful," Bones said. "The last thing you want to do is something stupid that draws the attention of the IRS."

His point was very well taken. Countless criminals from both collars of crime ended up in prison not for their crimes or their illicit gains but rather because they didn't know how to avoid paying taxes without alerting the IRS.

"The best thing to do is open safe deposit boxes in your real name. Keep the bulk of your cash in them. Keep enough money to live for three or four months hidden in your apartment. That way you won't have to go into your boxes more than you have to."

"What about buying a car?" I asked.

"Depends on the car. I know you like Porsches, but you can't just go out and buy one for cash. Any cash transaction for ten grand or more is automatically reported to the IRS."

"So how are we supposed to live? Like drug dealers?"

"More or less." Bones shrugged.

"So then we're eventually gonna have to get into money laundering and offshore accounts in the Cayman Islands."

Bones chuckled. "I like the Cayman Islands idea better. We might eventually have too much cash to launder."

"Sounds like we have a serious problem."

The conversation turned to Robin. It had already crossed my mind that she could become a serious security risk to the operation. Her end of these profits was $37,000. What would she do with her money? Robin was a compulsive spender. If she liked it, she bought it, no questions asked. I had explained to her not to spend large amounts of cash and not to use her own genuine credit cards excessively since their activity could be monitored by authorities looking for tax-dodgers and criminals, both of which she had become. She agreed to these discretionary tactics.

But what if she saw a car she liked as much as I did Porsches?

My favorite movie is *Goodfellas,* with Ray Liotta and Robert De Niro. Central to the plot is the real-life Lufthansa heist that occurred at Kennedy Airport in 1978, where millions in cash and jewelry were stolen out of the German airline's cargo hold. In the movie, De Niro's gang pulls the heist. Beforehand, he had warned each member to lie low once the booty was split up amongst them. "Don't bring attention to yourselves." But just days after the robbery, one of the gang shows up at their local hangout in a brand new Cadillac while another one's wife struts into the bar wearing an ostentatious mink stole. Upon seeing this, De Niro flips out and severely scolds his gang members.

I envisioned Robin doing something like that. She was certainly not beyond a blatant cash purchase. I would have to drill her on this again and again. My relationship with her was becoming knotty as she'd once again become my lover and was now my business partner. I would have to handle these complexities delicately. There was always the threat that Robin's fickleness might lead her to abandon her job at the leasing company, which would threaten our entire operation.

Back in San Diego, there were no less than two dozen messages on our scam house answering machines—all but one from bank security departments. We painstakingly called each one back and went through the questioning to satisfy their verification procedures. Again, it was the same line of questioning to ascertain that we were the people we claimed to be and had taken the cash advances of our own volition. The key piece of information each time was the mother's maiden name. Once the security person on the line heard it stated correctly, he was satisfied.

I found it amazing how unimaginative these people were. Couldn't any of them conclude that maybe this was a fraud where the perpetrators somehow got hold of the mother's maiden name? Perhaps the answer was that no one cared. It was just a job that each security person satisfied by following procedure.

The one odd call gave us a good laugh. It was from a bank wishing to make an apology to Mr. Carlson. He had applied to it for a Visa card, but the bank regretted that its $10,000 credit line was only available through MasterCard. Would that be okay?

"How insensitive of them," I cracked.

Bones immediately called the bank. He said, "I not only accept your apology but shall gladly accept the MasterCard as well." It turned out to be a $10,000 bonus we'd thought was a denied application.

The phone calls made, we turned our attention to the department stores. Each day, Bones and I hit the road with the van. There was no more personal shopping. Everything was now bought in view of carting it off to Alberto in Mexico. We already had such huge amounts of clothes, electronic equipment and miscellaneous bric-a-brac that it would be at least six months before we'd need to think of replenishing our personal wardrobes or anything else pertaining to our daily lifestyle. However, Robin always found a little something she wanted.

After work at the leasing company, she joined us for the evening runs through the stores. With store cards, there was no problem with each of us shopping individually with different charge cards. Department personnel generally did not care if the name on the card matched the sex of the person using it. If ever questioned, Robin would inform the person asking that she was the missus of the cardholder. In any event, clerks at the register never demanded ID.

In this manner, we blew through their departments like a cyclone, sweeping up everything in our path, loading shopping bag after shopping bag into the van outside. I'd risk saying it was the largest coordinated buy-up operation in department store history, legal or illegal.

At the end of the week, I called Alberto. He was quite interested to hear that we had $100,000 in retail merchandise, all of it designer clothing. I asked him if he could handle it.

"*Claro que sí*," came the response.

Bones and I loaded up the van with big brown garbage bags filled with designer merchandise. Ralph Lauren clothing as usual was the largest component of the shipment. But this time it was 70 percent women's apparel. We also packed Calvin Klein jeans, some expensive numbers from Pucci (about which I'd inquired to ensure Alberto wanted them) and various outfits from Liz Claiborne and Givenchy.

Robin had wanted to come along as she'd expected another trip to Ensenada, but we told her there was no time for pleasure on this trip. Besides, we were crossing into Mexico with $100,000 in ticketed merchandise. If stopped by Mexican customs officials, we'd have some explaining to do and didn't need her around in that instance.

We had discussed this possibility with Alberto. What was the risk of coming into Mexico with a truckload full of goodies?

Alberto had flashed his soft Latin smile. "Don't worry so much for that, *amigo*. They stop very few vehicles, and if they stop yours and send you to *secundario*, you just give them a few pesos."

Secundario was Mexican customs' version of their US counterpart's "secondary," the area to the right of the primary inspection booths where suspicious customs agents directed vehicles for further scrutiny. I, like everyone else who'd ever heard of Mexico, had heard the stories about epidemic levels of corruption within Mexican customs and police departments near the border.

Bones and I discussed it at length. If directed to secondary, we would subtly make it known that cash was available to speed up whatever delay we ran into. We'd also take along the receipts for all merchandise brought into Mexico, which would defeat or at least allay suspicions that the merchandise was stolen or obtained by some other illicit means.

Arriving at the border crossing in San Ysidro, we ran into the Saturday rush of Americans visiting Mexico. Although delays were always considerably worse on the way back into the US, where customs ran every vehicle through its computer and at least asked everyone the purpose of their trip to Mexico, weekend delays inbound to Mexico could be as long as an hour. At the point of entry a Mexican border guard with a thick black moustache who was eating a burrito summarily waved us through. He didn't as much as look at our van as he passed us through. From there, it took just fifteen minutes to get to the main drag and park. We walked to the Ralph Lauren outlet a few blocks away. We wouldn't bring the merchandise until Alberto said to.

Alberto wasn't there. Nina gave us a pleasant smile and said in perfect English, "Alberto is not here. You can bring your merchandise and put it in the storage room."

I didn't know if I was more surprised by Nina's perfect English or Alberto's absence.

"Where is he?" Bones asked. We hoped he was out fetching the $22,000 in US currency to pay for the goods.

Hardly. "He's in Acapulco on holiday."

Again I was hit by a double surprise. Not only was Alberto lying on a beach a thousand miles from where this deal was to go down, but his cousin Nina had been educated somewhere in the United Kingdom. This was evidenced by her usage of the word "holiday" for vacation.

At this point it was no longer necessary to proceed with caution in dealing with Nina. It was obvious that she was an integral player in the underworld dealings of the shop. It became even more obvious when we later learned she actually was the owner of the shop. Alberto was her right-hand man. Whether or not he was really her cousin was of no consequence.

"How are we going to be paid?" Bones asked sharply.

"I will pay you. Now would you please go and get the merchandise? Saturday is a very busy day in this store." Nina was just as succinct as Bones had been.

She instructed us to drive the van right to the storefront to facilitate its unloading. We followed her orders and double-parked it. It took us a bunch of trips to unload it all. Passers-by on the sidewalk didn't think anything out of the ordinary about two gringos hauling giant garbage bags into Tijuana's Ralph Lauren outlet shop. Neither did the customers entering the shop. Neither did the two foot-patrolmen who walked right by us as we dragged bags inside the shop. It wouldn't have surprised me if they'd offered to hold the door open.

When we'd finished, Nina laid a manila envelope stuffed with cash on the counter. There were two customers inside the store but they were either uninterested or didn't notice.

"You're not going to go through the merchandise?" Bones asked her.

"I don't have the time. What is its retail value?"

"A hundred thousand give or take," I said.

Nina nodded at the envelope. "There's twenty-two thousand there. Whatever the give or take is, we can settle it next time. That's if you don't mind running a temporary balance in either favor." Spoken like a true businesswoman, though this kid could not have been eighteen years old.

"Of course," Bones said, slipping the envelope off the counter. "Say hello to Alberto for us, and we'll be in touch soon. *Adiós.*"

"*Adiós.*"

"What was the purpose of your visit to Mexico?" the US customs officer said to Bones from his booth at the re-entry point. Our van was now empty.

"Just hung out and had lunch in Tijuana," Bones said.

"Bringing anything back?"

"Just indigestion."

The customs officer laughed and waved us through.

Explosion
United States, 1993-1994

BY LATE 1993, OUR IDENTITY AND CREDIT-THEFT OPERATION WAS booming like a proud skyscraper guarding a city's skies. This was a fitting analogy because we had expanded to several major cities and our national headquarters was now located in one of those skyscrapers, the Sears Tower in Chicago, which at the time was the tallest structure in the world.

The fraud that had ignited in San Diego blazed through Los Angeles, San Francisco, Phoenix and Denver like a wildfire out of control. Then the firestorm caught wind and burned a swath through banks from Minneapolis all the way to Houston. The major cities of the Eastern Seaboard, including the apple of the world's financial eye, New York, would soon be ours as well. Bones and I had become millionaires and the prefix "multi" would soon be attached.

Dozens of scam houses had been rented, used and discarded. More than a thousand credit and charge cards had surrendered their dignity and coughed up the cash and merchandise. Our wholesaling operation in Mexico was bringing in more than $100,000 a month, and Nina and Alberto only asked for more.

Two new and very innovative facets of our business were born in that time span. The first was Robin's idea. As her job in Taos, New Mexico, had been the gusher that sprung the Navajo rug scam, her current employment had given our identity theft business a major boost. She'd already run hundreds of credit reports on our prospective cardholders from her leasing firm, but doing so, we fathomed, was becoming risky. The sheer volume of these reports coupled with the lack of their subjects' leasing cars did not mix. Her superiors would start wondering why so many wealthy guys with good credit were stopping by their offices, filling out applications, but not signing leasing contracts. We needed another way of getting our hands on TRW credit reports without festering suspicion in a business where suspicion was bred on a moment's notice.

Robin came up with the idea. "Why don't you guys start up your own listing business?" she suggested one night while we barbecued in the back yard of our Phoenix residence, on a grill bought from the house and garden department at Sears. We now maintained a main residence in each of the scam cities from which no criminal activities were conducted. Each one was adequately furnished and decorated thanks to department store charge cards. We had the furniture delivered to one of our scam houses in the same city, then rented a truck to haul it to our residence.

"If you do that," Robin continued, "you'll be able to open up your own account with TRW, have them run credit reports for all your so-called clients."

After dessert, playing eight ball on a beautiful baize pool table purchased with a Big 5 Sporting Goods charge card, we discussed Robin's idea. The more we talked, the more we liked it.

We set down the pool cues and moved into the living room, furnished by the Broadway. A mahogany coffee table with a chessboard top fronted an L-shaped leather sofa. A beautifully lacquered wall unit housed a Sony hi-fi system and was filled with goodies ranging from Lalique crystal pieces to Bavarian Hummels. We sunk into the sofa.

Robin overheard us talking from the kitchen and joined us. "So what do you guys think of my idea?" she asked. "If you do that, I could quit that lousy job at the car-leasing place." She was currently on a week's vacation from it.

"Your idea is feasible," Bones said.

"We're gonna look into it immediately," I added.

A mail-listing business was in fact a great idea. All you did was compile lists for particular industries and send them to clients who wanted them. It was very easy to start up and give the impression that we were really doing business. We decided to start it right in Phoenix. We'd do what any legitimate would-be entrepreneur does: incorporate. We'd use the name of one of our stolen identities whose credit we would not touch. This way the listing business could continue functioning after the Phoenix portion of the scam was over and the scam houses abandoned. We also reasoned that it would be best to include the words "financial services" in whatever business name we chose. The logic was that in granting an account, TRW would impose less scrutiny on an entity engaging in financial services than on a business sending lists through the mail.

We went downtown to the city clerk's office, filled out the necessary forms and selected a business name. The only problem was that the first three we chose were already the names of established businesses. Before you became legally incorporated you had to run a business-name search to make sure the one you wanted to use was not already in existence. After the third name came up taken, I joked to Bones that maybe we ought to try "Identity Theft, Incorporated," as he'd joked on the beach when we'd first conceived the idea.

The name that finally cleared was "Cactus Financial Services." It had a nice ring of legitimacy to it. We paid the $200 fee demanded by the County of Maricopa to incorporate. After the clerk scrutinized Bones's flawless phony ID in the name of Eugene Wells, he proffered our new business certificate—stamped with the official seal of Phoenix, Arizona. We framed it and hung it on the wall behind Bones's office desk in the Phoenix residence.

A few days later, we found a small office for rent on Central Avenue. Mr. Wells signed the lease, and we moved in. We had a phone line installed and the number listed with directory assistance under the business name. Robin played secretary and receptionist. Bones called TRW and gave the required application information over the line. Then we put the Cactus Financial line on call-forward to the house. Each time it rang, Robin answered, "Good day, Cactus Financial Services, how may I direct your call?"

We were now a mail-listing and financial consulting firm, perhaps the only one in history that never had as much as a single client. In spite of that, Cactus Financial Services would become the instrument by which every major American city was ensnared in the nets of our identity theft operation.

TRW was glad to open an account for Cactus Financial. Upon checking up on its CEO, they learned that Eugene Wells was none other than the real CEO of an investment firm in Atlanta. I'd found him in the latest edition of *Who's Who in American Industry and Finance*. TRW's background check revealed that Wells was as respectable as he was financially stable; therefore, it had no qualms about doing business with him.

We did tons of it. Twenty credit reports a month. Never did we get back a bad one. Nothing but super credit ratings and timely payments for gold and platinum credit cards. If the old saying that money doesn't grow on trees was true, so was the new saying: "money *did* grow off the leaves of TRW credit reports."

The formation of Cactus Financial Services gave way to the operation's second innovative idea: form our own businesses across the entire nation for our identity theft operation. Instead of hiring answering services to front as our firms, we would establish real businesses and place our creditworthy applicants in their employ the way experienced headhunters did. Since we had successfully transformed the dermatologist Bloom into a TV producer and the lawyer Morra into a sports agent, we no longer had to rely on the practice of transferring businessmen from the concrete premises of their real companies to our multi-city concoction of phony branches and subsidiaries. We could simply create a new entity in each city, or several of them when needed, and just staff it with creditworthy "transferees" from the *Who's Who* pages. We'd learned that banks were not concerned about changes of location or profession, the latter of which they'd probably never know about anyway.

Soon we opened thirty businesses across the Western and Central United States. We had their presidents, vice presidents and CEOs crisscrossing the country in the mazes of jet routes mapped out in an airline's onboard magazine. Northerners were migrating south like a flock of birds; easterners were going west like a renewed gold rush. We had so many comings and goings we had to be careful of "midair" collisions. Scam houses followed suit. As fast as we paper-transferred these doctors, lawyers and businessmen, we had to find real brick and mortar scam houses for them to inhabit.

How we used these corporations and partnerships was the lifeblood of what became our colossal scam. It was obvious from the start that some air of authenticity had to be bestowed upon our bogus entities. The first things corporations usually have are functioning offices with employees. Not wanting to be noticeably different from any other business enterprise, we set out to do just that. In each city we rented the cheapest office space we could find. We had telephone lines installed, and then added the minimum amount of furniture.

We set out to hire real people to work in each "scam office," mainly women to answer the phones and supply banks and department stores with the verifications they requested. Like in any legitimate business, we would call them receptionist-secretaries to give respectability to the job function.

We placed ads in the Help Wanted sections of the country's newspapers. Bones and I conducted interviews with women who responded in the various cities. We often told them we were a certified public accounting firm whose accountants were always conducting on-the-road field audits. In some cases, we were traveling salesmen. In others, we got diversified and told them we were geologists who were abroad 95 percent of the time on Mideast oil and Australian Barrier Reef expeditions, or owner-operators of a long-distance trucking firm. Anything and everything that gave us the excuse to never be at our home offices. After all, if we didn't play it smart, our "receptionists" would surely start wondering why their bosses were never behind their desks.

In reality, these women were hired for only one—but extremely important—reason: to confirm dates and salaries of employment to bankers who called to verify what we declared to be true on credit applications. If, for example, we applied to a Missouri bank for a Visa in the name of Henry Kurland, the woman in our St. Louis office would be apprised of Kurland's employment with the company. When the banker called asking "Can you tell me how long Mr. Kurland has been with your firm and what his current salary is?" our receptionist would then become the secretary and open the employee file cabinet behind her desk. There she would find Kurland's manila employment folder neatly in line among dozens of others we'd planted in front and behind it to give the appearance we were a large firm with lots of employees. She would relay the information from Kurland's records to the banker, who would be satisfied because it corresponded exactly to what he read off the application. Any further checks made by the banker into our business itself would be satisfied by the Better Business Bureau of that city. We were, in every case, a business in good standing, even if we never did any business.

Just as much as we duped the banks, we had to dupe our real employees, the thirty *honest* women who worked for us. And they were honest, to the best of my knowledge. We didn't just hire anyone. I actually scrutinized *their* employee applications and checked the three references I'd required them to provide me. I spoke with these people on the phone, asked them various questions to assure myself that the women in question were not dishonest or involved in criminal activities. After all, I knew from experience that nearly every major criminal operation is busted for reasons that have nothing to do with the operation itself. With that in mind, I thought that if we hired a doper or some other type of illicit woman, she might lead the cops or FBI right to our office doorstep, especially if she used her *unsupervised* position to deal drugs or conduct other unlawful activities.

Another condition of their employment was that they be dependable. Almost as bad as a banker receiving conflicting information when verifying a credit application was his not being able to verify it at all. If, for instance, a banker called one of our scam offices for verification of an employee's application and received no answer or the continual recorded greeting of an answering machine, he would become negative and sooner or later suspicious. That would not only wipe out the creditworthiness of the candidate in question but also, and of much greater consequence, cast a shroud of doubt on the sham business itself. Such foul-ups would cost us a lot of time and money since we'd spent a significant amount of both to create it.

We were also an equal opportunity employer, and we paid our women well. Ten of the thirty were black or Hispanic; two others were Asian. Each earned $500 per week and none complained about the meager furnishings in her office. We imagined they were quite content with the privacy of their surroundings and the lack of someone watching over their shoulders, in addition to their paychecks written on perfectly legal checks against real accounts at major banks. Establishing these payroll accounts was the only instance where we dealt with banks on a non-fraudulent basis. We deposited the cash in business accounts established with stolen ID that was not used in the credit swindles. The last thing we wanted was to have one of our employees take heat because of a paycheck. We even had Federal Tax ID numbers.

One of our employees, a happily married woman named Wanda who answered the phones in our San Francisco office, told me I was the coolest employer she ever had and that she truly loved her job at "Bay Area Courier Services." This was because she spent most of her mornings reading magazines and the afternoons watching soap operas. Of course, I didn't object. Whatever it took to keep faithful employees behind their desks, ready to answer those bank-verification calls, I was all for it.

But it wasn't only bank calls the women in our offices received. We had to make them believe as much as the bankers that our companies, enterprises and businesses were all real. If one of them became suspicious that she worked for a counterfeit corporation or was part of an elaborate sham, we faced the danger that *she* would turn us in.

To protect ourselves from that lurking peril, we created the natural goings-on of business offices that ours lacked, mainly mail delivery and phone calls. In addition to the monthly haul of junk mail, we generated our own mail as we flew from city to city, sending it around the country to all our fictitious businesses. We designed letterheads and envelopes from companies with which we supposedly did business. Each scam office had a magazine subscription corresponding to the business it was supposedly in. Bogus checks that represented payments for services rendered came in the mail. Before long, we had significant trails of fake paper in multitudinous forms crisscrossing the skies above the entire USA and landing in our offices.

Then there were the non-bank phone calls. This was hilarious. Every working day, Bones and I would form a list of calls that had to be made to the scam offices. Then we would take turns running down the list and calling our receptionists in the various cities. Bones would call Minneapolis and ask for Mr. Guthrie, one of our cardholders who on paper lived in our Minneapolis scam house and worked at that Minneapolis office. The receptionist was led to believe that the call was coming from someone directly related to business affairs. Bones would say something like "Just tell Mr. Guthrie that we received delivery of the merchandise and we're very happy. None of the products are damaged." Or then: "Please tell Mr. Guthrie that I can't make that Denver convention next month. Something's come up." Then I would in turn call our offices in Dallas and Houston and go through the same spiel.

Each office received no fewer than a dozen calls per day. We changed accents frequently (Bones was a master at them, especially Asian ones) and even used a voice-changing gizmo we'd bought in a spy shop. Our phone bills climbed into the thousands of dollars (this was before cheap unlimited long-distance calling), but it was a prudent business expense, one that maintained the appearance of legitimacy, even if the calls interrupted *General Hospital* or *Days of Our Lives*. Not one of the women ever seemed suspicious, although I stumbled for an answer when our Atlanta receptionist asked me for the time and place of our office Christmas party.

With dozens of cities now entwined into our operation, we needed to implement an efficient system of internal control. We had begun working out of different cities simultaneously. Early on, we'd realized that the maximum number of stolen identities used for each city should not exceed eight. If we were going to remain steps ahead of the FBI and Secret Service, we had to continually move the scenarios of the frauds. Staying too long in any single location could attract the attention of the authorities.

We flew from city to city when setting up the individual frauds. In doing this we had to be careful not to make mistakes due to sheer confusion. There were the dangers of mixing up addresses and phone numbers of different scam houses in the same city, sending two applications to the same bank in the same name or listing an existing credit account belonging to one applicant on the application of another. The opportunities for mistakes were endless.

Certain fundamental precautions had to be taken when applying to banks. Since in many cases we had more than one applicant working for the same fictitious company, only one could apply to each particular bank. Two employees working for the same company suddenly applying for credit to the same bank in a new market where they had no financial history would appear suspicious. We also had to be aware of the credit card clearinghouse system. Back then, the entire system ran on a much more regional than national basis. Although that made the obtainment of multiple Visa and MasterCards much easier than it is today, we still had to be extremely careful because different banks often used the same clearinghouse. We learned this from the applications themselves. If the addresses on two different bank applications were the same, or if their bulk mail permit number was identical, then it was obvious that one central clearinghouse was processing both applications. In many cases, one major bank controlled the Visa and MasterCard services for several smaller ones. It was essential not to make an oversight here. Doing so would splatter red flags across computer screens warning banks of our impending depredations.

We also had to keep track of all places where we secured identity documents. First were the Department of Motor Vehicle stations we visited in each city. Despite our knowledge that their thumb-printing process posed no real risk of exposing us, we had to be on guard not to have Bones recognized by observant clerks, even if the likelihood of that occurrence bordered on zero. There, however, we were afforded the luxury of being able to use DMV facilities in outlying areas. Since driver's licenses were a state domain, you could secure one in any part of the state, no matter which of its cities you lived in. Nobody in the DMV offices asked why someone living in San Francisco was getting his driver's license in Sacramento.

Such was not the case with US Passport offices. They were always located in major cities. We had to be extremely careful not to have Bones recognized by federal employees. This is not to say that federal employees were more on the ball than state workers. Only that in comparison, US Passport offices were much smaller than state DMVs and employed fewer workers.

The tremendous expansion of our operation brought on the need for systematic record-keeping and filing. This is where our headquarters in Chicago came in. The offices we rented on the twenty-second floor of the Sears Tower contained all the files for the entire organization. It also had two distinct features on its walls. One was a huge map of the United States with different colored tacks indicating cities currently being scammed, those that had been scammed and those not yet scammed but in the planning stages. It looked like those huge military maps seen in World War II movies. The other was a giant blow-up poster of a platinum Visa card that represented our thousandth fraudulent credit card.

Records were of course kept in our residences in each scam city, but once that branch of the scam closed down, we transferred all its records to Chicago. This procedure may seem foolhardy, as it was of course storing criminal evidence that could be used against us, but we needed these records to marshal data on banks, credit card companies, department stores and whatever else might give us input as to how to improve and protect the operation. No one besides Bones and I ever stepped foot in these offices, and the file cabinets were kept double-locked.

Bones was by all accounts the most officious record-keeper of all time. Had he not been devoted to a life of crime, he most certainly would have qualified for a federal job at the General Accounting Office. His meticulous attention to detail was unrivaled. His system of internal control broke down into three categories: stolen identities, credit obtained and partners' distributions.

The first category was a file cabinet containing all the documents pertaining to each individual whose identity we stole. Inside each folder, alphabetized in the drawers, were photocopies of their *Who's Who* pages, official identity documents, and bills incurred in their names pertaining to the scam house and office in their cities. We even kept the actual identity documents, despite the fact there was never a need for them once the credit was burned up. I had questioned Bones about this. He responded that he just wanted to keep them, without giving a reason. I objected that it seemed imprudent. His rebuttal was that it wouldn't matter if we ever got busted. If the office were one day raided, he said, they would have enough evidence to convict us at least once for every identity we had stolen.

I couldn't much argue with that.

The second bank of file cabinets contained all the records for banks, department stores and oil companies, plus a research and development file for American Express and other credit card companies. We had been considering obtaining one Amex and one Discover card for each stolen identity, but had not as yet done so.

After receiving dozens of credit cards, charge cards and denials from each major bank, department store chain and oil company, Bones developed a rating system to denote their overall value to us. He set up spreadsheets for each entity the way that Top Ten CPA firms did for their clients.

He called them his master spreadsheets. They were color-coded and detailed all the pertinent activity concerning their issuance of credit. On the bank spreadsheet, Bones noted the size of each bank in terms of assets and how many branches it operated as well as its past performance records. When initially applying to banks in Herbert Trumm's name, we'd chosen banks based solely on size. Obviously we had no past-performance records to go on, so we selected the larger banks in the belief they'd be the most likely to approve the applications.

But now we were able to grade them in direct correlation to their willingness to grant credit and how much of it they consistently did. Bones used three levels to classify each bank. Following his idea of how TRW classified credit ratings, he classified banks AAA, AA and A. Citibank, despite the restrictions it imposed on cash advances against their Visa cards, was the ideal AAA institution. Any halfway decent applicant was a virtual cinch to receive a credit card with better than minimal limits. We assumed Citibank's sheer size was the reason for this en masse show of acceptance. Up until that point, we had a 98 percent success rate obtaining Citibank Visas, two denials out of 114 applications. That rate of success was so high we figured that the two denials may have been the result of computer error!

Bank of America, Wells Fargo and First Interstate Bank were also AAA banks. A few of the larger banks in the same class disappointed our expectations and were downgraded to AA. The medium-sized banks whose services were restricted to a single state were classified as AA banks, although a few of these were so cooperative with the extension of healthy credit lines that we upgraded them to AAA. By the same measure, medium banks not coming through with middle-of-the-road credit cards we stigmatized with As. Most of the smaller banks with few scattered branches were rated A, with one or two per city climbing the ladder to AA.

Some banks moved up and down our rating system like players in baseball's minor leagues. Some we dropped altogether when they came back with successive denials. We tried to determine why certain banks came through with $5,000 credit lines for one applicant and $2,000 for another, when both applicants appeared to be at equal strength in terms of creditworthiness. We wondered if there were details in the TRW reports we weren't reading correctly or not reading at all. We examined the reports countless times but never found anything that might explain why banks judged some outwardly equal applicants more creditworthy than others. When further investigation into it appeared futile, we just let it go and adjusted the ratings with each new batch of credit cards and denials.

Department stores and oil companies were not so exclusive or picky about how they issued credit. In similar fashion to our bank classifications, they were rated One, Two or Three. Neiman Marcus was obviously the king of the "Ones." Attaining the same distinction were Saks Fifth Avenue, Nordstrom and Bullocks. Department store issuance of credit varied less than banks. The high-end stores never missed with the $5,000 and $10,000 charge cards. The middle-end stores were consistently in the $2,000 to $3,500 range, and the low-enders routinely coughed up $1,000 to $1,500. The difference in performance between department stores and banks was that department stores never denied our applicants unless it was a question of excessive TRW inquiries.

Not a single oil company as of yet sent a denial.

When we weren't flying around the country setting up the overlapping scams, we were flying around the country scooping up cash and merchandise. Our assault was such that I couldn't help but envision a dragnet of Secret Service agents in place around every Comchek machine and ATM in the nation. We'd hit every Comchek in Vegas. Every cardroom in California. Every racetrack between Los Angeles and Chicago, and we were gunning for the machines awaiting us in the east. The ATMs were being pummeled as well. The truth was that the machines we hit greatly outnumbered the totality of Secret Service *and* FBI agents. It really was a cash-bash.

We did not let up on the merchandising end of the business, faithfully burning up department store cards, using gas cards to service our vehicles along the way. In every city we rented a van to transport the goods. Robin, who no longer worked thanks to the inception of Cactus Financial Services, opened two full-scale clothing boutiques in Scottsdale, Arizona and Chicago. Bones and I had been against her foray into retailing, but we could not keep her spirit down. We reluctantly agreed to supply her shops, both named "Robin's," with merchandise from high-end department stores. Lots of it came from Marshall Field's, which had given us a handful of $10,000 credit lines. She promised to take great care in destroying all the evidence of where the clothing came from and to properly re-ticket her items for sale. She hired three employees to work at each shop. Periodically, Bones and I visited the shops to make sure all items for sale were correctly ticketed and contained no remnants from the department stores.

We continued doing big business with Alberto in Mexico. Merchandise obtained from all over the country had to be shipped to the shop in Tijuana. Bones and I no longer had the time to do this, so we stored the merchandise in scam houses across the country, then hired legitimate trucking companies to pick it up and ship the goods to San Diego. We could not chance these truckers going into Mexico. Trucks crossing the border occasionally faced scrutiny from Mexican customs, but more of a factor was the threat of US Customs. Many people don't realize that US border agents regularly stopped vehicles heading into Mexico with close proximity to the border. When that happened, international permits and an assortment of delivery and insurance documents had to be presented upon demand. Questions about the companies being invoiced for the shipping and receiving of the goods might become pointed. None of that appealed to us.

Alberto proved relentless in his determination to cooperate with us. When we'd first proposed making San Diego the contact point, we'd anticipated a negative response on his part, or at least a decrease in the percentage of retail he was paying us. But he advised us that shipping the goods to San Diego was fine. He would come north of the border to pick up the consignments. All he had to do was sign the necessary papers, load the goods into his own truck and head back to Mexico. We were concerned that he might have problems, especially when entering the US, but like always Alberto told us, "*No ten miedo.*" Don't worry.

We wondered with trepidation how Alberto would be able to make repetitive border crossings without taking heat. Our first thought was that perhaps he was a US citizen. But we assumed he would have told us if he was. Then we figured he might have had people with connections to US Customs and Immigration. However, that was hard to believe.

Finally, a bit shaky about going through with it, I asked him inside his Ralph Lauren shop, "Alberto, how the hell are you going to cross the border every time we have a shipment? You're not a citizen."

Alberto smiled. "Gringo, of course I'm not a citizen."

"Then how are you gonna cross the border without ID?"

Alberto's smile broadened as he removed his wallet from his Ralph Lauren jeans. He flashed an identification card at me. Something about it reeked of familiarity. Then it hit me—it was a California Driver's license with his picture on it. But I didn't see the name Alberto.

"How'd you get that?" I asked with barely restrained curiosity.

Now Alberto laughed. "What's the matter with you, gringo? Haven't you ever heard of identity theft?"

A few bumps along the way
United States, 1994-1995

IN THE LATE FALL OF 1994, WE BEGAN OUR MOVE EASTWARD. IF the pickings had been ripe in the Pacific, Mountain and Central time zones, the true finest hour for our scam came with Eastern Standard Time. We started at the northernmost major city along the Eastern Seaboard, Boston, where we chartered a host of new banks and department stores. As in other areas of the country, we found our share of AAA, AA and A banks and stores to run our stolen identities through.

When we arrived in New York, we experienced two hitherto unseen "comings." The first was a $15,000 limit on a Chase gold MasterCard. The second was courtesy of Bloomingdale's, perhaps the finest and most well known department store in the country. They sent a beautifully embossed charge card in the name of William Mitchell to our Manhattan scam apartment (a tiny Greenwich Village studio). We'd been hoping they would fall in line with the rest of the country's top-end department stores and extend Mitchell $10,000. "Bloomies" didn't disappoint. They doubled it! A $20,000 charge account to support our Fifth Avenue shopping sprees!

Other stores along that fashionable avenue that authorized $10,000 were Lord & Taylor, Bergdorf Goodman, Bonwit Teller and, last but not least, Tiffany's. Even Barney's, which we had rated a "Two" department store, shocked us pleasantly with a $10,000 credit line.

After four of our identities made the credit rounds of New York, we realized that the city's financial and retail institutions having granted William Mitchell such magnanimous credit was no fluke. Nor was it the result of Mitchell's credit history being any more outstanding than the bulk of our identities. It was just the Big Apple's way of doing business. After all, New York was indeed the financial capital of the world.

Along with the addition of Philadelphia, Baltimore and Miami to our now completely national operation came problems we weren't quite prepared for. First off, we realized we couldn't handle the work anymore, not just the two of us. Robin was fully occupied with her boutiques and was actively pursuing her dream of opening her third one—in New York. The killer was that her boutiques in Scottsdale and Chicago were doing quite well. The zero-cost factor of her merchandise notwithstanding, Robin was unloading her goods at a rate competitive with reputable retailers selling similar lines. Bones and I were quite impressed by her sudden emergence as a retailer, though we really could have used more of her help with the operation.

We had come to the conclusion that unless we got outside help from people who would be privy to the scam, there would have to be a major slowdown in our illicit activities. If we wanted to involve other human beings, going about it wouldn't be as simple as we thought. It wasn't like we could take out ads in newspapers' Help Wanted sections recruiting "motivated individuals for growing fraudulent services company." We'd only be able to approach people we knew. Bones and I had worked with a dozen various acquaintances over the years in diversified scams, but involving any one of them in this "thing of ours" would have to be discussed in great detail before taking action.

In the meantime, we began running into operational problems and close shaves. The first close shave occurred not while draining credit cards for cash but rather during a New Jersey department store shopping spree.

We had received word from Alberto in Tijuana that he needed a large quantity of only Ralph Lauren's Polo line of clothing. He was specifically interested in shirts, trousers and jackets. His order was not difficult to fill inasmuch as all the middle and high-end New York and New Jersey department stores carried complete stocks of Polo merchandise.

At the time of Alberto's request, we had $250,000 in unused charge cards from stores carrying the merchandise. Before this particular order from Mexico came in, we'd had the habit of distributing our mass purchases throughout different departments. But this coordinated attack on one designer's wares through several department stores was sure to make noise. Even Ralph Lauren himself was bound to become curious as to why a certain autumn week in New York brought him a quarter million dollars in excess sales. And it wasn't even the week beginning Friday after Thanksgiving.

We decided to make our huge buys of Ralph Lauren merchandise into a skit. By playing it lightheartedly and charming salesclerks, perhaps we could deter suspicious thoughts on their part. I would pose as the nephew, and Bones would be the favorite uncle who could never say no to his brother's spoiled son.

The first target was Macy's. The limit on the charge card we used was $5,000. One thing I had to avoid was buying up clumps of similar merchandise with no attention to selection. Salespeople witnessing me grabbing an entire cubbyhole full of same-color but different-sized shirts had to wonder if I wasn't conducting a block-party raffle of Ralph Lauren clothing. With this in mind, I paraded through the department gathering up assortments of Polo merchandise that I lumped atop the counter next to the register.

When I had $5,000 worth, Bones showed up ready to oblige his "favorite nephew." While charging up my colossal purchase, he made a humorous comment to the salesman about how spoiled his nephew was and that he shouldn't be doing this. The man laughed, but his joviality was more in the delightful thought of his commission than Bones's good humor. He rang up the Polo shirts, pants, jackets and sweaters faster than I'd spilled them on his counter. I had the impression he wanted to get the transaction over with before "my uncle" changed his mind.

We followed this spoiled-brat-nephew routine in several different stores using different charge cards under different names. It worked without a hitch for three days. More than half the total charge limit for all the cards was eaten. We felt safe and far away from the risk of being nabbed by department store security men, who just might think something was fishy about our incredibly large purchases. Department personnel, however, never seemed to suspect anything. They were just happy to go along for the ride and garner their commissions. Bones began chitchatting with them unendingly as the store rampages continued.

But then we learned that anything could go wrong at any time. On that third day, we had shopped in the classy Lord & Taylor in Paramus,

New Jersey. While piling the mountain of merchandise on the counter, we made the very friendly acquaintance of Lora, whom we assumed to be the department's manager. She stood behind a male clerk who rang up and bagged the seventy-five Ralph Lauren Polo shirts I'd lumped on the counter. She even made the flirtatious comment that I must really fancy Ralph Lauren's polos, or that maybe I was a real polo player.

After the clerk had finished ringing up the purchase, Lora asked Bones what his name was. Bones introduced himself as Mr. Clarence Kowsowski, the same name he signed on the Lord & Taylor sales slip. The clerk thanked him, saying loudly in front of Lora, "We appreciate your business, Mr. Kowsowski." Lora smiled as we left, and offered her own farewell of "Hope to see you soon, Mr. Kowsowski." She, too, seemed to appreciate the $1,400 purchase of Ralph Lauren shirts.

The next day, we were in another Lord & Taylor men's department in a mall in Bridgewater, New Jersey, which was sixty miles from Paramus. There were four Lord & Taylor stores located between the two cities, so what happened next we would have thought very unlikely.

I was stacking high and wide still more Ralph Lauren items on the counter next to the register. As usual, the clerk had a smile on her face. She was in the process of ringing up the items when the unbelievable happened. Lora, the woman we'd seen and chatted with inside the men's department of the Lord & Taylor in Paramus, suddenly appeared behind the counter and stood next to the clerk. Here, in Bridgewater! She recognized us right away, which was okay except that this time the Lord & Taylor charge card that Bones was using for the purchase said he was Salvatore Giambi, not Clarence Kowsowski, the name inscribed on the card he'd used in Paramus.

I immediately shit a brick, as must have Bones. The name Salvatore Giambi was as ethnically distant from Clarence Kowsowski as you could get. Lora greeted us, and when she said with a grin, "On another shopping spree, Mr. Kowsowski?" I thought I'd drop a turd right in my pants. She remembered the name Kowsowski! And now if she saw the name Giambi on the charge card voucher, or heard the clerk address Bones by that name, we'd be in very deep shit and more likely than not have our first escape situation from a shopping mall.

The clerk took an agonizingly long time to finish ringing the sale, which maybe was for the better, for she didn't appear to be a very intelligent person. While Bones and I looked at each other, shivered and prayed, Lora went on with her small talk, several times throwing in a "Mr. Kowsowski." She didn't give the impression she was overly concerned with the mechanics of the transaction, but what both Bones and I were thinking was that the clerk would utter the name Giambi after that false signature was made. Something of the sort "Thank you very much, Mr. Giambi" or "Have a nice day, Mr. Giambi." And, we foresaw, with Lora's constant chirping of "Mr. Kowsowski," this clerk had to notice the discrepancy. Unless, of course, she was so deaf she couldn't hear the beeps from her computerized cash register.

When you're a thief you see, hear and witness even more incredible things than honest people do. During those very long, unbearable minutes at that sales counter, neither woman took note of the fact that Mr. Giambi had been Mr. Kowsowski or that Mr. Kowsowski was now Mr. Giambi, or whatever. They both thanked Bones again, neither including a name in her very pleasant farewell. We had a stroke of good luck that day, because it was still early in our operation, and had the shit hit the fan inside that Lord & Taylor men's department, I never would have had enough experiences to write a book about identity theft.

Another near calamity was the result of a foolish mistake we had made with our Detroit operation. In one of the city's two scam houses lived three automobile executives recently "transferred" from East Coast field offices. Bones had gone to three Michigan DMVs on the same day and obtained temporary driver's licenses for each. Michigan did not furnish newly licensed drivers with their permanent laminated licenses over the counter. They were mailed to the address matching that on the temporary.

On another similar day two weeks later, the three driver's licenses arrived in the mail. Bones and I happened to be sitting in the living room going over paperwork when the postman appeared on the landing. The front door that housed the mail slot had been open, so the postman stuck his head inside and said cheerily, "Anyone home? I got mail for all three of you."

Bones jumped off his chair and greeted the postman, who handed over the mail with a smile and left. It contained the three DMV envelopes and a few pieces of junk mail.

Bones fetched a letter opener and removed the three licenses. He laid them on a small table near the door. At that moment, the postman stuck his head through the door, an envelope in his hand.

"Sorry, forgot this one," he said, and moved to lay it on the table surface where Bones had placed the licenses.

I noticed a strange look narrow the postman's eyes. It disappeared quickly, and he said goodbye and left.

But he'd seen the three licenses. When it clicked in my head, my heart gave out a leaden, sinking feeling. The postman must have realized that he just delivered three official driver's licenses in three different names to the same man at the same address. He had to notice Bones's photograph on all three.

The threat of a serious problem suddenly loomed. Or did it? What had that postman actually seen? Did he absolutely see the photos clearly? He'd only glimpsed at them for a second, but the confused look on his face was unmistakable.

If his mind's eye told him that Bones was the recipient of three driver's licenses, then his brain would know he'd seen proof of flagrant identity fraud. That possibility chilled us to the bone. It wasn't like your cleaning lady seeing it. That postman was a federal employee. First thing he'd do was report his findings to the postal inspectors, who would make inquiries to Michigan authorities, who in turn would be working in tandem with the investigation division of the state's DMV. That chain of events would put us in a serious jam. There wouldn't be a motorcar in all of Detroit to get us out of there fast enough.

We anguished about it for the remainder of the day. Finally, we came to the conclusion that it was doubtful he'd had enough time to completely take in the discrepancy. We decided to stay on track with the Detroit operation, though we invoked security measures to protect us against a law enforcement setup. Each time we picked up the mail or went to the scam house for any reason, we drove by in different vehicles, satisfying ourselves no stakeouts were in place.

The operation reached its zenith without any incident, so either the postman hadn't registered the magnitude of what he'd seen or he never bothered reporting it to his superiors.

One miscalculation on our part did have disastrous repercussions. Although we were making millions of dollars, Bones and I, like any financial officers of legitimate corporations, always searched for ways to cut costs and increase productivity. The largest operating expense in our business was the rental costs for scam houses. The average monthly cost per house across the western and central states had ballooned to $1,600. This was mainly due to the setting up of operations in and around several major cities. San Diego, where we'd rented our first scam houses, had a lower cost of living index than Minneapolis and Chicago. Even in less affluent areas like Detroit and St. Louis, we paid higher rents because we had to seek out upper-class neighborhoods. This was not only because we wanted our addresses to look posh to creditors perusing our applications—it was also essential to the security of the operation. We did not want to deal with the crime and police presence in lesser-valued areas.

When we'd arrived in the eastern part of the country, those scam-house costs shot up even more. Boston and Philadelphia were bad enough, but New York was prohibitive. We would've preferred renting scam houses in the boroughs outside Manhattan, mainly Brooklyn and Queens, but the problem with that was the incomparable traffic you had to deal with when traveling in either direction between any two boroughs. Thus we were constrained to renting scam houses in Manhattan, which turned out to be $2,000-a-month tiny studio apartments.

After months of weighing the pros and cons for our drastic cost-cutting measure, we finally gave it the go-ahead. We would discontinue renting houses in favor of "rooms for rent." Proprietors of houses in the nicest sections of town often rented out rooms for whatever reason. The going rate was usually $300 a month, a mere fraction of the cash scam houses guzzled. By becoming one-room tenants, we could not only hugely cut costs but also in some cases increase the value of an address, which could amount to higher credit limits. Since banks only knew the address where its cardholders lived, not whether they rented or shared that address, this arrangement could serve us well. As with houses, all we needed to operate from a rental room was the address, a phone number and a mailbox.

Certain negatives had to be considered when renting rooms in lieu of houses. We'd be exposing our operation to the human element, since other people lived on the premises. Roommates might wonder at someone installing a phone line, receiving his mail, but never being there. And if it were known that more than one person was receiving mail in the same box, it would be doubly suspicious.

We had almost abandoned the idea when Bones enlightened me to a solution. We were driving south on I-95 on our way to Baltimore. We'd just left Philadelphia where we'd sold a half dozen Krugerrands to a coin dealer on Market Street.

"Buddies going through divorce proceedings against untrustworthy wives," he said, somewhat inspired by an offshoot version of *The Odd Couple*, or what would be in our case the "Odd Triple" or "Odd Quadruple." What Bones laid out was a plan where he would tell the landlord that he and his friends were all going through bitter divorces and wanted to rent a safe place where they could retrieve their mail and not have to worry about their wives tampering with it. He would point out that the arrangement was mutually beneficial: to the owner because he received the monthly rent and kept the room, having the option to rent it out yet again; to us since we'd get our mail and phone calls. All we'd have to do is pick up the mail and put the phone on call-forward to our residence. By this time, we knew that as long as we avoided sending applications to banks using the same clearinghouse, we didn't have to worry about different applicants having identical home addresses and telephone numbers.

The first "scam room" we rented in this fashion was in Cockeysville, Maryland, a nice Baltimore suburb. We installed three identities, then a phone line with the number call-forwarded to our Baltimore residence and a mailbox with a Master lock next to the front door. The family living in the house had its own mailbox.

There were no problems with that first scam room, so we rented a second in Washington, D.C., a third in Providence, Rhode Island, and four more scattered around northern New Jersey. The last of those Jersey scam rooms backfired on us.

It seemed perfect when we rented it. Three young men in their early twenties occupied the house. One of them was named Robby Parsons, and his mother, a divorcée, owned it. What we liked about the situation was that Robby said his mother never meddled in the affairs of the house. As long as the rent was paid on time, she was happy. She didn't care who her tenants were, so long as they didn't damage the house or cause any disturbances with the neighbors. She didn't even exclude pets.

Bones and Robby struck up a deal: $250 a month and no lease. If the tenant was unhappy with the premises, he could terminate his tenancy on the spot with the balance of prepaid rent pro-rated back to him. In the event the landlord wanted the tenant out, Mrs. Parsons had to give thirty days' notice.

Not unfair from the tenant's point of view. We were obviously delighted with the circumstances. Robby, too, seemed thrilled. He and his two roommates still had ample space to party and indulge themselves with New Jersey's young lovelies.

We affixed the mailbox and installed a telephone whose number was forwarded to our residence. Robby was given the phone number of Mahatsu Enterprises, one of our corporations serving northern New Jersey. Bones instructed him to call if any problems arose.

Three weeks later, as the first credit cards began arriving, we got a problematic call from Parsons. But not from Robby Parsons—Elaine

Parsons, the mother. I answered the phone, and she seemed very upset.

"What the hell is going on at my house?" she screamed in my ear. "It's all very fishy!"

"What's fishy?" I stammered.

"*What's* fishy!? I'll tell you what's fishy. The mailman put your mail in my son's box, and there's nothing but credit cards in there. Don't you think that's fishy?"

My breath caught. Bones and I had once discussed that possibility. I'd said to him, "What if the mailman accidentally puts our mail in the wrong box?" His answer was that it wouldn't happen.

Well, now it had happened, and the shit was hitting the fan. Bones was in the shower, so I had to play the part and try to calm down this very angry woman whose next call might be to the police. This was a "code red" danger that had to be diffused.

"Mrs. Parsons," I said very deliberately with the firmness required for her to understand. "I belong to a support group of men *and* women who are going through extremely trying divorces. We all give therapy and help one another, man and woman alike. We exchange ideas how to reduce the fighting and resulting damage. We learn how to protect ourselves. So what my two friends and I were advised to do, by a woman in the group, I might add, is rent a room where our privacy is not threatened." I didn't know how that crock of bullshit came to me so quickly, but I rattled it off like a machine gun.

"What's that all got to do with the credit cards?" she said in suspicious tones.

I frantically tried to latch on to thoughts shooting through my head. Finally I found one. I explained that my wife's behavior had been so malodorous that she took to coming over to the apartment where I'd been living since our separation, duping the landlord into giving her the keys, and then entering my home and stealing the cash and credit cards in my wallet. If that wasn't enough, she charged up thousands of dollars on the cards.

"So you see, Mrs. Parsons, we had to establish new credit accounts independent of wives. We're only protecting ourselves from financial harassment and embarrassment. Their flagrant misuse of our cards has nearly destroyed our good credit-standing. That can't happen again. We rented the room in your house for exactly that reason: just so we could have our credit cards safely delivered to us." I exhaled with relief when I'd finally finished.

But being a woman, Mrs. Parsons instinctively sided with the three imaginary women involved in the disputes. I could not alter her ingrained belief that men were pricks. She was a divorced woman herself, and obviously a bitter one.

When Mrs. Parsons begrudgingly said that for now she'd allow the arrangement to continue, it didn't make me feel any more confident when I ran into the bathroom to tell Bones what had happened.

"You did well, my son," he said, a towel wrapped around his waist, another one going through his hair. "We knew these rental rooms were a risk. Let's see what happens in the next few days before we make the decision to bail out of there.

When Mrs. Parsons did call two days later, she was even more frantic. This time her accusations were direct and far more venomous. Her fury could only be eclipsed by the hatred she must have felt for her ex-husband during their divorce proceedings. She screamed at me, "You're using my son in some kind of scam, and I'm going to report you to the police…!"

Now we had our own "New Jersey Missile Crisis." Mrs. Parsons' threat endangered not only our northern New Jersey operation but perhaps the workings of the entire national scam as well. And worse, we learned she had already called the scam office where the man Bones was impersonating supposedly worked and fired off a bunch of accusations at the legitimate receptionist we had working there.

It became a case for our bomb squad, and I doubted we could dismantle the bomb. I tried my best to offer Mrs. Parsons an appeasement, but all I got in return was the reverberating click of her slamming down the phone.

Bones and I immediately set an emergency meeting of our "security council." We had oftentimes strategized what we'd do in case of certain hypothetical catastrophes, but we were unprepared for one this explosive. After running out of feasible ideas how to deal with Mrs. Parsons directly, we settled on the only viable course of action.

Bones called up Robby Parsons. "What the hell is going on with your mother?" he demanded without preamble.

Robby was obviously not a man outside his youthful fun-loving world. He did not grasp the urgency of the situation. To him it was nothing more than an inconvenience, a nuisance.

"My mother's in menopause," he said. "She's been on a tear lately." His soft laugh further conveyed his thoughts.

Bones had to retain his grace. To alienate Robby was to cut off our only link to this terribly pervasive enemy who had sprouted up the way dandelions invade a healthy lawn. He softened his approach. "Come on, man," he said. "You told me she didn't meddle in your affairs. What's going on?"

"It's kind of weird, man. She's never behaved this way before. She comes over every now and then to clean up. She opened the box for my mail and found yours. She just flipped out."

"She threatened to call the police on me," Bones said indignantly. "That's ridiculous. I have enough problems with my wife hiring private dicks to snoop on me." Bones's hope was that Robby would appeal to his mother's better senses and get her to call off the dogs.

Robby dismissed his mother's threat. "Nah, she won't do that. Don't worry about it. She's happy enough to have your money."

"Well, do me a favor, Robby. Tell her to calm down. I'm only renting a room in her house, not making bombs in her basement. I'm strictly a legitimate guy. Please tell her to stop worrying. It's all nonsense."

"I'll tell her," Robby said.

We were still sweating profusely when Mrs. Parsons called the next day. She actually dialed the number we had in her house, which was forwarded to ours. This time she had calmed down but still made a pressing demand on us. Since we'd paid a month's rent, she said, she would allow us to maintain the tenancy with the phone and mailbox until the end of the month, which was five days away. Any mail arriving for Bones and his pals after that would be sent back to the post office with "Does not live here anymore" scribed on the envelopes. She would also pull the plug on our phone line.

Now the disaster was escalating. What Mrs. Parsons had threatened to do was irreversible. Credit cards were not forwarded. They'd be returned to the banks, and no second attempts would be made to mail them out. Trying to reclaim the cards was useless because the accounts would be cancelled out. Worse, bankers' suspicions heightened upon having a newly approved applicant's card come back to them. Why would somebody applying for a credit card give an address he knew he'd be leaving so shortly?

Bones tried every approach possible to reason with her. "My whole divorce case will go up in smoke if you don't allow me another month of tenancy," he pleaded. Then when he realized that using the divorce angle wasn't the best choice with someone who probably idolized Gloria Steinem, Bones switched to, "All my business deals will sour; I'll lose a fortune of money. That would be very unfair."

The bitch would not budge. Her "no" was as final as a hangman's noose. "I want you out of my house by the first of the month," she said coldly. "And, by the way, I have already notified the postman that neither you nor your confederates live here anymore."

That was the straw that broke the camel's back. The vision that crept into my brain was of an open suitcase filled with cash falling off a penthouse balcony, the windblown bills spreading like a mushroom cloud on their downward flight to the street, and me hopelessly bent over the railing watching them go. Not only was the money gone, but the future of our entire operation hung just as precipitously.

We scrambled desperately into damage-control mode. First off we notified the banks. Better they found out from us before receiving their cards back in the mail. On a piece of Mahatsu stationary carefully designed by a typesetter, Bones sent every bank we hadn't heard from a letter explaining that a gang of kids in the neighborhood was pilfering mailboxes, and one of them, as a prank, told the postman that the applicant no longer lived at the Parsons' address. Then the bank was asked to re-route the credit card to the Mahatsu offices. We didn't expect them to comply, but at least the letter might help prevent an investigation.

We thought of another move to salvage credit cards that had not yet been sent. We figured that banks would demand new applications with new addresses and telephone numbers that could be instantly verified. In order to supply them, we'd have to rent a new scam house right away. It would be worth the added expense if the banks agreed to send the cards there.

There were also the banks that had not yet made their decisions to accept or deny our applications. Perhaps they had sent correspondence indicating their need for additional information. This happened often enough, and by cooperating with their requests we ended up receiving approvals more often than not.

But the problem was that we had no way of knowing which banks were at what stage of the process. Before proceeding further, we needed more information. The only way to get it was to call each bank we'd applied to and request the status of the application.

On the very first call, I learned that our credit calamity had run head-on into Murphy's Law. When things go wrong in the fraud business, they get worse before they get better.

A Valley Bank operator connected me to the woman in customer service who handled applications for new MasterCard accounts. I told her I was Gilbert Braddock and that I had mailed in my application, but never received correspondence from the bank.

"But, Mr. Braddock," the woman's voice said in no uncertain tones. "Our records show that you've used your card right up to your credit limit. As a matter of fact, you've gone over your limit…"

"What!" My exclamation was involuntary.

"The bank granted you a five hundred dollar extension…"

"Five hundred dollar extension…!"

"My records show that our security department attempted to call you, but no one answered and there was no answering device for the line. Mr. Braddock, are you saying that…"

"How much was my credit line?"

"Ten thousand to start, then ten thousand, five hundred."

This was unfathomable. There was no way we had made a mistake as to which banks had sent cards and which hadn't. Bones's records were as accurate as those kept in the Library of Congress. Beyond that, I was a thousand percent sure we'd received neither a card nor a request for additional information about Mr. Braddock.

Something had gone haywire. I voiced my incredulity, but the woman assured me that no mistake had been made on the bank's part and the card had been used to the tune of $10,500.

"Maybe I should put you through to security," she said. "Your card must have been stolen from the mail."

My first gut instinct told me to hang up. For some reason I didn't. When the security director came on the line with a thick voice that went well with his title, I realized that the first thing I had to do was conceal the fact that the customer reporting the theft was the primary thief himself.

"My name's Jensen," he said. "Can I have your name and Social Security number please?"

I gave him both.

"Mother's maiden name?"

There it was again, the magic piece of information. Incredibly enough, it was Jensen. The Jensen on the line did not comment on the coincidence. But "Jensen" did satisfy Jensen that he was speaking with the real Gilbert Braddock.

I played the part of a victimized businessman. In all innocence, I said, "I can't believe this has happened! Who would actually steal and blatantly use someone else's credit card?"

Despite his tough voice, the officer was polite and seemed to take me for a genuine victim. "It happens all the time," he explained. "But I must admit,

I've never seen one misused for this much money."

He could never imagine the amount of money his and other banks' credit cards were being misused for. After asking a few routine questions for his report, Jensen informed me that the bank would mail documents stating that I had not executed the transactions against the MasterCard. I would have to sign it and send it back to him. He advised me that after his department's investigation was complete, a replacement card would be sent to me.

I told him that was fine, but I preferred to receive the documents at my business address. I could no longer have faith in the delivery of my mail to my residence. Naturally he understood.

Before I'd hung up the phone, I understood what had happened. Robby Parsons and his band had scammed us through the backdoor. They ripped us off of the credit cards we'd ripped off in the first place. Talk about audacity! They had shrewdly anticipated that if we were obtaining fraudulent credit cards, we had no recourse when they pulled the rug out and defrauded us.

We soon learned to what extent Robby Parsons had done a number on us. When the dead and wounded credit cards were finally accounted for, we ascertained that he and his cohorts had swindled us out of the seventy-five grand they spent on themselves plus the estimated hundred thousand we lost through banking administration, including cancelled accounts, cards destined for our mailbox that we never received, and cards the banks would have sent to the mailbox had the mishap not occurred.

When I told Bones about the reverse scam pulled on us, he flew into a rage. He even professed an actual deed of murder but I was able to calm him down. I convinced him that we had to accept the loss as a cost of doing business. The key issue was that our own scam was not revealed. Even though the banks had a massive theft of credit cards on their hands, they didn't pick up on the trail leading to the discovery that the so-called victims of the thefts were the world's greatest identity thieves.

Each document we received attesting to the theft of the cards was promptly signed and mailed back to the banks' security departments. In each case, the bank attached a replacement card application for the victim to fill out. Although we laughingly toyed around with the idea of actually doing so, we figured it was best to let sleeping dogs lie and get out of northern New Jersey.

Hot cars

California and Mexico, 1995

IN THE SUMMER OF 1995, WE FLEW FROM ATLANTA TO SAN Diego. Bones rented a car at the San Diego airport with a credit card and Georgia driver's license that said he was Harlan Abramson. We lodged in a hotel on the same credit card, then the next day we rented an apartment in Del Mar. We were loaded with credit cards that had come to us by way of three Pacific Northwest executives we had transferred to Atlanta. We did not return to California because we'd been homesick.

We had a new idea.

It was audacious, crazy and made "adventuresome" look like running a red light. In fact, it was life-risking. But we embarked on it anyhow. That it was my idea was not incredible. I was beginning to think I was indestructible.

After receiving a furniture delivery on yet another Georgia man's credit card, Bones and I drove into Mexico. We found our favorite parking spot along Tijuana's main drag. A few minutes later we stood in the Ralph Lauren outlet.

Alberto was surprised to see us; Nina wasn't there. "*Amigos*, you guys got another shipment so soon! I wasn't expecting you. Why didn't you call? I don't have the truck to go to San Diego today."

"Forget the truck," Bones said.

"No shipment?"

I shook my head. "Alberto, remember you told us you could arrange a buy for whatever merchandise we brought you?"

Alberto suddenly became rigid and took a step toward me. He gave a sharp chop with his right hand, the fingers fused together. "Hey, man, I don't deal drugs!"

Since I'd known him, Alberto never showed himself so demonstrative about anything. He'd always been as cool as a Mexican breeze. But now he got fiery, as if all of a sudden he'd found morals.

"Calm down," Bones said with authority.

"It's not drugs," I said. "It's hard merchandise."

"It's big," Bones added. "You said you could handle anything, big or bigger."

Alberto chilled out. "What the fuck is it, man, a yacht?"

Bones and I exchanged a glance and laughed. So did Alberto, but he thought we really were talking about a yacht.

"Almost," Bones said.

"Alberto," I said in a lowered tone, even though no customers were in the store. "I'm talking about a Rolls Royce."

"You mean like in luxury car?"

"Now we're connecting, Alberto."

"Can you set it up?" Bones asked.

Alberto gave us a smarmy look-over. "You want to sell a hot car?"

"For starters," I said slyly.

"You want to sell... *two* cars?"

"Let's start with one," Bones said firmly. "Can you set it up?"

Alberto laughed. "You two gringos are really something, maybe *loco*. You have the Rolls now?"

"*Si, señor*," I lied.

"Then I will set it up. Go to a bar and have a margarita. Come back in two hours."

We went to the bar and had two margaritas. When we returned to his shop, Alberto was all smiles.

"You know the race and sports book next to *Agua Caliente*?"

We knew it well. *Agua Caliente* was Tijuana's racetrack. If you didn't want to go watch the horses live, you could hang out and watch the simulcast at the race and sports book just down the road. The real draw, however, was that the facility took action on horse races and professional sports from all over the United States, just like the Las Vegas casinos did.

"Be there tonight at seven o'clock. Sit in one of the lounges away from the bar. A heavy guy with a sombrero hat will come and talk to you."

The guy wearing the sombrero hat had a lot more class than his hat. He appeared to be a wealthy Mexican gambler from Mexico City who was on a hot streak. He wore a striking beige summer suit and was the only guy inside the garish pink and red betting salon wearing the straw high-crowned hat. Plus he was heavyset, so it had to be him.

But he ignored us. He glided from gilded betting windows to velvet seats in front of TV screens showing races and baseball games to the fronts of busty cocktail waitresses who all seemed overtly receptive to his flirtatious gestures. When he finally parked his fluffy ass in the plush sofa on the opposite side of a small cocktail table, he laid a bottle of Dom Pérignon next to three glasses and invited us to join him.

"My long-shot horse came in and paid a huge price on my huge wager," he said happily, taking a healthy swig on the champagne. "Allow me to introduce myself. My name is Adnan Kashoggi."

That his name was Adnan Kashoggi was funny enough, but compounded by the contrast between his typical Mexican accent and that of any man of Arabic descent made it hysterical, let alone the one between him and the infamous Saudi arms dealer with the same name. Bones and I knew about the real Kashoggi. He'd been mixed up in tons of illicit weapons deals in the seventies and the Iran-Contra scandal in the eighties.

When this Mexican version of Kashoggi caught our amusement, he said generously, "You'd like to know why I call myself Adnan Kashoggi." Neither of us bothered nodding or saying yes, so he just went on candidly. "The source of my wealth is not from gambling. When I gamble, I lose like everyone else. No one makes money in casinos."

We begged to differ but remained silent.

"My money comes from my talent for arranging all kinds of illicit deals between all kinds of people, Mexicans and gringos alike. I am always the middleman. I don't touch the merchandise; I don't touch the cash." He let us digest that and then: "My associate Alberto tells me you have a deal that might interest me."

I spoke up. "Would you know of anyone in the market for a luxury car at a very modest price, say a Rolls Royce or Bentley for ten grand?"

Kashoggi's brows arched. "Are these cars new?"

"Not brand," I said.

"How many miles on their odometers?"

"I can't tell you that precisely."

"You're looking to sell cars and you don't know how many miles are on their odometers?"

Neither of us had an answer.

Kashoggi took pause and raised his champagne glass, motioning us to take part. We raised ours, and we all clinked glasses. "Well, where are these cars?"

That much we knew. "In California," I said, though I didn't know which city. "Do you know someone looking for a Rolls Royce or a Bentley?"

Kashoggi put down his champagne glass. "No."

Our hearts sunk.

Kashoggi smiled broadly. "But I may know someone looking for a Ferrari or Maserati."

I was glad that he didn't say Lamborghini, because those were difficult to find on the lots of Southern California's exotic car-rental agencies.

"Wait here," Kashoggi said, lifting his large frame from the velvet seat. He walked off and disappeared through a doorway adjacent to the bar. Bones and I didn't say much while he was gone. We watched the Dodgers game on a big-screen TV. We pretty much expected the encounter with the middleman to come off the way it did. The only thing mysterious would be the identity of the eventual buyer.

Kashoggi came back after fifteen minutes. "Tomorrow night you will meet the man who will buy your car if it's up to snuff," he said to both of us. Hearing him use the phrase "up to snuff" sounded comical, though I didn't laugh. He handed me a piece of paper. On it were written two words: Pink Rose. It was a typical name for a typical Tijuana bar.

"His name is Mendez. He will meet you there tomorrow night at nine o'clock. Don't be late. Don't be early." His gaze shifted to me. "Only one of you need be there." Apparently he expected that person to be me.

On the way back to Del Mar, we naturally wondered who this Mendez character could be.

"Only two possibilities," Bones pointed out just as we were waved through by US Customs. "Drug dealer or coyote." The latter was the term for illegal immigrant smugglers.

It made sense. No one else in Baja California would be in the market for hot luxury cars.

A Wild Ride with the World's #1 Identity Thief

I went alone to the divey Tijuana bar called the Pink Rose. It was a usual Saturday night in summer and the town was flooded with Southern California high school and college kids roaming the littered streets in search of cheap drink, whores or just plain old fisticuffs. I was slightly nervous going inside the place, which had the mixed décor of a beach bar and sawdust grind joint. It was wall-to-wall people, but I managed to squeeze into a stool at the bar. I ordered a White Russian. I loved the soothing coffee-taste of Kahlua and could drink the stuff like water, especially when it was as hot as it was in the place. A jukebox was blasting "Light My Fire" by the Doors, and a foursome of drunken Mexicans was falling over the pool table as they tried to play some game that might have been eight ball in better circumstances. Another foursome of rowdy white kids seemed to be waiting its turn to cue up.

The bartender poured me a second and third drink without my asking, nor did he ask for any money. Evidently, he knew why I was there or at least with whom I'd be meeting. Before he could pour me the fourth, two neat but slithery Mexicans, wearing hunky gold chains with open silk shirts, designer trousers and alligator shoes, came up to my stool and motioned me to follow them to a table tucked into the farthest corner of the bar.

I swigged down the drink and followed.

"When can you deliver the car?" the first one said with a Doritos TV commercial accent as soon as we were seated. There were no introductions, and despite the flavor of the accent, I knew this was serious business. I also knew that neither of the two was Mendez. They were his henchmen and would be handling the transaction for their boss. There wouldn't be any bullshit.

"Tomorrow."

"A 1995 Ferrari Testarossa?" asked the second one, more to confirm what I had told Kashoggi at the gambling place than out of doubt as to my capabilities. "You know the car? It's the one Don Johnson rode around in the *Miami Vice* TV show."

"I know the car, but I can't guarantee you it will be a 1995. But it will definitely be a late model Testarossa. I have to see what my people have coming in." I said this to give off the air that I was heading up a professional auto-theft ring. I certainly didn't want these goons knowing I would be out searching exotic car-rental agencies looking for their Ferrari.

"Mendez don't want it if it's more than three years old," the first one spat out.

"I understand that."

"Make sure you do," the second one said with some menace in his delivery.

"Does he have any color preference?" I asked quickly, much to hide the bolt of fear I felt going through me.

They looked at each other stupidly. Then the first one shrugged and said no. If Mendez had been a fan of *Miami Vice* and knew Don Johnson's was white, I guessed he didn't care whether his would be the same.

I nodded.

"We'll do the deal tomorrow night," he said. "Bring the car here but don't come inside. At ten thirty we'll be sitting in a silver BMW out in front. Honk at us when you see us, then follow us to where we take you."

I wondered where that might be but didn't ask.

"When Mendez sees the car for himself and approves, you will be paid ten thousand in American dollars. If he does not approve, you will drive the car back to San Diego and forget this meeting ever took place. Is this clear?"

"Yes." I figured that meant I would be meeting Mendez. The thought sent a quick shiver down my spine. Suppose they brought me somewhere to Mendez and he didn't like the Ferrari and got pissed off. Maybe *then* I'd get whacked. He wouldn't need me for any further car deals if he were unhappy with the first one. One thing I knew about drug dealers: there was no coming back for seconds if they didn't like the first product.

"*Bueno*," the second one said, and they got up and left me sitting at the table. I watched them disappear through clouds of smoke and then out the door. Suddenly, one of them slipped back inside and made his way back through the crowd to my table.

"Listen, *amigo*," he said hovering over me. "Tomorrow, when we drive on the highway, it's possible you'll be stopped by a *federale*. Make sure that when you show him your license and the papers for the car, you have a hundred dollar bill sticking out of your wallet. That's the way things are done here."

I nodded. Alberto had told me the same thing.

He turned to go but stopped and wheeled around with an afterthought. He reached into his pleated trousers and removed a wad of hundred dollar bills, dropped one on the table. "There, *amigo*," he said. "That oughta make it easier for you with the *federales*."

He disappeared again and neither of them came back.

A waitress came over with another White Russian. I gulped it down quickly to quench my thirst and soothe my nerves. Bones and I had been in the identity theft business for five years. We'd dealt with bankers, shop-owners, real estate and casino people, and salespeople. But drug dealers were not the same. They were a menacing breed. I really wasn't sure why I was letting myself get mixed up with them. We certainly had enough clever ways for making money off our phony credit cards and IDs. Why buck it? I guessed it was for the thrill. Maybe I'd been tiring of the ATM and Comchek machines we'd been hitting for the easy cash. Maybe I myself had watched one too many episodes of *Miami Vice*.

The next afternoon at five o'clock, just before closing, I appeared on the lot of Fantasy Rent-a-Dream in Beverly Hills. There were three dozen superbly gorgeous automobiles in three equal rows: Rolls Royces, E-Type Jaguars, Lotuses, Aston Martins and Panteras. One for every road dream imaginable. A shiny red Ferrari Testarossa sat in between a pink '57 Thunderbird convertible and a Corvette Stingray from the early sixties.

I smiled and went inside the office. A wispy, dour little man with an obnoxious manner was speaking with a young couple at his counter. It was somebody's wedding they wanted to go to in a Rolls Royce and then present it to the groom for the weekend as their gift. They made the deal, and then the little man turned his attention on me.

"What year is that Ferrari Testarossa in the lot?" I asked him.

"Ninety-four," he growled. "You wanna rent it?"

"Yes."

"For how long?"

"Just one day." Although the little prick would never see the car again, which delighted me, there was still no reason to have more than the minimum bite taken out of the credit card.

"That's seven hundred ninety-five dollars."

I laid the platinum Amex on the countertop. I had a matching driver's license in a stolen name with my photograph. It was the first time I had become somebody else. We'd been selecting some younger creditworthy men in the *Who's Who* volumes. It was also our first American Express card. We'd finally made the plunge in Atlanta, but we would not abuse Amex cards with the same ferocity we did Visas and MasterCards.

"You want insurance?"

"I'm already insured up to the yin-yang," I answered smartly. "My company covers me behind the wheel of *any* car."

"You got proof of that with you?"

I pressed my hand to my mouth as though I'd forgotten it. Of course I had personal insurance in my real name for my real vehicle, which by then was a Porsche Carrera, but obviously I couldn't show it.

"Sorry, then, Mr."—he looked down and read the name off the Amex—"Wilson. You're gonna have to take the minimum insurance. That's one hundred eighty-six dollars additional."

I grunted my acceptance.

"And that's if you're not taking the car into Mexico." His shiny, sweating pate popped up at me as he stopped filling in the boxes on the rental contract.

I swallowed a basketball.

"You're not taking the car into Mexico, are you?" He asked the question as if knowing I was, or so it seemed in my nervous state of mind.

I collected myself. "Of course not," I said as if the mere idea was ridiculous. "In fact, I'm heading in the other direction, to San Francisco. Going to a wedding."

"You, too!" he exclaimed, and I couldn't believe I'd said that.

He ran the card through the machine, I signed the contract and drove off the lot in the sharp Ferrari. I was in Mexico probably before that clerk sat down to dinner. I'd cruised down the 405 Freeway with the top down and blasted the radio. I exceeded no speed limits. Though for the time being I had broken no laws and only legally rented a car, I still had no desire to be pulled over and questioned by cops. And if that had to happen, I preferred it did with the *federales* in Mexico.

Naturally I was fearful, but in a fatalistic way. I'd have to handle this potentially dangerous operation by myself. Bones and I had discussed it at length during that morning's "board meeting." We decided that Mendez could be trusted to buy the car and not kill me. Why would he do so, we'd asked ourselves, if he could buy from us a $100,000 sports cars for a dime on the dollar? Besides, drug lords seldom killed people who were not a threat to their business. Rival dealers and hounding judges, yes, but not a small-potato American car thief, or whatever else they assumed I was.

When I crossed the border into Tijuana at seven thirty, the Mexican border guard gave me a contemptuous look. He was less than welcoming, but I knew why. After all, the vehicle he had just waved into his country was worth a hundred times the Mexican per capita income.

I had three hours to kill before the meet with the drug dealers. I'd thought of burning off the time in another bar on the main drag in Tijuana, but then thought better of it. I didn't want to park the Testarossa in the street and draw attention or, worse, have the car stolen. I pulled into the valet parking of the betting facility where I'd met Kashoggi. It was away from downtown; neither the car nor I would be noticed, at least by anyone other than the valet parker.

"Nice wheels, *amigo*," he said, his brows arched.

For some reason I replied, "I won't have 'em for long."

The Dodgers were taking the field on one of the giant screens at the front of the betting parlor. Just below it I saw the back of a huge sombrero hat and knew only the head of Kashoggi could be tucked underneath. He was smoking a cigar that stunk up the whole room.

"Ferrari Testarossa," he said knowingly in a conspiratorial tone as I sat down. "That's class."

"Don't know of drug dealers going in any other style," I replied smugly. I tried to read Kashoggi, to gauge whether or not I'd be facing danger in my dealings with Mendez and his men. Although he neither commented nor said anything to comfort me, I somehow felt reassured sitting alongside the pompous middleman from Mexico City. We watched the Dodger game, which ended at ten fifteen, perfect timing for my departure to the Pink Rose bar.

The silver BMW was sitting right where it was supposed to be, directly across the street from the entrance to the bar. I honked at it and recognized the guy behind the wheel when he turned toward me. He was the one who'd done most of the talking at our lounge table the night before. I didn't see the guy in the passenger seat's face but assumed he was the second of Mendez's men I'd already met.

The driver eased the BMW onto the road, and I followed. He led me through a few streets downtown, then up and around a snaking ramp to the highway. The BMW slid under the blue sign with white letters and an exaggerated vertical arrow indicating Ensenada. I wondered whether that was our destination. Who knew? For all I did, it was possible I'd be driving all the way to Acapulco.

I turned on the air and my favorite light rock San Diego radio station, settling comfortably into the ride, the BMW rolling along two hundred yards ahead of me. Ten miles out of Tijuana, I took note of the pretty Spanish-style haçiendas lining the darkened coast. Each house had a TV satellite protruding from its roof. I got the impression that most were owned by

American businessmen who came to their residences south of the border to relax and escape the surfers on California's beaches.

I was enjoying the sight of nearby dark islands protruding mountainously from the black sea when the smoothness of my ride was rudely interrupted by flashing blue lights splashing off my rearview mirror.

"Son of a bitch!" I shrieked aloud. The *federales*! And then I suddenly remembered that I'd forgotten to stick the hundred-dollar bill in my pocket. Worse, I'd left it in my apartment. All I had on me was forty bucks, and I wasn't sure how I was getting back to San Diego from wherever we were headed.

I eased the Testarossa onto the shoulder and prayed for the best. The *federale* who got out of the cruiser behind me and approached my driver's side window was a caricature of what you'd see in a B-movie. He was hatless with a big belly bunched into his uniform and funnily reminded me of the Dodgers' pitcher Fernando Valenzuela, whom I'd just watched pitch at the betting parlor while chatting with Kashoggi.

I quickly reached into my jeans pocket, extracted my wallet, grabbed the two twenties from the cash compartment and stuffed them inside the clear plastic fold containing my driver's license. Then I looked ahead to see if the BMW had stopped along the shoulder to wait for me. I didn't see it. I hoped the two dopers were aware I was being delayed and pulled off the road somewhere in the distance.

"*Buenos noches, amigo,*" the *federale* greeted me with a grin and crooked teeth.

"*Buenos noches.* What did I do, officer?"

"*Nada.* Nothing at all. Just a registration check. Can I see your driver's license and proof of insurance, too, *por favor*?"

"Of course."

I very carefully opened my wallet and removed the fold containing the license and money. Then, purposefully timed to avoid looking at him while he spotted the money, I reached into the glove compartment and pulled out the rental contract, which contained the proof of insurance. When I slid back upright in the seat, the *federale* burst out laughing. It was a real robust laugh with gusto. Naturally, I had no idea what was so funny, so I sat there with my mouth shut and waited.

"*Amigo,*" he finally said when the guffaw subsided. "That is not very much insurance you have there."

I knew what he meant, but didn't know what to say. Finally I said the only thing I could. "That's all I have."

He eyeballed me, the remnants of his laugh gone, then his eyes dropped down to my wrist and hands. A smile returned to his face. "*Señor*, that is a very nice watch you have there. *Muy bonita!*"

So he'd found my way out. I quickly unclasped the Cartier tank watch, which had been bought earlier in the week off another credit card, and dangled it to him. Had it been a solid gold Rolex, two of which had also been bought that month, one in Phoenix, the other in Santa Barbara, I would have let him impound the goddamned car and walked back to San Diego. But the Cartier was only a few-hundred-dollar item and would not put much of a dent in the ten grand I'd collect from Mendez.

If all went according to plan.

"It is very nice," he said for the third time, shining his flashlight at it.

"It's yours," I said with a forced smile.

"Mine!" he feigned his surprise.

"Yes, *la suya*," I remembered from high school Spanish.

"*Muchas gracias, Señor,*"

"Think nothing of it," I said with a touch of sarcasm, mocking either him or me. I wasn't sure.

"You have a nice evening in Ensenada," he offered with a final smile, then tapped the top of the windshield and added "Nice wheels" before he turned and went back to his cruiser.

I pulled back onto the highway. Ensenada. Was that where I was headed? Did the *federale* know it? Was he, too, on Mendez's payroll, or did he just assume I was headed to Ensenada because that's where a lot of Americans driving luxury cars southbound normally headed?

A few miles down the road, I spotted the BMW crawling along in the right-hand lane. As I got close, I gave it a flash of my brights and it picked up speed. We drove along for an hour and a half, but before we hit the outskirts of Ensenada, where the highway narrowed into a single lane in both directions, the BMW's right directional signal began flashing, which took me by surprise. I hadn't noticed there was an exit.

There wasn't.

It turned off onto a very narrow path lined on both sides by tall, camouflaging bushes of some cactus variety I couldn't identify. They, and the darkness, I imagined, could very well keep us hidden from aircraft patrolling above. That thought was confirmed when the BMW suddenly stopped a hundred yards into the bush. The Mexican in the driver's seat jumped out of the car and trotted toward me. And in the beam of my headlights I saw a machine pistol slung over his shoulder. I felt a lump in my throat, but at least it wasn't in his hands and pointing at me.

"Turn off your headlights and get out," he ordered me.

So here's where it ends, I thought, my heart now thumping with fear. I noticed the BMW's headlights were off. They were going to kill me and rob the car, after all. What else should I have expected from slimy drug dealers? Surely they didn't get rich from being honest and keeping their word.

The Mexican did not hoist the machine pistol off his shoulder. He said briskly, "Get in the BMW with Miguel." I didn't ask why or what was happening. I just obeyed his command while he climbed into the driver's seat of the Testarossa. Miguel didn't bother looking at me as he threw the BMW into first and slowly rolled along the gravel, in the now absolute darkness. His partner followed in the Testarossa.

The path was not a straightaway, therefore it could not be negotiated in total darkness without colliding against the brush, or whatever else might impede it, unless the driver was keenly familiar with its zigs and zags. After we'd traversed a bunch of them, I decided that they were not going to kill me. I assumed, correctly, that Miguel only wanted his partner behind the wheel of what would become his boss's newest luxury sports car. With me driving it through the blackness of that unfamiliar jungle, the risk of damaging the Ferrari was probably 100 percent.

We continued along in silence for nearly an hour. Miguel didn't say a word, nor did I venture a question or a comment. The only noise besides the engine was the crunching of gravel underneath rubber and the occasional swiping and scratching of branches against the fenders and windows. I guessed we'd gone about fifteen miles. I didn't dare lean over to get a look at the BMW's odometer. I certainly didn't want Miguel thinking I was nosy or maybe even a narc or something.

Then Miguel suddenly stopped the car and turned on the headlights, and I received a shock. We were sitting in front of a haçienda, a long, sprawling ranch-style haçienda with a marble statue pissing into a stone fountain in front and a sloping red stucco roof on top. Above it all were vast formations of spiraling foliage that made you feel as though the house were planted somewhere deep in an Amazonian rain forest. Before I got done admiring its façade, a man came outside through the front door. He was beautifully thin and wore a tapered shirt above jaunty slacks cut just below the knee. He had a shock of black hair that appeared less greasy than his comrades'. His gold chain was less thick and more refined than theirs. No doubt it was Mendez.

Miguel opened his car door and climbed out, motioning for me to do the same. Mendez walked quickly by us, muttering something in Spanish to Miguel that I didn't get but assumed was in praise of the Testarossa, and went to make a closer inspection of it. He did not demand of his other subordinate, still sitting behind the wheel, to pop open the hood, nor did he make any of the gestures normal people did when examining a used car they might buy. He only looked at the Ferrari's gleaming finish as he ran his hand along the side panel. After a minute, he smiled and said, "*Bueno.*"

I hoped the translation of that word in English meant "ten grand." With no problems. If one arose, it might instead mean "death."

Mendez looked straight at me for the first time. His eyes pierced mine like a pair of dark bullets. "Wait here," he said brusquely, and then with Miguel strode back past the fountain and into the house. The other Mexican got out of the Ferrari and joined me by the hood of the BMW. We both watched the statue pissing into the fountain.

"Looks like we got a deal, *amigo*," he said with a wide smile. For the first time, I felt really confident that we did. If they'd been planning on killing me and robbing the car, I'd already be dead.

Miguel came back out of the house alone. He walked up to me, and I could see a wad of folded hundred dollar bills squeezed in his hand. He handed it to me. "Ten grand," he said, in a tone that implied there was no need to count it. I didn't dare, and quickly stuffed the bills in my pocket.

"Mendez wants to know when you can deliver the next car?"

I looked in his eyes and shrugged. I didn't see any reason to waste time. "Tomorrow."

"Then do it tomorrow," he said with a curt nod.

"No problem. What kind of car does your boss want?"

"He doesn't care," Miguel responded, as if he didn't either. "Just make sure it's a nice one."

That was easy enough. Southern California was loaded with exotic rental-car agencies that were loaded with "nice" cars. Another two-and-a-half-hour drive for ten grand was well worth the trip. I'd do it until there was a reason not to.

"It will be just as nice as this one," I said, indicating the Testarossa with a head jerk. I was suddenly beaming with pride. In some perverse way it felt cool dealing with high-level Mexican drug dealers.

"Okay." He offered his hand and I shook it. He had a firm grip. He told his partner to drive me back to Tijuana in the BMW and I climbed back into the passenger seat. Again we traversed the long gravel road in darkness. At the intersection with the highway, he snapped on the lights. An hour and a half later, after speeding along the road without worries of *federales*, we were in Tijuana. He dropped me downtown, where I found a top-of-the-line fleabag and checked in. I spent the night, slept rather well and crossed the border on foot in the morning.

A curious female customs agent asked what I had been doing in Mexico.

I replied, "Yesterday afternoon I went to the racetrack. Then I spent the night getting drunk on White Russians with some friends. They went back yesterday; I checked into a motel."

For some reason she regarded me suspiciously while waving me through. After three paces inside the USA, I let out a sigh of relief.

"Hey!" the woman officer suddenly called out to me.

My face must have gone ashen as I turned around. "Yes?"

"Did you win?"

"Did I what?" My brain went foggy.

"Win. At the racetrack."

I was so nervous I completely forgot I'd told her about the racetrack. "Oh, win." Finally I collected myself. "Are you kidding? You know anyone who wins at the racetrack?"

She smiled and turned her head. I scurried back into California. I grabbed a bus to San Diego and hurried to our apartment. Bones had been waiting anxiously, but the grin on his face told me he knew it had gone all right. I tossed the packet of cash on the kitchen table. He glanced at it, and then made a note to enter it into the books.

I had a quick bite to eat while scanning the yellow pages. I picked out another exotic rental-car agency, and got there just before closing time. I rented a brand new Jaguar XJS convertible with a gold Visa that said I was Mr. Seymour Epstein.

In the next year, we hit two dozen exotic car-rental lots in Southern California.

Mendez and a lot of his drug-trafficking buddies were very happy.

Price Can't Be Beat Enterprises

Las Vegas, 1995-1998

DURING THE HOT CAR RAMPAGE, WE CONTINUED FLYING around the country attending to our other businesses. Our bank and merchandising scams expanded so rapidly that we needed faster sales channels just to keep up. The trucking system we used to ship the goods to Mexico was too slow, causing backlogs. So I came up with a telemarketing solution. Instead of shipping merchandise to Mexico, why not set up shop somewhere and hire people to sell our goods by phone? Potential buyers would be the entire United States of America, both residential and commercial.

But Bones and I did not have the time to set it up. If we were going to change the face of our business, we would have to bring in new faces. Firstly, we needed a trusted person to run a telemarketing room. I told Bones about a guy I knew from college whom we could trust. After much discussion, we agreed to approach him. He would not be told of the identity theft operation, just that we were a fencing operation that could get its hands on any and all merchandise.

Back in my days at Berkeley, I hung out and smoked reefer with a Jewish guy named Barry Horowitz who must have had Rastafarian blood running through his veins because he was just that mellow. During spring break in

Jamaica, he smoked every dude with dreadlocks we came across under the table. They all loved him. They invited him over to their clapboard houses to listen to Bob Marley and toke up. In fact, Barry was so mellow that I gave him a nickname: Bim. It stood for "being intensely mellow," and it stuck with everyone on campus.

After Berkeley, Bim had gone to Northern California, where he grew weed, became a vegetarian, got married, had two kids and turned into somewhat of a freak. I determined that when he told me years later that his twelve-year-old boy and seven-year-old girl had never seen a doctor, at least not since their births. That neither had ever eaten meat was by that time a foregone conclusion. If that wasn't enough, Bim's kids had never attended school. His wife taught them at home. If *that* wasn't enough, the last time I spoke to Bim, he told me that soon the vegetables would be out, too. He had found sun-gazing to help alter his diet, to the point where his consumption of food would be practically zero.

"What the hell is sun-gazing?" I had asked in disbelief.

"You gaze at the sun and suck in its energy," Bim said. He went on to explain that you had to do this just after dawn and just before dusk, when the sun's rays were no longer harmful to your eyes. By doing that, he assured me, you could eventually survive from the energy your body seeped up from the sun. You started your sun-gazing séances at ten-second durations, and then worked them up to two daily sessions of twenty minutes. That's what it took to reach the point of no food. He capped off this enlightening discussion by comparing it to Indian yogis who subsisted on water and a few leaves a day.

My first question for Bim was "What happens when it rains?"

"Oh, that's no big deal," Bim said. "You can still derive some energy through the clouds. But if it rains too many consecutive days, you gotta pack up and go somewhere in the desert. Or you have to go back to eating vegetables until the weather clears."

I just hoped he wasn't putting his kids through the same routine. Especially if he didn't believe in doctors and modern medicine.

That I knew Bim was fried did not deter me from seeking his aid to work with us. One of his traits, probably a by-product of his mellowness, was his ability to stay cool under pressure. I'd noticed this when the Berkeley campus police came crashing through his apartment door with a search warrant. Bim didn't bat an eyelash. He'd been doing a little dealing and had some stash hidden in a few boxes of cereal, but the cops didn't find it.

When I detailed my plan, he was all gung-ho. His only concern had nothing to do with the risks of the telemarketing scheme. When he expressed it, I had the perfect solution.

"Don't worry, Bim," I assured him confidently. "You'll be able to do all the sun-gazing you want! We're setting up the telemarketing offices in Las Vegas. You'll be right in the middle of the desert!"

Las Vegas, Nevada, was the capital of the world for two industries. The first everyone knows about. The second was telemarketing. Thousands of telemarketing operations sprouted up around Sin City like cacti in the desert. Most of them were fly-by-night, here today-gone tomorrow, but many were thriving businesses and practically all were at least on the fringes of legality.

Our telemarketing firm, which we named "Price Can't Be Beat Enterprises," had one huge advantage over any other that sold merchandise: our price could not be beat. Therefore, we could sell any kind of merchandise carried by department stores, which was practically everything, at prices significantly lower than those selling even stolen merchandise. This was true because firms buying stolen goods for as low as ten cents on the retail dollar were still paying *something*.

Most telemarketers worked with "leads," names of people or companies that had previously bought over the telephone, or were judged likely to buy based on certain social and economic criteria. Our callers would be calling without leads and banking on happenstance sales due to our incredible discounts. The motto of our company, as unoriginal as it was fitting, was "We'll make you an offer you can't refuse."

Our offer really couldn't be refused. We weren't restricted to hawking particular items. We were selling *everything*. People on the phone customarily rejected telemarketers in saying "I don't need this" or "I don't need that," but they couldn't say "I don't need *anything*." Our sales pitch would basically let people know that we could supply them with anything they needed within days, at (of course) the lowest price possible in all markets. This was like offering people dictionaries containing only the words they wanted to look up. It was perfect.

Bim stocked up his large kitchen refrigerator with enough dried fruits and vegetables to last the wife and kids a month, then kissed them all goodbye and flew to Vegas. We rented a 10,000 square-foot office for the operation, installing fifty phone lines. We anticipated hiring lots of employees. Bim conducted the interviews and hired ten people to start.

IDENTITY THEFT, INC.

Using the utmost discretion, we trained our telemarketers to inform potential customers of our unusual capability to provide them with almost anything without sounding like they were advertising a national clearinghouse for stolen merchandise. Bones and I worked long and hard to devise a pitch to subconsciously coerce people into believing we only manufactured goods vital to their particular business or home. Then by using scores of business cross-referenced directories categorized by type, location and longevity, we customized sales pitches to fit a particular business's needs. An appliance store in Tennessee was told about our massive close-out sale on boom boxes. A clothing boutique in St. Louis learned about our leftover inventory of designer suits that had to be gotten rid of before the new seasonal line came out. A bicycle shop in rural Wisconsin was informed about the surplus of Schwinns we had in stock.

Nobody, of course, trusted an unheard-of company enough to prepay orders over the telephone, but everyone gladly did business cash-on-delivery upon seeing *they* were practically stealing the merchandise. Did you ever notice how people flock to parties offering free food and drink? Well, that's about the same way it went with discounted goods we shipped across the country.

The last line of the sales pitch Bim taught his employees was "And if you don't like what you see, tell the driver and he'll deliver it right back to us at no cost to you." Naturally no one ever sent back our products. We were selling merchandise to businesses at prices they could never get from legitimate wholesalers.

It worked like a charm, though we still had to be extremely careful to avoid federal heat. When selling illegal merchandise to legitimate people who are not aware of the illicit nature of the transaction, certain rules apply. First and foremost is to never undercut their current suppliers by too great a percentage. If a clothing store is paying $4,000 a gross for designer shirts, sell them your gross of the same product for $3,500. If you were to sell it at, say, $2,000, you would be inviting suspicion, because even the most naïve merchant had to know that a jobber cutting his supplier's price in half was dealing in hot merchandise.

At the same time, it was important that the discount you offered was significant enough to grab the merchant's attention. By offering that same gross at $3,800, the merchant might not want to bother changing his supplier. Business people who'd established long-term relationships with suppliers preferred keeping them intact, unless, of course, a new supplier came along with a significantly better price while upholding the merchant's confidence. A buyer of merchandise at 10 or 15 percent below wholesale was likely to consider his new supplier a good find rather than a questionable purveyor.

Sometimes people we telephoned questioned our ability to sell goods so "reasonably." We had Bim train his telemarketers to respond that such information was a "trade secret." Such a response nipped any further inquiries in the bud.

Like legitimate retailers, we were able to furnish buyers of hard goods with manufacturer's warranties. Every TV, hi-fi system and washing machine purchased from a department store came with warranties. All we had to do was transfer those warranties to our customers. When they received the goods, they simply filled out their warranty cards and sent them to the manufacturers courtesy of the Postal Service's "No postage necessary" envelopes.

Warranties were not necessary for soft goods. Buyers of clothing were shown the garment inspection sticker inside the sleeves or pockets of whatever garment they were purchasing. In the world of designer clothing, there were so many below-wholesale suppliers that retailers very rarely questioned us.

Before long, Bim had fifty telemarketers manning the phones. Unlike most telemarketing businesses, we managed to hold onto employees. They were set up with generous commission schedules, and bonus incentives popped up all around them. A handful of the best "closers" were making as much as five grand a week. Their function was to close out deals after the initial caller had hooked customers but couldn't reel them in. They would come on the line and, speaking in quick bursts, tell the potential customer whatever it took to swing the deal.

The money rolled in. Sixty percent of it was in cash, and the rest by certified check, or by regular checks from repeat customers. These checks were deposited in legitimate bank accounts we maintained for the business in Las Vegas. Few of them bounced. In fact, we were completely legitimate within the banking end of the operation. We had a federal tax ID number, and we even paid business taxes, though of course no personal income tax returns were ever filed.

Many of our repeat customers were personal accounts. They presented us with a particularly humorous dilemma: they wanted to pay us by credit card! At first we declined, but upon the loss of hundreds of customers who would only do business with plastic, we realized that we had to accept credit cards. So like any other retailer, we joined the Visa and MasterCard association, although we stayed away from American Express. I never would have dreamed that we would be on the merchant's end of credit cards, but that's what happened. And we enjoyed a great business relationship with the banks and credit card companies.

A few of our smarter employees sensed that we weren't exactly an aboveboard operation. This we'd expected, as people who floated in and out of telemarketing rooms were often criminals themselves. These boiler-room operations did not conduct background investigations into employees. Those employees who grew suspicious kept their mouths shut to protect their own jobs. After all, what did they give a shit whether we were on the up-and-up? They were smart enough to know that they had lucked into great jobs, and that discussing them with anyone else outside the room was counterproductive to their own financial security.

Occasionally a curious employee asked about the production end of the business. Bim's response was to remind them that sales, not production, was their only concern. This gave the impression that Price Can't Be Beat Enterprises was run by serious entrepreneurs who had no time for dealing with questions not pertaining to the bottom line.

The business got so lucrative that we printed up customized catalogue booklets and sent them to our repeat customers. Businesses ordering electronic equipment were sent catalogues displaying TVs, hi-fi equipment, computers and electric typewriters. Those that ordered blouses and dresses received our catalogues featuring designer outfits for both men and women. Sporting goods companies received pretty pamphlets with overlays of baseball bats, basketballs and hockey sticks. The idea was to expand the types of merchandise our customers were buying.

Our marketing concept worked so well that soon we were receiving orders we couldn't fill. Despite hundreds of department store charge cards pouring in monthly, we couldn't come up with five hundred computers or three thousand CD players. Those customers that we couldn't satisfy, we lost.

One of our telemarketers was connected with a large chain of New York camera shops. The owner was delighted that we could supply Nikons and Canons at 15 percent less per gross than his current suppliers. Only problem was that he wanted 10,000 assorted cameras.

I happened to be in the office when this happened. The young girl who'd made the call came running to Bim, who came to me. I told the girl to inform the guy that we could supply him with 500 cameras a month, maybe 1,000. To do so we would have to direct the totality of our charge cards to that end in those department stores that sold cameras. But the guy ended any further speculation when he said he couldn't be bothered with the savings on such small lots. These losses of potential customers were a fact of life we had to swallow, just as a restaurateur had to digest turning parties away from his packed dining room.

After a year in the telemarketing business, we left its reigns entirely in Bim's hands. He proved efficient in running it, and was extremely well-liked by the employees. His staff of fifty worked full-time Monday through Friday. A skeleton crew worked on Saturdays. United Parcel Service shipped all of our orders. We had opened a business account with them, and they billed us monthly just as they billed tens of thousands of other customer accounts.

In Cleveland, where we had two scam houses going with six identities, I thought of another crazy scheme. Actually, it was a version of the decades-old garage sale. Except that ours was a bit unique, more like selective merchandising. Instead of used clothing, TVs, stereo equipment and lawnmowers, we would offer but a single item for sale—though it was gigantic.

It started with regular-sized Sony nineteen-inch Trinitron TVs. We bought a dozen of them in department stores at $800 a pop. The idea was to sell them all in one fell swoop, without having to transport them the way we did with the telemarketing room merchandise. That's where the garage-sale idea came in. Why not have our customers come to us?

We put an ad in the *Cleveland Plain Dealer* classifieds: "Brand new Sony nineteen-inch Trinitron, $500." The phone at the scam house started ringing off the hook. Obviously the general population knew that Sony televisions had the best reputation in the industry, and they jumped at the chance of buying one for 37.5 percent off. The first question people invariably asked over the phone was "Do you still have the TV for sale?" The second was "Why are you selling it?" Our stock answer for the first was, of course, "Yes," although we peppered it with "But someone is coming over to see it tomorrow." Naturally that response was geared to get the caller over to look at it *today*. The questions about why we were selling it were met with assurances that the set was brand new and still in the unopened box. We gave excuses of urgently needing money, suddenly being forced to move out of Cleveland and whatnot.

Once again, we'd found another efficient way of turning merchandise into cash. However, this was the first time we had succeeded in moving bulk hard merchandise as easy, if not easier, than soft goods. After three weeks of this, we transferred the operation to our second Cleveland scam house. We also changed the Sony. Why not buy the absolute top-of-the-line product?

At the time, department stores were just beginning to sell giant-screen TVs. The huge seventy-inch monsters first appeared in specialty "Big Screen TV" stores and were not available elsewhere. We hit the appliance departments in the major department stores and bought up as many super TVs as our charge cards allowed. They did not come cheap. Between $5,000 and $7,000 was the price, which meant each TV burned up the limit of a charge card. The positive was that we only had to make one purchase, plus the department stores delivered the giant novas to the scam house.

With four in stock, we placed the ad in the *Cleveland Plain Dealer*. We had an address and phone number that differed from those used in selling the nineteen-inch Sonys. The first gentleman who came to see the set we had priced at $3,500 exclaimed, "What's the matter, aren't you a football fan?" To which I replied, "Sure, I am, but I have a family of four and don't need this thing clogging up my living room." He nodded and gave me the cash.

Bones handled the second sale while I was closing up the other scam house. It seemed for some reason that prospective buyers were more inquisitive about why we were selling than they'd been for the smaller TVs. Bones used the "unwanted wedding gift" rap. He explained to people that he and the new missus were just starting out and needed cash to buy other more necessary items for their household. A few people declined, but eventually he sold the second of our four sets.

The third one went to a bunch of college kids from wealthy Shaker Heights families. One of them reminded Bones of Robby Parsons from the New Jersey disaster. They said they wanted the TV for the common room of their fraternity house at Boston University. Since they were renting a truck to transport their belongings to the frat house, adding the giant TV to its load would not complicate matters or add to the cost.

The transaction for the last of the four big-screens was the one that sent a shiver down my spine. It had been sitting in the scam house's garage, still in its protective packing. I was upstairs going through a very difficult bowel movement when the doorbell rang. I'd forgotten someone had called to say he was coming over early in the evening.

I whispered an expletive, wiped my butt, pulled up my pants and ran to the door. What I forgot to do was close the partition that closed off the dining room area from the living room. In that space was a stack of boxes containing much smaller televisions. We did have some "front furniture" in the living room, but the only eye-catching decoration in the house was that stack of TV sets sitting in unopened boxes. I didn't realize it until it was too late. I had already opened the front door.

The middle-aged woman standing there in front of her husband struck me immediately as someone who asked lots of questions. I was not wrong. The first thing she asked upon entering the house and giving it the look-over was "How long have you been in the neighborhood?" The neighborhood was just on the outskirts of Shaker Heights.

"Only two months," I said, noting that the husband didn't seem interested in small talk.

"What do you do for a living?" was her next question.

My mind said, "I'm doing it, lady!" But I told her I was a certified public accountant, which I really had to be to count all our goddamned merchandise.

"Oh, that's nice," she said, then proudly added, "Our son's currently at Northwestern studying to be an accountant."

"Oh, really!" I feigned polite interest.

Finally, the husband got me off the hook. "Let's take a look at the big screen," he said rather curtly. He was a burly, bull-headed guy. I noticed his eyes catch sight of the stack of televisions in the dining room. With great concentration, I held my attention away from them as if they weren't there. I led them out to the garage and unwrapped the video monster. The man was impressed. He immediately asked how much I wanted for it.

I went into my usual sales pitch. Indicating the sales ticket attached to the wrapping, I said, "I paid seven thousand for it, and as you can see, it's still in the box." I paused a moment. Then: "I'll take half." Like always, I was careful not to sound slick when giving the price. I would never use the word "grand."

"Why are you selling it?" he asked. He wanted to know, even though he didn't want to grill me like his wife did.

"It was a wedding present from my wife's aunt. We just don't need it. Nor do we have the room for it."

The woman refused to give me a break. "Oh, you're married," she said. Her tone implied that for some reason I either shouldn't be or didn't merit a wife. "How come your wife isn't here? It's already getting dark outside."

I had it in me to say "Because she's out getting her ass screwed off by my best man," and even the husband rolled his eyes in mock impatience with his wife's prying, but I simply told her my wife was an early-evening jogger. Then to my utter amazement, she asked how many miles my wife ran. Either this woman was an ex-investigator of some kind or watched too many cop shows. I answered that she was doing a lot of running lately because she planned on entering the Cleveland marathon. I didn't know if there was a Cleveland marathon, but at least it moved the conversation back to the big-screen TV.

The husband liked the big TV and offered $2,500 for it. We had gotten $3,500 for each of the other sets, but I just wanted to make a deal and get these people out of the scam house. Despite that, I said that $3,500 was a very low price. The man offered $2,750 and we haggled back and forth before settling on $3,000. He went out to his car to fetch the cash. He said it was locked in the glove compartment.

While he was gone, his wife said, "Oh, my husband will just love this TV. I'm so happy for him. He works so hard during the day. Coming home to watch his baseball games on that set will just light up his life."

I was thinking that she certainly couldn't. Then for some reason, I idly asked her, "What kind of work does he do?" I certainly couldn't have cared less.

She looked at me askance, as though I should have known by what means her husband made his living. "Oh, you didn't know? He's the chief of the Shaker Heights Police Department, Chief Barnes."

That knocked my socks off! I managed to blurt out, "The… Shaker Heights Police Department?"

"Been so for seven years," she affirmed proudly. "Been with the department for twenty-seven."

About the same number of years I might be facing in prison if Chief Barnes ever found out the truth about his big TV. I mumbled, "That's wonderful," as I began wondering if he had gone out to his car to get a warrant instead of the cash.

But Barnes returned with the cash in his hand. He proffered the bills. I was scared shitless to take them. The whole thing could be a sting operation, I warned myself. Perhaps someone had informed the Shaker Heights Police Department to the strange activities transpiring at our scam house. It could have been one of the previous buyers, or perhaps just a nosy neighbor. Had this indeed occurred, then all the chief needed was for me to accept the money and, bingo, I was busted, in the same manner drug-buy setups went down.

Suddenly I faced a dilemma. I truly didn't know what to do. One thing I knew I couldn't do was to call Bones. The ball was in my court. Either I dribbled it or turned it over. I had to decide then and there if this cop was a genuine buyer or if his three grand was dangerous money.

He caught on to my hesitation. "What's the matter?" he asked in a good-natured but disturbing voice. "You changing your mind? You don't think three grand is a fair price?"

The way he said "three grand" made me go for it. The fact that I had avoided the same term in order not to sound sly told me he would have made the same avoidance had he been setting me up.

"No problem," I said with mustered confidence. "We have a deal." I took the cash, still worried he would grab my wrist to slap on the cuffs while a team of the chief's officers crashed through the door and wrestled me to the ground. I actually squeezed my eyelids shut stuffing the bills in my pocket.

But none of this happened. Barnes and his wife thanked me very much. I was greatly relieved and thought it was all over when we shook hands. But the chief asked, "Would it be all right if I came back early tomorrow morning with a department van to pick up the set? It's getting late and I can't fit it in my car."

I hadn't planned on returning to the scam house the next day, but I didn't have a choice. I wanted neither to piss off the chief nor stir dormant suspicions. I told him he could pick up the set the next morning.

Back at our residence that night, which happened to be an exclusive rental apartment in Shaker Heights, I worried again that the scenario was a setup. I concocted visions of Chief Barnes getting his warrants overnight and returning with the rising sun to bust me.

Bones wouldn't hear of it. "Kid, you're always worrying too much," he scolded me. "Just don't sweat it. It's nothing. The chief went bargain-hunting like everyone else does. He's probably a Cleveland Indians fan and wants to catch their games on the big screen."

At least that corresponded to what his wife had said. "I don't know," I said dubiously. "You would think that Barnes would've come prepared to take the set if he were legit."

"He gave you the cash, didn't he?" I nodded. "Then he's legit. If it were a setup, you'd already be busted... And so would I for that matter."

"Just tell me one thing, Bones. Where does a cop get three grand for a television?"

"You said he was chief, right?"

"Yeah."

"Then if his salary's not paying for it, something else is. Either his wife or he's just as corrupt as we are."

The next morning at seven thirty, Chief Barnes rang the bell of the scam house. I looked out the upstairs window and saw the police van in the street. On its side was the unmistakable insignia of the Shaker Heights Police Department. I raced down the stairs in a hurry to get this over with. When I opened the front door, the rush of early morning light was like fire on my eyeballs. Squinting, I looked beyond Barnes. I was relieved to see no other vehicles besides his van.

I led him to the garage, and then helped him load the TV into the van. Before departing, he looked me straight in the eye and said, "Son, it was a pleasure doing business with you."

I watched him drive away. When he turned a corner and disappeared, I still stood there several moments. I was in a state of disbelief. We had just sold a giant-screen TV bought on a giant-limit charge card that was part of a giant criminal operation—to the chief of police.

What could be next?

A pair of phony high rollers

Las Vegas, Atlantic City, Puerto Rico and the Caribbean Islands, 1995-1998

WHAT CAME NEXT WAS NOT ONLY INCREDIBLE, BUT ALSO MY most enjoyable experience as a master identity thief. It came to me in the place where it should have come to me. The same place that inspired my earlier brainstorm to use Comchek machines: Las Vegas.

Bones and I were in Vegas visiting Bim, who continued his success with our telemarketing operation. One night in his apartment, the conversation turned to casinos. I had visions of the tons of easy cash that had come from casinos' Comchek machines. Although still generating lots of cash with Comchek, we had abandoned the machines in Vegas. We'd hit them far too many times. We'd become fearful of being set up in a casino by the Secret Service or FBI with the aid of the various Nevada law enforcement agencies that policed casinos, including the Enforcement Division of the Gaming Control Board. But the conversation in Bim's apartment gave me another idea.

"A big credit scam in the casinos," I said excitedly to Bones in our hotel room in the biggest one of them all, the MGM Grand.

"That's hairy," Bones said. "Lots of variables. Lots of uncertainties. And worst of all, lots of undercover cops and security people running around casinos."

"And lots of money running around, too," I added.

Bones slung his head in agreement. "Can't argue with that," he chuckled. "But how do we do it?"

I thought about it. A big credit scam in the casinos was the ultimate. It had the allure of a James Bond movie. A little bit of Frank Sinatra's *Ocean's Eleven*, too. I had always known about the huge amounts of credit casinos extended to their patrons. I remembered reading that people gambling on credit made up nearly 40 percent of casinos' gaming revenue. The credit instrument used by casinos was called a "marker." Once a casino's credit department approved you, you could obtain gaming chips by signing a marker, which was a saw-toothed document that greatly resembled a bank cashier's check. You would ask for a certain amount of gaming chips limited only by your assigned credit limit, then sign the marker at the blackjack or crap tables and receive your chips.

But how did it work? Was obtaining casino credit along the same route as establishing credit accounts with banks and department stores? When you borrowed money to gamble and then lost, when were you expected to pay it back? And if you won? Were you obliged to reimburse the casino immediately, before leaving town?

Bones agreed that a casino "bust-out" operation was worth looking into. I did the research. First thing I learned was that establishing credit in casinos was even easier than for banks and department stores, at least in terms of what you had to physically do. There was no need to fill out applications. All you had to do is call a casino's credit department. The entire process was handled over the phone.

Since Caesars Palace was my favorite casino, having been the first place we hit a Comchek machine, I decided to make my initial fact-finding call to its credit department. I had in front of me all the information pertaining to our latest identity, an accounting professional from Salt Lake City, Utah, who had been born the very day I was, same year and all. I found him in the *Who's Who in American Finance* at the University of Nevada Las Vegas library.

I asked the Caesars switchboard operator to put me through to the casino's VIP services. I figured that if I came off as a very important person, they would take me for one. A woman identifying herself as Dotty came on the line.

"I'd like to apply for casino credit," I said politely. "I understand I can do that over the phone."

"Yes you can," she said amiably. "I can take all the information from you now and pass it on to the credit department. They'll get back to you within three business days."

"Great."

"Okay then. Let's start with your full name, date of birth and Social Security number."

I wondered if my assumed mother's maiden name would be next. "Steven Tyler, August 17, 1942." I gave her the real Steven Tyler's Social Security number.

"Your current address?"

"Seven Timmony Circle, Boca Raton, Florida, three-three-four-three-two." We'd selected Boca Raton for a reason: it was one of the richest enclaves in America. The address would look great to the casinos. We had already set up two scam houses there.

"Telephone number?"

I gave her the number of our first Boca scam house.

"Employment?"

"I'm the comptroller of the Tropicana Electronics Company in West Palm Beach." I gave her the address of the business we opened under that name and the phone number connected to the address.

"What is your base salary, Mr. Tyler?"

"I earn seven hundred fifty thousand dollars a year." I listened for a reaction, but there was none. Obviously there were a lot of high rollers with big salaries who gambled their bonuses away at Caesars Palace.

"I need one checking account that's been open for at least six months," Dotty explained.

So there was the kicker for establishing casino credit. You had to give them a bank account that had been in existence for six months. And I understood why. People looking to obtain casino credit who already knew that credit departments demanded banking information could easily run to their bank, open up a checking account, stick a large amount of cash in it, and then empty it once their credit line was approved. By stipulating that the account be aged by at least six months, casinos virtually wiped out that possibility. And by doing so they avoided being stung by those credit-seeking fly-by-nighters whose debts often proved uncollectible.

I was thoroughly unprepared for Dotty's request. There was no way I could furnish the necessary information at that moment, so I feigned an interruption and advised her I'd call back. She thanked me, and I broke the connection.

Leaving Bones in Vegas, where he kicked back for a few days at the MGM's reservoir-sized swimming pool, I flew to Florida to set up the first of our casino-credit scams. With the necessary ID that I had previously obtained in that state, I opened a checking account in a Boca Raton bank in Tyler's name and made two deposits three days apart of just under $10,000 to safely remain exempt from the IRS cash-reporting law. Then I made a small third deposit to round out the account's balance to $20,000. A month later, I returned to Boca, and over the course of two weeks deposited another $30,000 in the account.

During the next six months, we never let that balance dip below $50,000. In addition, we created banking action by writing checks into and out of the account, making it look like Steven Tyler was a big-time check writer, a real mover who never stopped replenishing the funds in his account.

At the end of the six months, I made my second call to the Caesars Palace credit department. The woman on the line was not Dotty, though I would have hardly cared had she been. She welcomed me and said her name was Cynthia.

This time around I was highly prepared. I had Steven Tyler's actual interest-bearing checking account names and numbers in front of me. I also had his tax returns. For this new operation, we'd made our first direct foray into the IRS's records. By sending $4.25 and copies of ID documents in Tyler's name along with IRS Form 4506, we received copies of Tyler's tax returns in the mail.

Because the bank accounts paid Tyler interest, that interest income appeared on his return. I couldn't be sure of the total amount of funds in the bank, but based on the interest earned I could estimate the balances.

Cynthia asked me if I had ever applied for credit at Caesars Palace before. At first I was not sure how to respond, since I had been in the middle of applying, but ultimately decided to tell her exactly what had transpired. "Several months back I called your department, but I changed my mind and never finished the application process."

"Let me see if I have your name in our computer."

It turned out she did. Caesars probably figured Mr. Tyler would be back looking for a credit line. Cynthia quickly went through the information she read from her screen to verify it was current. Then she arrived at the banking section. I gave her the pertinent information for an account whose balance I estimated at $50,000. It was one of the accounts from Tyler's tax return.

"Is this the account you're going to write checks against to pay off casino markers?" Cynthia asked.

Now it was my turn to throw the Caesars credit department a curveball. "No," I said. "That's the account my wife knows about. For Caesars Palace I'm going to use a different account." Trying to be cute, I added, "My wife won't notice when money disappears from that one."

But Cynthia must have heard that one before. She didn't as much as chuckle. Behind the joke was implied seriousness. People working casinos' VIP services were well trained in the art of discretion. They understood all the crap about men gambling behind their wives' backs and juggling around funds in bank accounts, usually associated with a mad scramble to pay off casino markers. Thus giving Cynthia two checking accounts was quite natural, the reason obvious.

After the bank information request was satisfied, Cynthia double-checked the entire application, then promised that she would personally call to let me know the credit department's decision. Bones and I evaluated the situation. We felt our chances of being approved for a generous credit line at Caesars Palace were strong. The strength of Tyler's application was that we supplied its credit department with one of Tyler's real checking accounts, one that had probably existed for years. Had I only given Cynthia the one checking account that had been conveniently open for exactly six months, the minimum time allowable for approval, Caesars may have been reluctant to give Tyler a full credit line. We later learned, through repetitive credit-requests, that the casinos' practice was to extend credit in the amount of verified funds in the checking account you planned to use for paying markers. One verified checking account could secure credit lines in several casinos, depending on how quickly their credit departments reacted to whatever measure of excessive inquiries they went by. We didn't know it then, but casinos had a central computer networking system much the same as the banks'. Any individual credit department in Las Vegas could key in a person's name and view his casino credit history not only in Las Vegas but in other gambling areas where casinos were allowed by law to extend credit to their patrons.

Only one item concerning the real Steven Tyler was bothersome: Did he already have a credit line in any casino? Fortunately, Cynthia had not asked me this. Despite changes in Nevada law that made collecting gambling debts legal, information for casino credit accounts did not appear on TRW reports, therefore I couldn't know the right answer. If it turned out that Tyler did have casino credit lines, we could have a problem as the discrepancy between his genuine Utah address and our Florida one would show up in the system. However, given the fact that the real Steven Tyler lived in Salt Lake City and was undoubtedly a Mormon, the chances that he mixed gambling with the Church of Latter Day Saints were remote.

Cynthia called to inform me that I had been approved for a $50,000 credit line. She told me to page the casino host when I arrived at the hotel. He would "take care" of me. I would be given RFB privileges, which meant my room, food and beverage (except champagne) costs would be taken care of by the casino, as long as I showed the pit bosses the required gambling action. She instructed me to bring proper identification and an unsigned blank check from the account I'd be paying markers against. I assured her that not only would I bring the ID and the check but also that "my gambling action will even entitle me to free champagne."

A stretch Cadillac limousine rolled to a stop under the bright golden light filling the entranceway of Caesars Palace hotel in Las Vegas. The chauffeur parked behind a second black limo against the white marble steps that led to an armada of pearly glass doors into the casino. With the help of a Caesars valet, the limo's rear door swung majestically open and out stepped yours truly in the company of a glamorous woman I had met a week before.

She was Bim's wife, and I'd had no idea she was so glamorous. Despite the fact that she was a vegetarian and an animal-rights-protecting sun gazer like her husband, Deborah Horowitz was as hot as any caviar-eating bejeweled princess wearing a mink shawl Las Vegas had ever seen. I had not known this until Bim introduced us at their apartment.

With Steven Tyler's $50,000 sitting in the Florida checking account we had opened six months earlier, Bones and I had put our entire operation on hold—with the exception of the telemarketing scam—to design our casino-credit-fraud operation. We knew it would need several people involved, as it was far too complex and demanded too much physical maneuvering to be carried out by just three people. Bim's wife Deborah was actually the last of five new people we recruited to participate in the scam.

She and her children had moved into Bim's Vegas apartment. The kids suffered a major culture shock, although they were not enrolled in public school. As the scam would only be worked on weekends, Deborah would still be able to take charge of their reading, writing and arithmetic courses. In fact, she insisted on it. The only way to get her involved in the scam was to guarantee that her kids would stay out of school.

Deborah happened to be a natural scammer, despite her intensely clean lifestyle. She had an old-fashioned larcenous heart. So much so that she even agreed to wear a mink stole into Caesars Palace. Without the promised land of *mucho* bucks on the horizon, Deborah wouldn't be caught dead wearing anything that once had the ability to bite. Underneath the lush stole was a $2,000 Sonia Rykiel matching outfit fit for a princess. Salvatore Ferragamo shoes completed the look.

I wore an expensive, exquisitely tailored Armani suit that we'd bought with a Neiman Marcus charge card. Hand in hand with Deborah, we had all the air and sophistication of contemporary grace. Only we knew that beneath all the dazzling glitz, we were nothing but a pair of high-rolling con artists.

On the top step before the handsome doors, I paused to light a cigarette with my Dunhill. I had taken up part-time smoking just for this occasion and those to follow, if only to bring into evidence my gold lighter and French cigarettes. After a puff, which I hardly inhaled, I blew out the smoke and escorted my "wife" into the dark seduction of the casino. Cheers from crap tables wafted up from the pit, accompanied by the constant metallic beeping of slot machines.

We stepped into the sunken, domed pit and walked through sentinels of horseshoe-shaped blackjack tables. We skirted around one end to make our way to the main casino cashier cage. I picked up a house phone and asked the operator to get me the executive host's office. Sal Imperatore, Caesars's big honcho host, was expecting me. When he came right on the line, I said with the haughty confidence of the strip high roller, "Sal, Steven Tyler here. I'm in from Boca Raton."

Sal Imperatore spoke with the jocular familiarity that casino hosts use on complete strangers. It was a privilege in the casino business. It was also a polished method for ingratiating people out of their money.

"Been expecting you, Steve. How was your flight in? Stewardesses take care of you all right?" He chuckled obnoxiously. "If not, we'll find you some better ones on the ground." The host, so caught up in his own bullshit, had forgotten that his newest high roller was in town with his wife.

But I rolled along with the gig. Bones and I had rehearsed my act a hundred times. The difference between swindling casino machines and casino personnel was night and day. Whereas with bank cards we spoke to Comchek operators on the phone before heading to the cage to pick up the cash, we were now dealing with actual casinos whose money we would be stealing. Our entire stay there would be scrutinized by a wide array of personnel, everyone from hosts to pit bosses to unseen surveillance people. I had to be sharp. One little fuckup and they'd get on to me real fast.

"Thanks, Sal," I said, real chummy. "But I'll take the broads some other time. This trip I'm stuck with the wife."

"I'm very sorry to hear that, Steve, but we all learn from our mistakes." Sal continued pouring it on, and we hadn't even met yet. I gave him my best version of a fake laugh.

"Hey, Steve, you ever hear the slogan 'What goes on in Vegas stays in Vegas?'"

"Sure thing, Sal. I'll take you up on it next trip," and I would. If the casinos wanted to lay a few babes on me at their expense, why the hell not? Bim's wife Deborah certainly wouldn't care. "Hey, Sal, could you come over to the cage right away and get my credit fixed up? I'm really itching to play a little before I take the lady upstairs." That was my cue to cut the bullshit and get down to business.

"I'll be right over," Sal said. "We'll take care of everything, and you got full RFB."

"Great, Sal. Thanks."

While Deborah and I waited by the casino cage, I thought of all the planning that had gone into this operation. Besides Bones, Bim, Deborah and myself, four people joined our ranks for this scam. The most important was a New Yorker who once dated the same chick I did while at Berkeley. Neither of us knew we were being two-timed, but the love triangle eventually collapsed into a simple line of friendship between the two of us. The guy's name was Richard Marcus, and he was really cool. He was also a big-time gambler who'd moved to Vegas to count cards at blackjack. He told me he made a great living at it.

Richard and I had hit it off from the get-go. He didn't catch me with Valerie, and I didn't catch him with Valerie. One day, Valerie invited me over to her campus apartment. When I got there, she said she had something to tell me, but it had to wait until the second guest got there. The second guest was Richard, who'd arrived five minutes later. Valerie introduced us. At first I thought Richard was her brother; she did have one I had never met. Richard later confided in me that he'd thought *I* was her brother.

Before the whole thing turned into a farce worthy of François Truffaut's *Jules and Jim*, Valerie sat us down and said simultaneously to each man in the room, "I've been cheating on you."

Well, Valerie may not have been the free spirit in Truffaut's film, but she certainly was one of the freest at Berkeley. Richard and I simply looked at each other and laughed. Valerie laughed, too, but I think deep down we both hated her for it. Valerie ended up splitting town for the weekend. Richard and I went out and got drunk.

A true friendship was born. He told me over beer mugs how he'd quit Boston College, where he'd been studying physics, to be a card-counter in Vegas. I found his life story fascinating, though I didn't know much about gambling. Two women in the bar were also interested enough by it to join us. We ended up in a foursome, during which neither of us missed Valerie.

Richard periodically came up to Berkeley from Vegas. We partied, chased women and had a blast, even though he didn't smoke pot. In fact, he had never tried it. I tried to get him to since, after all, we were at Berkeley during the seventies, but I didn't press it. In spite of his not getting high, we had many intense conversations about everything from political turmoil to our mutual fascination with ants. It never ceased to amaze me how advanced ant civilizations were. My standout memory with Richard was of a hiking trip where we fell upon a massive army of ants that stretched a mile and must have numbered in the billions.

After I dropped out of Berkeley, I lost contact with Richard. Over the years I occasionally tried to locate him, but I had no leads and his name was quite common. When Bones and I decided to move ahead with the casino scam, I thought of him again. I'd said to Bones, "This guy knew everything about casinos. He had ways to avoid heat when he beat them counting cards at blackjack. I'm sure he knows the intricate workings of casinos." I told him how Richard and I had been cuckolded by the same babe.

Bones seemed impressed. "Can you trust this guy?"

"First I have to find him."

"Then find him."

"How?"

He looked at me silently, and then snapped his fingers: "Private investigator."

I hired one in Las Vegas and paid him in cash. He did not accept credit cards, which was a first for us—but it didn't matter, because three days and 1,500 bucks later, he found Richard.

He was game to join us right away. He'd long ago given up card counting and had taken to gambling on horses and sports. He hadn't fared too well, so he jumped at the opportunity to make some "serious money."

I only told Richard what he needed to know. I said we had paid for some ID documents and used them to establish credit in casinos. I mentioned nothing about our huge ID theft-credit scam. I only said that the IDs we had were perfect phonies and would not draw any heat in and of themselves. I let him know we could obtain as many as we needed.

Richard whistled in awe. "You guys could make a fortune in these joints," he gasped.

"And we want you in on it," Bones said with enthusiasm.

In the course of a month, Richard gave us a thorough lesson on how casinos worked. He explained the entire marker system. He taught us how casinos keep track of their players and are constantly on the watch for phony gamblers. One scam they were constantly on guard for was people feigning to be high rollers when in reality they were just hustling comps (freebies) from the casino. He showed us how they used "offset" procedures to con the casino into thinking large sums of money were being wagered when in fact the bets only cancelled out. A favorite method of this was done on crap tables, where one guy would bet on the "Pass Line" and another the same amount on the "Don't Pass Line." Most people doing that, Richard advised us, were sure to be caught before they even got a lousy hot dog out of the casino, let alone a free room.

In order for our mammoth casino-credit scam to work, we would have to perfect Richard's offset procedure to the point where we could implement it for thousands of dollars on every roll of the dice without giving ourselves away. But Richard said that craps was not the ideal casino game to do it on. "Baccarat is better," he said, "because there you usually have an equal distribution between people betting on player and people betting on bank, the two main bets in the game."

He taught us everything about baccarat. It was the game of choice for super high-rolling jetsetters. Baccarat salons were always tucked in exclusive corners of casinos. They were all elegance with glittering chandeliers above the groomed heads of the casino's best-dressed players. By the time I spoke to Sal Imperatore on the house phone, he knew I was a baccarat player.

Sal Imperatore looked like a beautifully polished bowling ball that someone rolled down an interstate alley from Chicago and into the gutter at Caesars Palace. He was all smooth hustle, with that put-on personality that he could turn on faster than a light switch. His suit was expensive, perhaps as expensive as my Armani. His black shoes were shiny but not as shiny as the elastic skin that stretched over his sleek face. The dark hair was slicked back to oily perfection. But still, he was one of those guys that no matter how much he spent on grooming his body, he could not escape that he was pudgy and crusty like an Italian loaf of bread.

Before I could open my mouth, Sal swept me into an embrace, his heavy arms locked around my shoulders. "Steve, it's so nice to see you at last!" He said this as if we'd been pen pals for centuries and had finally crossed a desert without water to see each other. Once he released me, he didn't waste any time getting me closer to the gambling tables, where he thought I would lose my money. He escorted me to the VIP window at the cage.

"How are you, Mr. Imperatore," the woman cashier greeted him.

Sal just nodded. Then he said to her, "This is Mr. Steven Tyler from Boca Raton. He's a new player at our casino, and I want you to set him up right away. He has full RFB privileges in the hotel."

The cashier went into the rear of the cage and removed some paperwork from a file. She laid my file card on the counter in front of me. "How do you plan to pay off your markers, Mr. Tyler? Cash or check?"

"I will pay by check within thirty days," I guaranteed her confidently.

"May I see some identification please?"

"Would you like my driver's license or passport?"

"Either will do, sir."

I gave her the Florida driver's license with my photo next to the name Steven J. Tyler. She compared the photo to my face and wrote the license number on her file card.

"Have you brought a blank check for the account you'll be using to pay off markers?"

"I have." I slid it along the counter to her. She paper clipped it to the file card. Then she had me sign two separate signature cards. Each time I signed a marker, she explained, the signature on it would be compared to the one on the signature card. She told me that I would be required to give casino personnel in the gambling pits my date of birth when requesting a marker. She let me know that my birth date was the first line of defense against someone impersonating me and fraudulently obtaining credit from the casino. I would have loved to let her know that my birth date was my first line of *offense* in fraudulently obtaining credit from the casino.

Finally, she informed me that my brand new credit account at Caesars Palace would be activated in fifteen minutes, at which time I could sign markers as I pleased up to the limit of my credit line.

As soon as business at the cage was done, Sal began his less than tactful retreat. Other high rollers had to be met and pampered. "Well, Steve," he said, "I wish you the best of luck during your stay. I hope you beat us for fifty grand."

I thanked him while mumbling under my breath, "Count on it."

Fifteen minutes later, Deborah and I were standing at a busy crap table watching white-dotted red dice tumble across the green felt layout. People where cheering and hollering with their fortunes. We looked like the typical Vegas high roller and his wife.

A sexy cocktail waitress sauntered over and took our drink order. Of course, Deborah didn't drink alcohol, so she opted for grapefruit juice. I thought that maybe she would order a soda, but then remembered she didn't take caffeine either. I ordered a White Russian, momentarily reflecting on that first night in Tijuana when I met the drug dealers. The waitress flashed her artificial smile and was gone.

The time had arrived to commit our first casino crime, the actual obtaining of money under false pretenses. I called over the pit boss, who'd been shooting the breeze with another casino employee at the podium inside the pit.

"Yes, sir?" he said promptly.

"Give me a marker for five grand," I said without preamble.

"What's your name, sir?"

"Steven Tyler."

He suddenly looked at me funny, and a bolt of panic flashed through my gut. "You're not *that* Steven Tyler, are you?"

It didn't hit me, but Deborah, who, like her husband Bim was a faithful Deadhead who'd followed Jerry Garcia around the country before marrying, knew the pit boss was referring to Steven Tyler from the band Aerosmith.

"No, I'm not him," I said to the pit boss, who excused himself and instructed the table's box man to have the dealer cut me out five grand in black one hundred dollar and purple five hundred dollar chips. A few moments later, a pit clerk with a clipboard in her hand approached me. Attached to it was the credit slip I had to sign. It was saw-toothed and looked just like a bank check. I signed it, thanked her, and she walked off.

Although Richard had said that baccarat was the best game to implement the offset procedure, we decided to stage our first bout of phony gambling at a crap table. The reasoning behind it was that in the fancy baccarat salon we'd be under more scrutiny, therefore, any mistakes we made would be more perceptible to casino personnel. Since Bones was the only one among us besides Richard who had considerable casino gambling experience, it was best we learn the casino ropes at the crap table before adventuring onward to baccarat.

I placed two black chips on the Don't Pass Line. Deborah, merrily laughing as though she were having the time of her life, did the same. At the other end of the table stood Bones and Bim. Bones was with Jackie; Bim was with Naomi. Deborah had brought these women into the operation. They were friends of hers from Northern California. They were told that Bones, Richard and I were professional gamblers and that all they needed to do was help us make strategic bets. They were completely ignorant to the ID-credit scam. They would pose as wives and bet alongside their husbands.

Following Richard's offset procedure, Bones and Bim placed identical bets of a hundred dollars, four green $25 chips. Jackie and Naomi followed suit. The total effect of our betting scheme was that we had $400 in black chips on the Pass Line and $400 in green chips on the Don't Pass Line. This was a perfect offset. When one bet won, the other lost, except for 2.8 percent of the time when one bet lost and the other pushed (tied). In that case, we'd lose half our total wager. This was the only money the casino would win from us. We treated it as a business expense. The entirety of all other expenses would be comped by the casino.

Richard's having Deborah and I bet the Don't Pass Line, on which only 10 percent of crap players wagered, was strategic. Since I was the high roller being watched by the casino, I should be the one betting the side least often bet. In this fashion, I was the oddball. Only I would be noticeable to the casino's eyes. Had the situation been reversed, where I was betting the Pass Line and my cohorts the Don't Pass Line, *they* would stand out to pit personnel. A sharp pit boss might notice that their $400 was offset by my $400, especially if my bet was the only large one on the Pass Line. The coup de grace of this scenario was that we had four people offsetting two. Normally, as Richard had explained, people using this method of trickery to fleece the casino worked in pairs, one offsetting the other. And, for disguise, we could always shift the offsetting alignment. We could have three offsetting three, even one offsetting five, adjusting each bet so that the total on each side remained the same, or close to the same.

From an adjacent crap table, Richard stood watching ours. His job for the entire casino scam was to oversee its operation. Our success—and freedom—hinged upon his ability to spot any heat we might draw from the casino and to evaluate it. One thing he told us was that once casinos caught on to scammers of any genre, their surveillance departments immediately galvanized into a full investigation spearheaded by their multimillion-dollar video systems. "They watch you in the dark and you don't ever notice," Richard had said.

He should have known. He'd been chased around casinos for years by undercover security agents bent on stamping out his card-counting career. We had worried that security people might recognize him in the casino and then tie him into us. Richard reassured us that he'd always worn disguises and been away from casinos long enough for them to forget him. We accepted his reassurances, and even Bones, who had never ridden shotgun in any criminal operation he partook in, deferred to Richard inside casinos.

We all liked Richard's current girlfriend, Carol, a sparkling blonde. He'd been with her for years in Vegas, and she was already casino-wise. Richard vouched for her caginess and said she could be trusted.

After a few rolls of the dice, Richard and Carol made a pass of our table. Richard gently rubbed his chin to indicate that everything was going smoothly. We had developed a series of signals for non-verbal communication inside the casino. Whereas it was fine that casino personnel knew each man was with his woman, they could not know that each of the couples knew one another. Allowing that would blow the cover for the offset procedure.

Richard's signals were those he had used with his teammates in his card-counting operation. Had he gently rubbed his nose instead of his chin that meant that a problem had developed which we needed to discuss immediately. In that event, we would suspend play at the table and meet somewhere outside the casino.

But for now, things were going well. Deborah and I varied our bets, as did Bones, Bim and their ladies on the other side of the table. The cocktail waitress returned with our drinks and again flashed the smile she reserved for high rollers. After two hours playing craps, I was broke. The fifty black chips given me by the casino had now become theirs again. But on the other side of the table, our foursome had won $4,800. The cost of our first gambling skit was $200.

I playacted my disappointment at losing five grand in front of the pit bosses and promised I'd return "to win back my money and then some." This parting gesture was made to give the impression I was a lousy gambler who did nothing but lose his chips. Deborah scolded me on cue, saying for everyone to hear, "Darling, I hope you're not gonna blow fifty grand in here." Then I made some affected crack for her to keep her mouth shut, and we left.

Across the street from Caesars Palace was a little casino called O'Shea's. In its rear was a food court loaded with the usual eateries. We may have been a bit overdressed to be gathered in a Burger King, but that's where we sat to evaluate our first offsetting session at Caesars.

According to Richard, it had gone great. The casino bosses loved my action, and had completely bought my act. He had stayed behind after our remaining players left the table. He heard one of the bosses comment on my play, saying that their new player Tyler looked like a "real steamer," a term casinos used to denote bad gamblers who chased losing bets. Richard said that Deborah and I had played the part perfectly. He saw no reason why we shouldn't go right to the baccarat pit. The time was ripe for the second stage of the operation. Our goal for the weekend was for me to lose $50,000, the entire amount of my casino credit line. The reason it was necessary that I ended up a loser was that I couldn't repeatedly sign markers while winning. Doing that would give casino bosses the impression I was hoarding chips, and maybe even lead them to think I was doing what we actually planned on doing, but at a much later date.

The Caesars Palace high-roller baccarat room was tucked into a private alcove off the main casino, enclosed by an elegant royal gray railing and a uniformed security guard. Comfortably nestled in their velvety chairs around the long oval baccarat table, underneath big chandeliers, was an assortment of immaculately dressed men and women of different colors and races who all wore expensive jewelry and spoke several foreign languages amongst themselves. The green felt table was guarded at each end by high-towered chairs. Seated in these chairs were the two laddermen who verified the dealers' payoffs and gauged the players' large bets at the table. Their hawkish concentration was only thinly disguised by their evening dress, and it seemed much more intense than anything I had seen in the casino's main pits.

Bones and Bim, who ostensibly didn't know each other, took the first two chairs that opened up on the big table. The action was high; the table minimum was $200, the maximum $8,000. Instead of risking $400 on each hand of baccarat, Bones simply offset Bim's bet by wagering $200 on player while Bim bet $200 on banker. As Richard had said, the bets between player and banker were equally distributed, unlike in craps where one side had most of the action. Here, we didn't have to worry about who bet which side. We had adopted a strategy whereby everyone occasionally changed sides and fluctuated the size of their bets once we were all positioned around the table. With the eight of us at the table, there were literally dozens of combinations we could use to attain the desired amount of money bet on each side.

Deborah and I were the last to be seated. Buoyed by the confidence carried over from the craps pit, I summoned the pit boss. He instantly came around from behind the tuxedo-clad dealers to place his hand on my shoulder.

"Yes, Mr. Tyler?"

I was impressed that he knew my name. He must have been notified by the clerk in the crap pit prior to my arrival in the salon: A big baccarat player named Tyler was on his way.

"I'd like a marker, please."

"How much, sir?"

"Twenty thousand." It was time to get the show on the road.

The pit boss nodded obediently, then instructed the dealer to issue me $20,000 in chips. "How would you like that?" the dealer asked.

"Just give me five hundred and one thousand dollar chips."

The dealer's polished fingers dipped into his rack and removed stacks of princely $500 purple and $1,000 yellow baccarat chips. He pushed twenty purples and ten yellows across the layout to me. As at the crap table, the pit clerk appeared with her clipboard. I signed the chit and thanked her.

My mission was to lose the twenty grand as fast as I could, without making it obvious. I couldn't just bet the table max of $8,000 because our offset against my bet would appear obvious. Also, at that betting rate, I could be broke in three hands, which would look peculiar to casino personnel. High rollers did not comfortably sink into their velvet chairs around the baccarat table only to leave broke five minutes later. Thus for the duration of the scam, we had to maintain a delicate balance between exhausting credit lines and how long we took to accomplish that.

My cohorts all had black chips. They had bought in for cash. Before entering the casino, Bones had distributed $10,000 to each player besides me. No one would run out of money. Whatever bet I made, they would offset it with the total combined sum of their bets. Deborah would only bet when I instructed her to. When betting high, I could use her to partially offset me. Sometimes gambling wives liked to bet against their husbands, although it was usually a smaller amount. In any case, her betting against me would draw no suspicion from the casino. Pit bosses saw this "connubial play" often enough.

I had placed my first $500 bet on the Player betting circle when the distinguished-looking pit boss came around and placed his bejeweled hand on my shoulder. "Would you like tickets for the show tonight?" he asked graciously.

"Who's playing?" I hadn't noticed the neon marquee when we'd arrived in the Caesars limo, which had picked us up at the airport. Of course, we hadn't flown into Vegas. Bones simply dropped Deborah and me on the arrivals curb, where we met the limousine.

"Julio Iglesias."

I wasn't a big fan of Julio's, but maybe Bim and Deborah wanted to go. "What time does it start?" I asked.

"Ten o'clock."

I looked at my diamond-studded watch. "That gives me two more hours of gambling. Sure thing." I exchanged a glance with Deborah. She nodded happily. "We'd love to see Julio."

"How many tickets would you like?"

"What?" My first thought was that he somehow knew Deborah and I were not alone.

"Perhaps you have some guests you'd like to have accompany you."

Wow! Not only was I relieved, but the offering of additional tickets knocked me right out. If one thing was evident up to that point, Julius Caesar himself must have believed I was a high roller!

And I went with it. "You know what," I said to the pit boss, "I'll take eight, if you will. Three couples I know from Boca are staying at the MGM. I'd love to invite them."

"No problem, Mr. Tyler. Eight tickets to the show will be waiting for you at the box office. If there's anything else I can do for you, just let me know."

I thanked him, and he patted my shoulder before walking off.

Two hours later, I was ahead $9,600. The total amount of money lost by Bones, Bim, Richard, Jackie, Naomi and Carol was $9,900. This $300 overall loss was added to the $200 we lost playing craps. The $500 total loss for the evening was in line with what we had expected. Richard had made calculations based on estimates of the total amount of money we'd put into play coupled with the house advantage working against us. In fact, he had made similar calculations for projected losses in the long-run. He'd said rather amusingly, "If this thing lasts long enough, we could end up losing a million bucks."

But if we lost the million, we'd have ten times that in profits.

Going into the Circus Maximus showroom, around a bend from the main casino, was not as easy as it appeared. Not when you're scamming the casino for big money. Since I was the high roller accompanied only by my wife, it was imperative to the security of our operation that Deborah and I not be seen in the company of our cohorts who'd played baccarat with us. What enabled us all to see the show without being together was that the tickets left for me at the box office were not part of a seating arrangement. They were casino VIP tickets. You presented them to the showroom host at the door, with a gratuity, of course, and he led you to the best tables in the house, usually right up against the stage.

So I went alone to the box office, picked up the eight tickets, then passed them to everyone outside the casino. We re-entered as four unassociated couples at five-minute intervals. Being the high roller, I slipped the host a fifty dollar bill and was led to the front row. According to plan, Bones, Bim and Richard tipped twenty dollars, and were seated with their companions a few rows behind us. When the show ended, we gave the casino more baccarat action, then called it a night.

There was one non-casino related detail we had overlooked while planning the whole operation. Caesars Palace had furnished me a comped room. Now that they had, I was obligated to sleep in it. Part of the charade was to completely live the Vegas life of a high roller. If I went to the apartment we'd rented, leaving the hotel room vacant and the casino found out, they'd get edgy.

On the surface this posed no problem. Sleeping in a Caesars Palace hotel room couldn't be half bad. But when Richard told us that I had to stay overnight in the room with "my wife," Bim nearly had a heart attack.

"You never know when they're watching," Richard advised us as we walked along the neon-washed strip after the show. "They've got cameras everywhere. If they see you entering a room with a woman other than your wife, they may begin to wonder."

Deborah was a real knockout, and I did like her. But we both promised her husband that nothing would happen between us. Bim reluctantly accepted the arrangement, but not before insisting that either Jackie or Naomi exchange roles with Deborah the next night we'd be sleeping at another hotel.

It was two in the morning when Deborah and I arrived at the room. Room? It was a magnificent suite! Upon opening its double baroque doors, a beautiful living room with dangling chandeliers, plush carpeting and an array of lavish furniture overwhelmed me. There was a movie screen on one wall and a small collection of impressionist paintings on the others. In the center of the room was a handsome blue baize regulation-sized pool table.

Stepping inside, Deborah said humorously, "Who gets the bedroom? You want to flip a coin?"

"No, let's do odd-finger."

"Okay."

We shook our fists, and she called, "Even." I stuck out my index finger, and so did she.

"Well," she said with a laugh, "maybe tomorrow night you won't have to play odd-finger with Jackie or Naomi. Which one is gonna play your wife, anyway?"

I really hadn't thought about it, but upon inspecting the bedroom, with its king-sized bed and silk sheets, I was leaning towards Naomi. To Deborah, I said, "Well, at least Bim will be happy to know we had a suite tonight."

The following afternoon, we played three hours of baccarat. I managed to lose $25,000. Then, after dinner, I lost $30,000 more, which wiped out my credit line. Mission accomplished. Our actual losses to exhaust my credit were $1,700. This was a little more than we wanted to lose, but it was unavoidable. Whatever losses we incurred would come back to us exponentially.

Deborah and I checked out of the hotel. At eleven p.m. Bones dropped Naomi and me at the Las Vegas airport. Minutes later, a long stretch limo pulled curbside and scooped us up. This one was from the Las Vegas Hilton, another behemoth gambling resort on Paradise Road a block off the strip. Our suite there was also a paradise.

The Hilton host who greeted me at the casino cage turned out to be a hostess, and she had a lot more class than Sal Imperatore at Caesars. She was a good-looking Eurasian woman with high cheekbones who introduced herself as Vanessa. We engaged in some small talk, much of which was about Boca Raton, with which she was familiar. She said she had relatives living there. She even mentioned particular restaurants and clubs she knew. Despite the fact we had opened scam houses and offices in Palm Beach County, I was not very familiar with Boca. The bulk of our criminal operations in Florida took place in Miami. But I knew Boca just well enough to stick with the flow of Vanessa's conversation. Basically my responses consisted of "Yes, I know it well," "I love the food there," etc.

IDENTITY THEFT, INC.

She led me to the VIP area of the casino cage and instructed the teller to process my credit account. Again I showed my Florida driver's license and handed over the blank check. My ID for the Hilton was Paul McIntyre. According to the Las Vegas Hilton's credit department, Paul ran a discount brokerage house in Palm Beach. I had pulled his name out of the *Marquis Who's Who in the South*. His current address was our second Boca scam house. His business was located on Worth Avenue in Palm Beach. The man himself was now wearing zeros (eyeglasses with no ocular power), and his hair was cut short and slicked back. He looked nothing like the man Caesars Palace knew as Steven Tyler.

The teller had me sign the signature cards, then advised that my account had been instantly activated and I was free to sign markers as I pleased. I thanked him, told Vanessa it was a pleasure meeting her, and headed up to our penthouse suite overlooking Las Vegas. Its view was panoramic. Looking down on Sin City, I truly felt like I was king of the world.

When our team gathered around the table in the Hilton's grandiose baccarat salon, we all looked wildly different than the night before. The three women had colored their hair and changed their styles, as well as their clothing. Bones also wore zeros. Bim and Richard donned Hilton baseball caps and windbreakers purchased in the hotel gift shop. Although it was not as important to disguise their appearances as much as mine, we took the added precaution. You never knew who might show up in the Hilton baccarat salon and recognize the same group of people from Caesars Palace. Richard had told us it was commonplace for casino people to visit other casino people at their workplaces. The last thing we needed was for a Caesars baccarat boss to spot me playing at the Hilton and then learn I had another name. If that weren't enough, upon seeing our entire crew he'd have to be an idiot not to know a major scam was in the works.

My credit line as McIntyre at the Hilton was $35,000. I had asked for an initial line of $50,000 but was told my play and payment history would have to be evaluated before that increase could be made. That was fine. The whole premise of the casino-credit scam was to pay off markers punctually while getting the credit limits for each identity in each casino raised repeatedly up to a ceiling point. Then we'd stiff them on the markers and abscond with the cash. What that ceiling point would eventually be and how long it would take to get there, we did not yet know. However, we were prepared to dig in for what might be a long credit war against the casinos, one that would take place in several locales besides Las Vegas and force us to make a tremendous outlay of cash.

It took the rest of Saturday night and all day Sunday to exhaust my credit line at the Hilton. We only lost $900 of our own money.

The last phase of the weekend mission was turning the chips we accumulated into cash. As I had lost $85,000 in credit between Caesars Palace and the Hilton, my cohorts had recouped more than $80,000 of it. That's a lot of chips to cash out. It was also the most difficult and dangerous phase of the operation.

The first rule Richard taught us was to never cash out $10,000 or more in chips at one time. At that number, casinos, like banks, were required to fill out a cash-transaction report for the IRS. Needless to say, we did not want any federal agency being made aware of our activities, even if they were being conducted in phony names with phony IDs. Any reports sent to the IRS could lead to all kinds of federal investigations, any of which might expose our operation.

Richard instructed us to cash out the chips in numerous trips to the cage. His preferred method was to have everyone cash out in lots of less than $2,500. At that amount, Richard explained, tellers asked people cashing out where they were playing. If you answered "In the baccarat salon," they called the baccarat boss to verify you played there. They gave a good physical description and told the boss how much in chips you were cashing out. The boss then gave his approval over the phone—if satisfied that the player in question was legit. If not, the boss came right to the cage to see you. If he did not recognize you from the baccarat room, the payoff would be held up while you were questioned.

We did not need any of this. Not only because our action was a sham but also because each person cashing out aside from myself was always a winner. Repeat winners make casinos very suspicious. So if Bones, Bim, Richard, Deborah, Naomi, Jackie and Carol were making constant trips to the casino cages with large winnings, the bosses would want to know who these people were and how they were winning all the time.

In keeping the cash-outs limited to less than $2,500, the only question tellers asked was "Do you have any markers to pay?" In my partners' cases, "no" was the truth, so there was never a problem. When it was my turn to cash out chips and answer the same question, my response was "Yes, I have markers but I'll be paying them by check." This was fine and appeared normal in the casino since the value of the chips I was cashing out was just a small fraction of the amount I owed it.

IDENTITY THEFT, INC.

After that first Vegas weekend of the casino scam, Bones and I flew to Boca Raton to do the books. We wrote two checks: one to Caesars Palace from our Steven Tyler checking account, the other to the Las Vegas Hilton from our Paul McIntyre account. We mailed them to Las Vegas. One practice we adopted was making sure we mailed all our casino payments from the city in which our gamblers lived. We were thinking that a curious investigator noticing a sudden increase of new credit players sending in payments from cities other than their own might become suspicious and launch an investigation.

Richard had schooled us in how casino credit departments handled the collection of unpaid markers. First of all, they did nothing for two months. Gamblers were given a thirty-day grace period to pay their debts, just like banks offered to cardholders. But the casinos were more discreet. They did not bother you with a late notice until a second month without payment had elapsed. Then they sent a reminder. When that did not produce payment, they sent a third letter two weeks later. Only after three full months did the credit department make a phone call to a player's business or residence. This was because gambling debts were highly likely to be sensitive interfamily issues. Husbands could lose wives and vice-versa due to gambling losses. Businesses got wrecked, people committed suicide. Heck, casino gambling debts in Nevada were not even legally collectible until the mid-eighties.

When they finally did telephone, they politely reminded the customer about his "unpaid obligation to the casino." In our case, we wouldn't be answering phones since both the scam house and office would have already been abandoned, but not the actual telephone lines. They would be put on permanent call-forward to an answering service. We would receive the message and then call back the casino credit department to say we needed more time. That routine bought us another month, sometimes two. Then, when successive phone calls bore no fruit, casinos took to dunning late notices that were sent by certified mail. When they were informed by the postal service that "Alice does not live here anymore," they finally realized they'd been had. That wouldn't be for a minimum of six months after they got busted out, even longer for casinos in Puerto Rico and the Caribbean. By the time the FBI got involved, it could be nearly a year after the crimes were committed, at which point all traces to the fictitious imposters would be galactic dust. The fallout would only lead investigators to the real people whose identity we stole and whose credit we abused.

The next weekend we were back in Vegas. Again I was Tyler at Caesars and McIntyre at the Hilton. I had no trouble blowing $50,000 at Caesars, most of which my cohorts recouped, but at the Hilton my luck ran too good. No matter how I maneuvered my bets, I couldn't lose. Too bad it wasn't for real. Even one of the pit bosses commented on my lucky streak. But what he didn't know was that my partners betting against me lost more than I won.

Before leaving the Hilton, I made sure to pay my markers at the cage. They only amounted to $10,000 since I'd been winning. Since nearly all credit gamblers leaving Vegas winners squared up before heading to the airport, I had to do the same. The most crucial aspect of the scam was to never exhibit behavior deviating from what casino bosses saw every day.

We treated casinos uniquely in the course of our scams. Unlike banks and department stores, whose credit and charge cards we immediately maxed out, we worked in the casinos slowly like a precious violin. The key was patience. Whereas the banks set rigid credit limits and were pains in the ass when it came to issuing increases, casinos freely increased your credit line if you faithfully paid your markers.

Under Richard's invaluable guidance, we laid down the greatest credit scam in casino-gambling history. In cyclical fashion, we worked the major casinos in Las Vegas, Atlantic City, Puerto Rico, the Bahamas and Aruba. There was no time for Reno, Lake Tahoe or any of the smaller gaming areas. We jetted from one place to the other, working the casinos strictly on weekends when they had the most action.

In the Caribbean, we had a great time working. We went jet skiing, parasailing, scuba diving and sipped daiquiris while watching sunsets. The best part of it was that we charged everything to the casinos. They gladly paid.

The casinos in Vegas couldn't do enough to keep their high rollers happy. Before long, they were not only picking us up at airports but also paying for our flights. Air tickets were sent to the scam offices whose addresses appeared in credit department files. We received invitations to casino functions, offers to fly us in for them as well. A few even offered to send us on paid vacations to non-gambling venues! As our credit lines went up, so did their desires to please us.

Naomi had slipped shamelessly into the role of my wife, and she was very good at it. Not only was she convincing at the tables, but her performance in the suites' bedrooms was worthy of an Academy Award—if she had been acting! We grew very close during the scam, and after a few weekends playing the part with Naomi, I no longer missed Robin.

Naturally, the atmosphere of the world's ritziest casino resorts helped fuel our relationship. I mean, come on, you're with a hot woman scamming the pants off casinos, and all the while they're bending over backwards to make you feel like a king and queen. What healthy man or woman without serious commitment to one of the opposite sex isn't going to take the plunge? Even Bones and Jackie had gotten a thing going, and they were only staying at our apartment. I'm not trying to make this sound like something out of Caligula, but when you're in the company of an attractive member of the opposite sex and surrounded by all that opulence, it's hard not to get sexual about it. We were having too much fun.

When we weren't gambling at a particular casino, Naomi and I could be found dining in one of the hotel's gourmet restaurants, soaking up the sun's rays around its marble-tiled swimming pool, or up in whichever luxurious penthouse suite we occupied, relaxing, making love or sleeping.

All this came at the casinos' expense. They paid for our every indulgence while we robbed them blind. Naomi loved massages. They paid for one every weekend. Her facials, too. When I played golf with Bones, there were no greens fees. They even paid for my lessons with hotel golf pros. I wondered how far casinos would go to court high rollers. One thing was for sure, I took more pleasure out of bilking the casinos than in any other part of the operation. I convinced myself that they deserved it. Of course, I was wrong, but I didn't realize it then.

As the months rolled by, we balanced out the Vegas attack with a multi-front offensive establishing beachheads in Atlantic City and the Caribbean. The scam became an overlapping process of gamblers raiding the system. As Tyler and McIntyre continued gambling in their respective casinos, I activated credit lines in other casinos under different names. Then older gamblers personified by Bones reinforced the invasion. We marched up and down the Vegas strip as a tandem of casino credit-playing monsters with incredible endurance, backed up by our army of well-trained soldiers. Amazingly, we never took heat. As long as the markers got paid, the bosses in the casinos treated Bones and me as their most valued high rollers.

Soon pit bosses on all three shifts were routinely welcoming us like old friends, with a "Good to see you again, Mr. Fishback" and a "Good luck this time in, Mr. Morrison." We accepted it all gracefully and continued staging our acts as carefree high-rolling losers, all the while recovering our visible losses in the dark at the other end.

After three more weekends at Caesars Palace as Steven Tyler, each of which I was largely greeted by the casino host, Sal Imperatore, I informed Sal that I'd like a credit increase to $100,000. He advised me that he thought this would be no problem and brought my request to Caesars's credit executives. I knew that they would delve into my short history as a casino credit-player and like what they saw. I was both a consistent loser and quick payer. Each Monday morning after a weekend of losing tens of thousands at the baccarat table, I sent off the check from Florida. Then why not, they would ask themselves, double my credit line so I could lose twice as much?

They followed this logic.

And so did we. After two months of this charade, they upped my line to $150,000, regardless of the fact my bank account only contained $50,000. They were sold by our elaborate setup and my seemingly endless capacity to lose and then pay. Having a credit line of $150,000 in Caesars Palace earned me the title of casino "whale." That was the special term reserved for super high rollers, the cream of the cream of the crop, that small group of elite gamblers for whom any casino would bestow every artificial luxury imaginable, in anticipation that each whale in return would leave a million bucks in the casino's coffer every year.

While this onslaught went on at Caesars, other casinos got the same treatment. We'd spend six hours in Caesars, where I signed markers, gambled and lost as Steven Tyler, then six more at the Tropicana, where Bones, as James Howell, did the same. Then it would be off to the MGM, where one of us became someone else and set in motion the same revolving-door credit scam. We seldom worried about personnel from one casino coming into another and spotting us at the baccarat table. Vegas had become so huge, its football field-sized casinos so thronged up with people, that the odds of this rivaled the town's biggest longshots. And even if a Caesars Palace pit boss coming into the Hilton baccarat room to chat with an acquaintance did spot us, he'd probably only say or nod hello to us. Discretion was a cardinal rule observed religiously in the flashy and often secretive world of casino gambling.

A funny thing happened one night at the Monte Carlo casino. Bones was playing high stakes baccarat as a certain Mr. Shahidi, a wealthy Lebanese-American oilman we had stolen from the *Who's Who of American Industry*. Well, lo and behold, sitting right next to him at the table in the posh baccarat salon was Adnan Kashoggi. Not the pudgy middleman we knew from the sports book in Tijuana, but the real Adnan Kashoggi! The Saudi Arabian arms dealer was shooting missiles in the form of $10,000 bets. What added to this comic drama was that Kashoggi tried to engage Bones in conversation. In Arabic! Bones did have aquiline features with a swarthy Middle Eastern sheen to his skin; plus Kashoggi heard the pit boss tactlessly address him as Mr. Shahidi. Thus Kashoggi took him for a real Arab. Bones graciously informed Kashoggi, who was all done up in his sheik's regalia, that he was first generation American and regretfully did not speak his mother tongue. To which Kashoggi shook his head and ignored him for the rest of the night at the baccarat table.

When Steven Tyler, after two years of faithful gambling in the Caesars Palace baccarat room, during which casino bosses bestowed upon him every casino gratuity imaginable, had finally reached that credit-line plateau of $1 million, he simply busted out the casino. This means that he bade the pit bosses and Sal Imperatore farewell, and never returned. Nor did he pay his markers. Through our elaborate cash-out procedure under Richard's supervision, we turned all the Caesars chips we'd accumulated into cash. By the time the Caesars scam was over, we'd cleared more than $800,000 from its casino. The net profits from the seven other Vegas casinos we bilked ranged from $500,000 to $700,000. The total take from the worldwide casino-credit scam was in upwards of $10 million. Not bad for a couple of phony high rollers!

Riding high in April, shot down in May

United States, 1998-1999

TO SAY THAT WE WERE RIDING HIGH AFTER OUR GREAT CASINO scam would be the understatement of whichever timeframe you choose to categorize it. We all had a terrific time traveling through the casinos and stealing their money. It had been a whirlwind of sheer joy, and each of our personal cash reserves was riding nearly as high as us.

The $10 million profit was split according to the deal we'd all agreed to before embarking on our first casino excursion. Bones and I received $2.5 million each; Richard and Carol were paid $2 million together, Bim and Deborah $2 million, and Naomi and Jackie $500,000 each, and they never knew what had actually happened. During that whole time she played my wife, Naomi believed that the dozens of names Bones and I used to sign markers were an exercise in discretion by casino bosses to protect our anonymity. We had told her and Jackie that it was commonplace for high rollers to hide their true identities in casinos, which in fact was true.

When the scam was over, Richard and Carol moved to France. They had been there together years before on a summer trip. Both had expressed an interest in the French language and culture, and Carol also had a fear of getting caught by an ensuing investigation into our scam.

Naomi and Jackie returned to Northern California. Whatever they did there, legal or illegal, didn't concern me. If busted, they could never give me up. That's because they never knew my real name. Neither did they know Bones's, Richard's or Carol's. The only participants whose true names they did know were Bim and Deborah. That did not worry me, for I was certain Bim and his wife would never give us up.

There wasn't much of a tear-jerking goodbye between Naomi and me. As the thrills of the casino scam had nurtured our romance, its ending wilted it. Perhaps in its aftermath I had the first inklings of sorrow for all I had done. The complete demise of what had seemed to be a true-love relationship opened my eyes to the shallow side of human existence. I saw that once the juice of the scam stopped running through our veins, so did the feelings. Naomi ended up buying a condo in San Francisco. We kept in touch for a year or so, but I never saw her again.

Bim remained in Vegas, and his family stayed with him. They bought a house on the west side of town. They even enrolled their kids in public school. Money has a way of changing not only things, but also attitudes. Once Bim and Deborah had enough of it, their devotion to the pure and natural way of life was washed away by the flooding excesses of Las Vegas. They did, however, remain faithful to their vegetarianism, although they gave up on the sun-gazing. In time, Bim also allowed his kids to see a doctor.

In the following months, there was a lull in our activities. In the course of the casino scam, we had accumulated more bank and store cards, but not as many as before. Whenever we had time during the week, Bones and I accumulated department store merchandise to keep Bim's telemarketing business thriving. But we were getting tired. Bones and I had been wanting to take some time off. We'd been in the ID theft business for eight years; it was time for a break. We decided that in the summer of 1998 we would take a European vacation. Neither of us had been there, and listening to Richard and Deborah speak so highly of France, we decided a nice trip abroad would do us good. We had worked extremely hard to make Identity Theft, Incorporated a huge success. But what good was it if we weren't enjoying the fruits of our labor?

But we didn't get the chance, at least not in 1998. Earlier, I spoke about how nearly every major criminal operation gets busted for deeds not directly related to the crimes. Protecting yourself from that ever-present threat is difficult, especially when you don't know the form it takes.

My first premonition that something was wrong with IDT came from

Bones's behavior. He'd been acting strange lately. He seemed irritable at times I would have expected him to be cool. I noticed that when we hung out at the apartment pool, he was reading less than usual. Bones was an avid reader. Everything from *Playboy* to the *Wall Street Journal*. Often he solved the *New York Times* crossword puzzle. But now he seemed totally preoccupied.

One day lounging at the pool, Bones said abruptly, "There's something we have to talk about."

This was unusual. Bones was not of the habit to preface something on his mind. If he had something to discuss, he just went into it.

"Okay," I said agreeably. I figured it had something to do with the operation. Maybe he wanted to pack the whole thing in. We each had plenty of money and surely didn't have to do it anymore. But then again, Bones loved the scamming action even more than I. At this point, neither of us were in it solely for the money. We had already reached the pinnacle of organized criminality but still wanted to go higher.

"Not now," Bones said. "When I get back from Chicago."

I didn't object. We had just finished with a Kansas City operation. Bones was flying to Chicago the next day to file the records pertaining to it.

I began thinking it was something of a personal nature. Maybe he was sick. Could Bones be dying? He hadn't looked so great the last few months. I had attributed it to stress or plain exhaustion. Bones was now on the wrong side of sixty. The traveling during the casino scam had been grueling and taken a toll on him. But maybe it was more than that.

The next morning, I dropped him off at the airport. Getting out of the car at the curbside, he flashed a smile and said he'd call later that night. Pulling away from the terminal, I thought his smile was forced.

That evening on the couch, I was engrossed in the movie *Scarface*. Al Pacino's performance was so good, I hadn't thought of Bones not calling. But by eleven p.m. he still hadn't. It was midnight in Chicago. Bones should have called by then. That he hadn't added to my speculation about something being wrong.

I had a premonition that he had a woman in Chicago. He'd been going there often enough. Maybe he'd met a woman with whom he was having a relationship and never told me. Maybe he was out carousing with her and was either having too good a time to call or simply forgot. Thinking of Bones with a woman, I had a sudden urge to call Robin. It had now been months since we spoke. She was still running her boutiques, and we still supplied her with the merchandise, but it was Bim who handled her deliveries through the telemarketing office. I called her house in Phoenix.

"Long time, no speak," Robin said the moment she recognized my voice.

I responded, "How's business?" I couldn't think of a better way to begin the conversation.

"Starting to slow down for the summer," she said. "Is your little junket finished?"

Whenever we spoke on the phone, we didn't mention specifics about anything. Her inquiry into my "little junket" was her way of asking if the casino scam was over. I told her it was and that all had gone well. Robin had never asked for a piece of that action, and we had never offered.

When the conversation turned to Bones and I told her of my suspicions, Robin's voice took on a note of worry. "What's the matter?" I asked her.

"I don't know. Call it a woman's intuition, but it's not like him to forget to call. He's always so precise. Even if he were ill, he'd call."

Now I worried, too. When I hadn't heard from him by noon the next day, I really became anxious. Where the fuck was he? I thought of calling the cell phone he'd just begun carrying, but incredibly I didn't have the number handy. I'd written it down somewhere but couldn't find it. At the time, cell phone service was neither as cheap nor ubiquitous as it is today. Whenever one of us traveled alone, we communicated by regular land-line phones, from one scam house to another. In fact, I had never dialed Bones's cell phone number.

By that evening, I was beside myself. Bones still hadn't called. There was no longer any doubt that something was wrong. My theory that he'd been out cavorting with a woman no longer held water, certainly not into a second day.

I called Bim at his home. Perhaps he'd heard from Bones, though I seriously doubted it.

"He didn't call here," Bim said. "What's up?"

"I don't know. He took off for Chicago yesterday morning to close out some business affairs. He told me he'd call last night. He still hasn't called."

Bim couldn't make any sense of it. How could I expect him to? I knew Bones a lot better than he. Calling Bim was foolish on my part. It could only serve to spread my panic, and panic is very contagious.

One of the worst feelings when you're a criminal is sensing impending doom creeping over you. No matter where you are, no matter what luxuries surround you, you feel like you're in a prison cell, and it's getting smaller and smaller. Our apartment in Vegas was no Shangri-La, but in spite of its relative comfort, I now felt as though its walls were converging on me.

By the third day, I couldn't take it anymore. I'd been sleepless all night, mulling over whether I should fly to Chicago or not. My greatest fear was that I'd be walking into a trap. If Bones had been arrested and the authorities discovered our headquarters in the Sears Tower, they might have it under surveillance and be lying in wait for me. But if they hadn't, the incriminating records there had to be destroyed.

By seven o'clock that evening I was at O'Hare Airport in Chicago. I jumped in a cab and headed directly to the Sears Tower. Feeling the tenseness in my bones, I showed the night guard my building pass. I wore a ball cap and zeros to disguise myself. I took the elevator to the twenty-second floor. When it pushed upward, there was a lump in my throat to go with the churning of my stomach. I watched the yellow indicator pass through the floors above the doors. Then came the ding and the doors slid open.

I stepped out and walked down the long corridor to our offices. "IDT CORP" greeted me proudly on the glass as I fitted the keys into two locks on the door. I pushed them open and entered in a flurry, my eyes darting from side to side in the darkness. I steeled my body as if preparing to be jumped. But no one was there. I breathed a sigh of relief and turned on the lights. I quickly walked through, checked the hall closets and then pushed open the door to the inner office, Bones's private sanctum with the giant platinum Visa poster and Scam Cities, USA map on the wall. Again I braced for an unseen attack, but it didn't come.

Time to clean up shop. Moving like a whirlwind, I tore the map and poster off the walls. I jerked open the file cabinets and dumped everything into two large empty boxes that had been in the hallway closet. I knew while doing this that there was a chance it was all for naught. The possibility that this whole disaster was nothing more than my paranoia still existed. But I couldn't take the chance. Even though Bones might flip out if my actions proved unwarranted, it was better to be safe and face the wrath of my senior partner than that of the United States government.

After I'd gathered and boxed all the files, I laid the boxes outside the offices in the corridor. Then I went to the bathroom next to the reception area, removed a towel from its rack, wet it and went to work wiping down the entire facility of fingerprints. It took three hours, after which I was certain not a single latent fingerprint remained in the offices of IDT. By midnight,

I was safely tucked away in a Sheraton hotel room a few miles from the airport. The front desk clerk had regarded me strangely when I checked in with two boxes but no suitcases. I didn't know exactly how I would destroy the evidence. I sure as hell couldn't start a fire in the hotel room. First thing in the morning I'd rent a car, drive to some remote area and burn the files.

I was terribly exhausted by the three-day ordeal. Although still very fearful, I managed to fall asleep. My last clear thought before closing my eyes was wondering what twist of fate had put our entire operation in jeopardy.

The twist of fate, I would learn later, was that Bones had walked into a McDonald's one afternoon in Dallas and ordered a cheeseburger and fries to go. The young girl who handed him the bag and his change was an adorable raven-haired Texan with a lovely smile. Bones, who'd been yearning for real female companionship since his fling with Jackie in Vegas, was immediately smitten by her. Hearing her southern drawl, which only enhanced the attraction, sealed his fate.

He asked if she would have dinner with him that night. She smiled broadly and accepted.

Darlene Perkins was nineteen going on thirty. Blessed with that mixture of natural sex appeal and charming innocence seen in so many Texas lovelies, Darlene was a perfect candidate for the Dallas Cowboys cheerleaders. But she had spurned their offer in favor of a hotel management career, for which she currently attended the University of Texas at Austin. Now between her freshman and sophomore years, she was working at McDonald's for the summer to earn extra money for the fall semester.

Darlene was not from a wealthy family, so the array of expensive gifts from a much older suitor was exotic to her. Bones escorted her through department stores, charging her presents to his cards. He bought designer clothing for her wardrobe, fashionable gold and diamond jewelry, which he had the pleasure of fastening around her slender neck and wrists, and a parade of fancy bottles of perfume. After the day's shopping spree, he took her to Dallas's best restaurants and hottest nightclubs.

Bones courted Darlene in this fashion for a month. Naturally she was curious to know what her new beau did for a living. Of course Bones did not tell her the true nature of his business, but somehow he wasn't convincing when he claimed to be a traveling salesman. He was not concerned by the possibility that she knew he was full of shit. She loved him, and she loved his way of fawning over her and lavishing her with everything money could buy.

Exactly a month after that fateful cheeseburger, Bones proposed. He started by begging her to quit her job at McDonald's, and then stretched that to dropping out of college. In the course of his feverish pleas, Bones imparted a little too much about what his travels as a salesman entailed. To this day I don't know exactly how much he told her, but it was certainly at odds with his constant diatribes on trusting women with compromising information and how most men in prison got there because of women who'd betrayed them.

Bones must have felt that Darlene would never betray *him*. That's because she said she wanted to marry him. But what Bones hadn't taken into account was that Darlene Perkins was a law-abiding, God-fearing Christian young lady despite her occasional lascivious behavior and love of material gifts. Her father was a hardworking blue-collar man who had saved up the balance of the tuition his daughter's scholarship didn't cover. Her mother had worked part-time as long as Darlene could remember, and then took a full-time job once she was out of the house like her older brother, Roy.

Darlene said she would discuss the marriage proposal with her family. Bones was thrilled to death. However, there were two things Bones didn't know. The first was that while he was showering after they'd made love, Darlene was no longer able to restrain her curiosity and had a peek inside his wallet, which Bones had left in his pants. At first glance, she smiled with satisfaction because the Texas driver's license she saw said Bones was Gerald Kelly, the name by which she knew him. But what made Darlene suddenly frown was the second Texas driver's license in the padding behind it. That one had the same picture of her beloved, but the name next to it was Raymond Martin. If at that moment any chance of an acceptable explanation existed, the next totally dismissed it. The third license behind the second one called Bones "Robert." Not only was the last name different, it suggested another ethnic group altogether—the third identical DMV photo was of Robert Sanchez. Maybe she should have surprised him coming out of the shower by calling him "Roberto."

The second thing Bones didn't know was that Darlene's brother Roy was a cop with the Dallas Police Department. It's not that Darlene ever tried to hide that fact; she was proud of it. But it just never came up in conversation. They were always too busy talking about each other when not buying up expensive merchandise in department stores. Darlene was close to Roy. She told him about her older suitor with a seemingly endless supply of money, or at least charge privileges in department stores.

Roy did not become suspicious that Gerald might not be Gerald, but he did council his younger sister not to marry someone more than thirty years her senior. But when Darlene told Roy that Gerald was also Raymond, who was also Robert, Roy had some stronger advice for his sister about the man who'd asked for her hand in marriage—it was "Don't ever see him again. I'll take care of it."

I didn't actually find out that Bones had been busted until Robin phoned me in Vegas two days later. She had gone to Chicago to tend to her boutique there and had seen something on the local news she thought would interest me. She recounted how a joint taskforce of FBI and Secret Service agents raided the offices of some company in the Sears Tower, arresting its owner and charging him with multiple counts of credit card fraud and impersonating numerous people. She said the guy's name was Gerald Kelly, and when the news program showed him being taken into custody, he had a suit jacket raised over his head to hide his face. She asked me if Kelly might be Bones.

The question was not as dumb as it appeared. Robin never knew of our Chicago headquarters. She had no need to. Keeping its existence from her and everyone else involved in the scam was part of operating under our "need to know" policy.

The real Gerald Kelly was in fact a banker from Milwaukee who we'd moved to Dallas. He'd come out of the *Marquis Who's Who in American Finance*. I have to admit that in spite of my receiving the dire news from Robin, it was kind of amusing that it was a banker who finally did us in. We had been ripping off banks for eight years. Never once until I came across Kelly's name in the library had we used a banker. And then when we at last steal a banker's ID, he bites us on the ass.

"Yes, Robin, it's Bones."

"What!"

"I'm afraid so."

"What does this mean for my boutiques?"

I could see she had no concern for Bones. That pissed me off. "I guess it means you're gonna have to find a new supplier. Or maybe you can start manufacturing your dresses yourself…"

As the shock wore off, I wondered how Bones got busted as Gerald Kelly. We'd closed down the Dallas scam house and office a month earlier. The Dallas files had already been transferred to Chicago. So why was Bones carrying ID in Kelly's name? There had to be a reason for this lapse of security. At the time, I was unaware of Darlene Perkins.

But now I had to act fast. In a devastating situation like this, the only thing a white-collar crime boss can implement is damage control. There were two distinct operations that had to be put into effect immediately. The first was to abandon the scam houses; the second was to recoup as much of the cash we had in banks as possible. Close to a million bucks used to set up the casino scam still sat in banks in several cities.

The day I learned Bones got busted, we had eight scam cities operating across the USA. They were in various stages of production or pre-production, but it didn't matter. Everything in progress had to be dropped. Documents had to be destroyed, fingerprints wiped away.

There were direct threats to my safety emanating from the scam houses. The first was our telephone system. Every single phone in every single scam house operated 24/7 on call-forwarding. All calls from banks and department stores were routed to Las Vegas. If any scam house were compromised, the feds would be able to trace me to Vegas through the phone system. I immediately called each house and deprogrammed the call-forwards, but the calls to our Vegas number could be identified through telephone-company records.

I also worried about potential physical evidence found in the scam houses. As Bones and I had regularly traveled to them all, I had to assume that a scent leading back to me in Vegas might be sniffed at any of them. We had so many crisscrossing facets of the operation that it was impossible for Bones and me to remember every detail concerning individual cities involved in the scam. There were bills pertaining to the houses themselves, other loose documents, anything and everything that could put the feds on my tail.

Bones had a habit of mixing things up when he made trips to multiple scam houses. There were times he'd flown into Boston, checked up on the scam houses there, then caught another flight to Philadelphia and later the same day a train to New Jersey. Recalling that, I thought of the possibility, albeit remote, that when Bones got busted he had something on his person pertaining to our Vegas residence. I sure hoped not. The thought of abandoning the apartment for a hotel room crossed my mind, but I let it go.

Next I telephoned Bim. He was in the middle of dinner but took the call anyway.

"Bim, I got some bad news for you."

With an absolute calm, Bim asked, "We're out of business?"

"How the hell did you know?" Despite the calamity I nearly laughed.

"I didn't," Bim said. "I just couldn't think of anything else you would have prefaced with 'bad news.'"

I told him what had happened. He took the news that his telemarketing business was suddenly gone in stride. He'd made a small fortune working with us and had no complaints. Together with his share of the casino rip off and his house, Bim was worth more than $3 million. A month later, he sold the house and moved his family back to the boondocks in Northern California. I imagined that up there with his kind of money, Bim could live like a king. I just hoped he didn't return to his old habits of sun-gazing and strictly vegetarian delights.

Recovering the funds we had on deposit in banks was much easier said than done. They were sitting in checking accounts that had suddenly become very vulnerable. In order to recoup the cash, each bank involved had to be visited by the person bearing the ID of the account holder. This had to happen very quickly, before the authorities had the chance to either freeze the accounts or stake out the banks. Assigning the time limit for this was the crucial decision. Basically it was like a losing hand at poker. You had to know when to fold 'em. I decided right away that the time to fold 'em was after two days. I'd spend forty-eight hours chasing after the money and then take the loss. Cash that could not be pulled out of the accounts in the allotted time would remain in the banks until the US government decided what to do with it.

Fortunately, most of these checking accounts had been opened in the names of men whose identities I used to scam the casinos. While in Chicago, I had the presence of mind not to destroy the ID documents pertaining to those accounts, therefore, I could enter the banks with matching ID documents and withdraw the cash. The $200,000 in accounts bearing names of men whom Bones had impersonated was not recoverable because those IDs had Bones's photo on them.

I hurried to the airport and flew to Portland. After closing out an account there, I hopped a plane to Seattle. Then it was on to Denver, Albuquerque, San Antonio and Houston. In each case I went to the main branch of the bank involved and demanded cash, telling concerned bankers I had no compunction complying with the IRS cash-transaction reports. I had to wait a few hours for some of them to gather the cash, but the duffel bag I carried with me filled up in increments of greenbacks. It took three days instead of two, but I encountered no problems.

Back in Vegas, Bim and I donned rubber gloves and wiped the telemarketing office clean of fingerprints. We pulled the fifty phones from their jacks, wiped them down and loaded them along with the business records into our van. We drove to a local garbage dump, tossed the phones into a heap and burned the records. Any raid occurring at Price Can't Be Beat Enterprises would find a large 10,000-square-foot office that looked as though it hadn't been occupied in years.

Bim dropped me at the airport. My second mad streak across the friendly skies was to each of the scam house cities. I entered the houses, gathered the records and burned them at garbage dumps. My last stop on this tour was to see Robin in Phoenix.

Robin sadly had to give up her career as a high-end retailer. Whatever merchandise she had left in her two boutiques, besides what she wanted for herself, she sold at flea markets. While she ran her shops, she'd been renting a condo in an exclusive Scottsdale development. She had gotten very involved in the wealthy town's social scene. Too many people who had shopped in her boutiques befriended her, and now they posed a danger. Robin was reluctant to flee Arizona, but I was able to convince her it was in everyone's best interests, especially hers. Before splitting town, we went to the offices of Cactus Financial Services and destroyed the credit reports we had on file there. Robin ended up moving to a beautiful part of the United States we never touched: Hawaii. I never saw her again.

Within a week after Bones's arrest, all our scam houses were empty. Every sheet of records had been burned, anything incriminating destroyed. The only evidence the feds would get was what they had obtained from Bones. With that in mind, I could rest assured that it would take a considerable length of time before the FBI and Secret Service connected the dots leading to me. Bones was not about to help them. If one thing were sure, Bones would sooner do a long stretch in prison than cooperate with any investigation.

That investigation took shape after Darlene Perkins told her brother about the multiple identities carried by the man she knew as Gerald Kelly. Roy Perkins did what any good cop would upon hearing that his kid sister was involved with a major criminal: he told his superiors. The Dallas police then notified the Texas Attorney General's Investigations Unit. Its investigators linked Gerald Kelly's credit abuses to those of Raymond Martin and Robert

Sanchez, and three other men who had Texas driver's licenses with Bones's photograph that Darlene had never seen. When it became clear to those investigators that a major credit card fraud operation was in the works, they contacted the FBI and the United States Secret Service.

Bones was not arrested in Texas. Instead, he was prudently placed under 24-hour surveillance by a joint team of FBI and Secret Service agents. Meanwhile, the FBI had located the real Gerald Kelly, who was living in Seattle and had never been anywhere near Dallas. Since Kelly had not yet heard anything from the nation's three major credit bureaus, he had no idea that someone had perpetrated a major fraud in his name before the Secret Service told him. In the coming days, the Secret Service would locate Martin and Sanchez in other parts of the country far from Texas. They, too, would be shocked upon learning that debts over $100,000 in their names were outstanding.

Bones had remained in Dallas for two days before flying on to Chicago. Authorities in Texas had already known about Darlene's multiple-identity suitor for several weeks. Fortunately, though, Darlene had told Roy about him after Bones had left Dallas the last time he'd been with her. That meant the authorities had to wait until Bones returned to Dallas, since he had never given Darlene a way to contact him. At least, in hindsight, his traveling-salesman rap prevented us from being set up in Vegas, which would have been a far greater disaster and led to a much earlier release of this book (which would have been written in prison). During their romance, Bones always telephoned Darlene, who'd never pressed him for his phone number. Perhaps she'd thought he was married and preferred not to infringe.

Another fortunate event was my rushing to Chicago, which turned out to be a day before Bones led the surveillance team there. Had he gotten there before me, the feds would have seized the two boxes full of documents that I burned in the woods near a rest area on an Illinois expressway. This did not mean that they would never uncover the entire operation. Once the evidence from banks and credit card clearinghouses came to light, they would know that the scope of the fraud was gigantic. Then there would be the tie-in to casinos defrauded out of millions more. I didn't know how long casinos kept surveillance tapes before either reusing or discarding them, but if the feds ever got to see the tapes, they'd have enough casino crime on screen to surpass *Ocean's Eleven, Twelve* and *Thirteen*! If not, they'd put it all together from the photos on ID documents. But all this would take months if not years. I would have ample time to make my escape.

Bones was charged with conspiracy, forgery and racketeering, the latter being the most serious crime because it fell under federal racketeering statutes (RICO). Conceived by the government to clamp down on the Mafia, the RICO act empowered judges with strict sentencing guidelines to mete out long terms in federal prisons. But Bones was saved from RICO by the government's lack of evidence. While awaiting trial, Bones's lawyer negotiated a deal with federal prosecutors that spared him a long prison stretch. He pleaded guilty to one count of conspiracy, one count of forgery and one count of credit card fraud. He was sentenced to fifty-eight months in federal prison.

In the month following the demise of IDT, I wrestled with decisions about what to do with my future. The first thing to decide was where I would live. Then I had to find the best way to get my money there. I had over $4 million in cash in safe deposit boxes in a hundred banks in twenty cities. Every one of them had been rented in my true name: Glenn Hastings. Since I had never committed a crime in my own name, which appeared absolutely nowhere in relation to our operation, I was as safe as you are from the FBI's and Secret Service's investigations of it. Not only that, I had never even gotten a parking ticket. The only documents attesting to my true existence were a California driver's license and a Social Security card. I'd never been fingerprinted except for a lone thumb print taken by the California DMV. None of the IDs I impersonated were set up in that state.

However, I was not totally free from risk. I could still be connected to Bones and the operation in the event Bones gave me up. Even though I considered that nearly impossible, the thought was enough to solidify my first decision. Remembering Richard and Carol's yearning to live in Europe, I decided it was time to practice my French. The first week in June 1998, I threw four large duffel bags in the trunk of my Porsche and headed for the open highway. One contained clothing and toilet articles, another the $800,000 in cash I'd withdrawn from banks. The last two were empty.

I crisscrossed the country, stopping in cities where my money was stashed. I systematically emptied out the safe deposit boxes and packed the cash into the duffel bags. Each night upon checking into a motel, I took them into my room. When I reached the last city on my map, New York, I sold the Porsche to a used car dealer at a dirt-cheap price.

On July 1, 1998, I took the biggest risk of my life. I flew out of JFK to Paris. I checked four padlocked duffel bags at the Air France check-in counter. The attendant informed me that I was one bag over the limit and had to pay a $100 surplus charge. Considering that the contents of three of the four duffel bags were $5.2 million, I thought it was a pretty fair deal. I could not take any of it as carry-on luggage because it would be X-rayed. So I made the decision to check it. Since New York to Paris was not considered by customs to be a drug route, the chances that my bags would be searched were remote. There was always the possibility that dishonest baggage handlers would have a peek inside. However, my duffel bags were far more nondescript than their contents. There was plenty of Gucci and Louis Vuitton luggage to attract the eyes of potential baggage thieves. Besides, I'd had no other choice. With Bones locked away in jail, there was no one I could trust to safeguard my money. I was not about to leave it with Robin, who could always end up busted as well. I may have been a real gambler at heart, much more so than the dozen high rollers I impersonated. But this gamble was one I really had to win.

While watching my duffel bags disappear through the flaps hanging over the conveyor belt, I thought how sadly ironic it would be if my luggage did not meet me when I stood by the luggage carousel at Charles de Gaulle Airport in Paris.

On the flight over, I felt strangely alone. My plan was to rent a car with a credit card in my real name and drive along the French countryside. I really had no ideas beyond that. But now as I looked out the porthole into the darkness, I reflected on Bones and realized I would never see him again. It saddened me greatly. In many ways he had been a father to me. He was also a man of remarkable intelligence and insight. His weakness was that he'd always been vulnerable to his own powerful personality. Though his strength and arrogance instilled confidence in people, his savage affection for those close to him was sometimes more harsh than loving.

Though I did not know it then, his having been taken down by a woman was not that surprising. During the course of our travels, I'd learned that Bones had never married. He didn't talk much about past relationships with women. I didn't know for sure if he'd had any. The only examples of his behavior towards women he wasn't conning were the times he shacked up with Jackie during the casino scam. He seemed happy in her company but never made any overt statements concerning their relationship. I had always felt that Bones was "desperately seeking Susan," or whoever she might be.

Thus I assumed that Darlene Perkins triggered some latent zest for life deep within Bones's being. Having made all that money in the scam, he still had to come to grips with advancing age and mortality. Bones had never been rich before IDT, even if he ought to have been. He never really had the chance to enjoy the fruits of his previous criminal endeavors. When that luck and opportunity for easy living finally arrived, Bones must have decided that he wanted to share it with a woman, obviously a much younger woman. This desire was so strong it caused Bones to desert his lifelong stance of never revealing his illicit activities to a woman. He completely broke down and discarded the rules of criminal life he'd so often preached to me. Whether or not a certain part of him did that willingly, I could never be sure. Perhaps when he left his wallet for Darlene to see while he showered, he did so consciously in the hope she wouldn't turn him in. Perhaps he even knew her brother was a cop. With Bones it was difficult to say. He was a complicated individual, as most criminals are.

When we landed in Paris, I jumped up as the plane taxied to the terminal. I wanted to be the first passenger out as to be the first in the baggage claim area. A stewardess had to reprimand me back into my seat until the plane came to a complete stop. When I finally did disembark, I ran feverishly to baggage claim hoping to attract as little attention as possible. My heart was pounding as if it would explode, but I kept moving.

Of course my bags were not among the first load arriving through the chute above the carousel. Of course I began imagining the worst. And of course when one of my duffel bags finally showed up, it was the one packed with my personal belongings, not cash. Then when I spotted the second, after a few minutes that seemed like hours, my eyes played tricks on me. It looked much less packed, even empty, as if someone had cleaned out the cash. When I grabbed it, it seemed lighter. I thought I would keel over and die. Either that or fly back to the States as a stowaway and turn myself in to the FBI. Or just try jumping out of the plane.

But it had just been my imagination. The duffel bag looked less full only because it had been flattened in the course of the voyage. The locks were in place, and I breathed a deep sigh of release. Then the two remaining bags arrived intact. I grabbed a luggage cart and went to customs. French customs officials at the time were notoriously lax. I passed through mumbling "*oui, monsieur*" a few times and headed to the Hertz counter. I rented a compact, drove ten hours to Nice, and with my four bags checked into a discreet hotel on the French Riviera. The next morning I put them back in the trunk and took a scenic drive along the Mediterranean looking for a place to live.

I found it in Menton, an old-world but expensive town just twenty minutes from Monte Carlo. I rented a small one-bedroom from an older gentleman who bought my rap that I was an American author sojourning in France to write a book. Believe me, I had no idea that I would one day actually write a book. Saying so then just served as a good reason for my being in France for an extended period of time.

I'd been a little ignorant to summer rental rates on the French Riviera, perhaps the highest in the world. When Monsieur Pinot told me the going rate for a one-bedroom was 25,000 francs ($5,000), I thought he meant for a month, which was expensive enough. But that was the weekly rate. When I swallowed my surprise, he said that if I wanted the apartment year-round, he'd give it to me for the 25,000 francs a month.

Although confident that my true ID would remain hidden from the American authorities and that I'd be able to live my new European life to the fullest without fear of extradition, I encountered some problems living abroad that I was not well prepared for. The first was what to do with my money. I couldn't keep $5 million in cash in a giant garbage bag under the kitchen sink.

My first thought was to open up a checking account in a French bank and then secure a safe deposit box. When I'd made my hasty decision to expatriate myself in France, I had enough sense to check into French visa requirements. Any American wishing to remain in France for more than ninety days needed a visa, but as long as I didn't legally work there, I could skip it. My US passport would get me a quick pass if ever stopped and asked for documents.

But I overlooked French banking laws. I'd thought my passport would be sufficient to open an account. I was wrong. Foreigners had to establish legal residency in France to establish bank accounts. To get that legal residence you first needed a visa for permission to be in the country legally.

That was all a big zero. I didn't want my name skipping across desks inside the American consulate. I decided to run the problem by Monsieur Pinot, who loved telling me war stories in broken English about his experiences on Omaha Beach during the D-Day invasion. I served him some cognac *chez-moi* to get him talking. After some genial conversation about how I liked his apartment, Pinot found the solution for me.

I was not the first "wealthy American" to have rented from him, he informed me. One common practice among his ex-tenants was to keep valuables in private guarded vaults that were not part of the state banking system. Many tourists who were not French residents took advantage of these facilities to protect their cash and diamonds from French cat burglars who trolled the Mediterranean in summer like bees swarming honey. Box rentals were not cheap, Pinot let me know with a typical Gallic shrug, but they were safe. The vaults were guarded twenty-four hours a day, if open only eighteen. In his long memory, Pinot only recalled one burglary at a French Riviera vault. One night while it was closed, a band of Italian thieves tunneled their way into the interior from a sewer pipe and drilled open the boxes.

Those odds were good enough for me. The next day, I drove my rental car to one of these vaults in Nice, filled out the application, showed my passport and rented the biggest box available, just large enough to store $5 million in cash. I was given one of the two keys needed to open it. It worked just like safe deposit boxes in US banks. I packed the box with all the cash except for $200,000, which I'd keep hidden in the apartment.

Next, I dumped the rental car and leased a brand new but nondescript Peugeot convertible for a year. Even in France I was not about to draw attention to myself. You never knew. I'd heard stories about conspicuous American white-collar criminals on the lam getting rounded up in Europe. I would keep my wealth to myself. I'd live well but low-key.

In the following weeks and months, I settled into my life as an American living in France. I enrolled in a French language school and made a serious effort to attain fluency. I actually liked it. I made friends, even the short-lived acquaintance of a charming young Frenchwoman named Nicole. She was enjoying lunch with another attractive woman at a sidewalk café while I sat at an adjacent table with some Germans from the language school. I tried speaking French to Nicole without making an idiot of myself. She ended up saving me by replying in excellent English. Over cappuccino I asked her out, but she declined even if she thanked me graciously. I told myself that if ever I saw her again, I'd give it a second shot.

After six months of living in Monsieur Pinot's Mediterranean apartment, I'd come to love France. My French had climbed to an elementary level, and I was able to use it in charming a few *mademoiselles* on the beach. One day lying on the sand, I thought I had spotted my casino mentor Richard from a distance. I called out, but the guy didn't respond.

As time went by, I thought less and less about my illegal activities spanning two decades. If I truly missed one aspect of it all, it was the casino scam. The thought of being wined and dined like royalty while cleaning out their coffers was too much.

But bygones were bygones. I had been reborn as Glenn Hastings. My life finally appeared to be on the right track. I imagined I could easily live out the remainder of my life overlooking the Mediterranean. There was a whole continent to see, then other hemispheres. I could travel at will, do it all. I had the cash. Nothing could stop me. I was happy as a lark.

But I made one mistake that would eventually suck me back in. I did not know it was a serious mistake even when I compounded it. I wouldn't realize the true damage for more than a year. It would force me once again to shed the skin of Glenn Hastings for those other people who would become the breadwinners of IDTA, Inc.

Identity Theft *Again*, Inc.

Getting the digits

Europe and the USA, 2000-2002

I SHOULD HAVE NEVER GONE INTO LE CASINO DE MONTE CARLO.

But I did. The first time was in the summer of 2001. I had been living in Menton for three years. Monsieur Pinot had gladly renewed my lease twice, for 2,500 francs more each time. My French was now conversational, and I had a handful a friends with whom I practiced it. I also had another handful of female friends with whom I practiced other forms of French communication, though none of these relationships developed beyond that. Perhaps the reason was that I had been showing more faith to the principality of Monaco's casinos than to its women.

It was a balmy Mediterranean night the first time I walked inside the elegant casino at the front of Monte Carlo's fabled square. With its high ceilings, red carpeting, Renaissance paintings and tapestries, the interior was quite impressive, if not altogether regal. The baccarat game at which we'd scammed the casinos in Las Vegas was called *chemin de fer* among the jet-setters who played it here. It translated to the English word "railroad," and I soon learned that its European enthusiasts called it "chemmy."

Well, chemmy was my downfall. I was immediately seduced by the dark green oval table underneath a low-slung, brilliant chandelier, croupiers in tuxedos and a clientele made up of some of the wealthiest people in the world. The five mil I had stashed in the vaults back in Nice was chump change to this immaculate façade of people.

The true elegance of the game was evidenced by the way it was conducted. The croupiers used lacquered wooden rakes to push cards and chips around the table. The chips were not really chips but rather plaques resembling small bricks. It was total opulence that outdid anything I had seen in Vegas and Caribbean casinos.

I got carried away. I started playing chemmy as though I were Steven Tyler or Paul McIntyre back in Vegas. Here, though, there was one significant difference: I was Glenn Hastings, and when I lost my bets there was no cohort winning on the other end of the table. And lose I did. That first night gambling in Monte Carlo, I lost as if winning had gone out of style.

Earlier that afternoon, I had gone to my vault in Nice and removed $20,000. While living in France, each time I needed cash, I took American bills from my stash and changed them to francs at currency exchanges. Most Americans abroad simply took cash off their credit cards at Cirrus ATM machines. Obviously, my case was a little different.

Since the twenty grand I'd taken was for the express purpose of a gambling stake, I'd changed it in the casino for 120,000 francs in *chemin de fer* plaques. I'd sat at the table at nine p.m. By midnight I was broke. And then I was off to the races.

My first Côte d'Azur gambling binge lasted two weeks. I made so many trips back and forth to the vault that the guards both inside and out began frowning at me. By the sixth day, I had lost half a million dollars. At the end of two weeks, my losses reached the full million. That was 20 percent of my total net worth hidden in the vault.

Those first three years in France, I'd spent approximately $350,000 on living expenses. I lived very well, but not like a king. Had I continued the same lifestyle without gambling, I would've had enough cash reserves to squeeze out forty years.

But suddenly my financial planning went up in smoke. I tried to stay away from Le Casino de Monte Carlo. I did, but unfortunately the French Riviera was loaded with casinos. Two of them in Monte Carlo, Le Café de Paris and the Sun casino, were American-styled. I decided to try my luck at those casinos, which were less fancy and more Las Vegas-like in atmosphere.

The result was the same. I got buried. I quickly progressed from a problem gambler to an absolute degenerate. Soon I was going to the Monte

Carlo casinos every day. Practically all my waking hours were spent chasing one losing session after another. The pit bosses in all the casinos knew me by name and bestowed upon me the same excessive pampering I'd received in Vegas, but this time my part in it was not an act. I was a real super-high roller bleeding rivers of cash to the casinos.

New Year's Eve, 2001, I sat at the roulette table in Le Casino Monte Carlo. I had given up on *chemin de fer*. Like the Russian writer Dostoevsky, I had turned to roulette in a craze. I'd adopted system after system in vain attempts to predict on what numbers the little ivory ball spinning around the cylinder would land. Each lost more than the last. I was pathetically wrapped up in the throes of gambling.

Just when the clock struck midnight and the international set around the table wished each other a happy New Year, I came to the stark conclusion that I had better make a New Year's resolution right then and there: Stop gambling.

When I finally did, I had but $500,000 left in the vault in Nice. Though a long way from broke, I was just as far from retirement. I certainly could not live the rest of my life on the Côte d'Azur with that amount of money. Even in the States, I'd be hard pressed to survive forty years on a half-million dollars earning no interest and thus being devalued by the second.

The grim conclusion was that I had to go back to work. What that actually meant at the time, I didn't know. Thankfully, I still had enough cash to reflect on possible life choices. As long as I stayed away from gambling, something would come along before I became destitute.

That something turned out to be David Woo. In March 2002, after a few months of recovery from gambling, I went on a ski vacation with Jean-Pierre, my closest friend in France. I hadn't skied but a few times since Taos. I was really excited about the chance to take it up again. It would do me a world of good. The fresh mountain air and smooth powdered snow of the Alps were sure to cleanse my system.

We went to a charming ski resort called Bettex, just on the other side of Mont Blanc from the famed celebrity-studded ski town of Chamonix. Both of us being advanced skiers, Jean-Paul and I opted to ski off the marked trails onto virgin snow covering steep inclines. Cutting through the snow down the steep mountain with breathtaking views of lakes and villages below, the last thing on mind was identity theft.

But that changed in the ski lodge after sunset. In a cozy restaurant warmed by a crackling stone hearth fire, sat a group of young Americans on vacation. They were eating and drinking *vin chaud* (hot wine) while laughing about some experiences they'd had on the Internet. At that time, I was only vaguely familiar with the web and its explosion into everyday life. Living on the beautiful Mediterranean, I'd been prone to enjoy the scenic outdoors. Being cooped inside on a computer never appealed to me.

What really drew me to their conversation was when I heard a Chinese guy among them start bragging how he'd cheated in online poker. Despite my having become an inveterate gambler, I had only read about online gambling in newspapers. I had never played with it nor had I ever seen it. But when I heard the Chinese kid say, "It's so simple to cheat and win a lot of money," I was suddenly interested.

I also overheard which trails they liked skiing at Bettex. The next morning when I told Jean Pierre that I was going to ski the resort's trails instead of the unmarked terrain, he was surprised. We agreed to meet up for lunch.

I spotted the Chinese kid on the lift line. He was a snowboarder. I realized immediately that I wanted to go up the mountain in the same chair with him, but I was too far behind. When I got to the top, I pulled a Bode Miller and ski-raced down the slope to catch him at the base where the lines were forming to go back up. I managed to get next to him in the line. It was perfect because it was just a two-seater and the ride up the mountain would be nearly ten minutes.

"I couldn't help but overhear you last night," I said to him just as the chair chugged out of the station, my skis resting parallel to his snowboard on the foot bars. "I've been getting killed gambling in these casinos, and I found it so interesting how you're beating online poker."

David Woo laughed. I could see at once he was a real talker. Before introducing himself, he said with a chuckle, "It's what paid for this vacation."

"Are you a student?" I asked.

"Yeah, Stanford."

I nearly fell out of the chair. "I went to Berkeley."

"You don't look like the type," he said, and we shared a laugh.

"What are you studying?"

"Computer programming and communications."

Sounded better by the minute. "Tell me, David, how do you cheat online poker? Don't they have some kind of security system?"

David laughed again. "It's easy. But I don't know if I should tell you.

How do I know you're not a cybercop?"

I would have loved to tell David Woo at that moment that I was perhaps the world's greatest identity thief. But it would have to wait. "Do you think that if I were a cybercop, I would've admitted having gone to Berkeley?" I smiled at him.

He laughed back. "Well, I started by writing a program that actually plays for me. It's like a computerized robot. I install the program to my machine and it plays the hands with 100 percent efficiency, much like the chess and backgammon programs you play against on your computer."

"Robots?"

"Actually they're called 'bots' for short. And they give you a hefty advantage against human opponents."

"Is that legal?"

"Not really, but there isn't much the online poker sites can do about it. They've got their hands full with more serious problems."

"Like what?"

"Like hackers breaking into their systems, cracking security codes and messing with their shuffling algorithms, which usually operate in sync with their internal clocks."

It sounded like gibberish to me, but the only word in that high-tech mishmash that interested me was "hackers."

"You mean like hackers who break into banks and transfer money?"

David's hands-up, "wait-a-minute" halting gesture coincided with the jerk of the chair as it docked into the station at the top of the mountain. "I haven't done *that* yet! But, yeah, the same hackers capable of breaking into bank and government files are the ones who can really clean up at online poker."

That was a double bombshell! Bank *and* government files. I was thinking that if those two elements showed up in an equation, the equal sign would be followed by "identity theft."

"Well, nice chatting with you," David said. He suddenly pushed off and shot down the mountain like a kamikaze. If the guy was as good on the keyboard as he was on his snowboard, he might prove to be the solution to my future. But that was a big "if."

In any event, I was not about to drop this meeting with David Woo. I had ascertained from their dinner conversation the night before that they were at Bettex for a week. I'd have plenty of time to cultivate a relationship with him. Instinctually, I sensed he was the type of carefree kid who would be game to some serious hacking for big money. He reminded me a little of me.

By the third day of the trip, we were skiing together. Seeing how skilled he was on his snowboard, I convinced David to come with Jean-Pierre and me on the naked trails outside the ski resort. He'd never ventured there before, heeding the advisories for dangerous avalanches, but decided if I could do it so could he. We actually did witness a few small avalanches tumble down the mountain in dusty, white mushrooming balls, but none got close to us.

"That was awesome!" David exclaimed with that typical college energy at day's end. "I don't think I'll ever ski marked trails again!"

Jean-Pierre, who knew nothing of my indecent past, wondered why I encouraged this much younger American to tag along with us. I told him I was homesick, to which he smirked.

The night before David's departure, we hung out in the chalet's bar drinking glasses of hot wine. A combination of French tunes and rock music piped in from a radio station. We were talking about David's return to Stanford when he suddenly asked me, "So, Glenn, what is it you're really into?"

I had indeed told him my real name. Not that I wouldn't have, but since Jean Pierre knew me as Glenn Hastings, it would serve no purpose to adopt an alias. When David put forth that question, my mind shifted back to that fateful day at the Miami Airport when Bones approached me. Now I was more or less in Bones's position, with David in the role I had been in with Bones: that of potential recruit.

Jean Pierre had gone up to the room with an Italian woman he'd picked up a few nights earlier. So I came right out with it to David. "I'm into identity theft," I said, looking him straight in the eye but with a trace of a smile.

He nodded. "I kind of thought you were some kind of white-collar criminal."

"Yeah, but I seldom wore the white collar." I went on to inform David that I had never used the Internet in my business. The only computer connection to my identity thefts had been to the TRW credit system. David evidenced some knowledge of the credit world when he commented on Equifax, one of three major nationwide consumer reporting agencies that had eradicated TRW's virtual monopoly on the industry.

"Did you make a shitload of money?" he asked with a sparkle in his eye.

"Enough to pay for this vacation," I quipped, and we laughed remembering how he'd said the same thing about his online poker cheating profits. I did not divulge the grand scale of the operation I ran with Bones, nor did I tell him of its many facets. I just wanted to feel him out, see if he was interested in doing something illegal in a big way. Also, I sought his input. I really had no idea what an identity thief could do if he were a hacker or teamed up with one.

"What year are you in at Stanford?" I asked him.

"This is my last year."

"Oh, you're a senior then."

He cocked his head. "I didn't say that."

He had me puzzled for a second. "Are you dropping out?"

"Depends what you have in mind." This kid was as glib as he was Asian.

"Let me ask you something, David," I said, resting my glass on the bar, turning completely toward him. "You said before that guys hacking online poker games also hack into bank and government files. What about you, David?" I paused for a moment. Then: "Do *you* know how to hack into bank files?"

One distinguishing trait about David Woo's personality was that he was precocious beyond his years. Then again, weren't all computer geeks seemingly that way?

"It's not whether I can hack into those files," he informed me in a somewhat condescending manner. "It's whether I can do so and then hide the fact that I'd been there."

I nodded slowly as I started to understand and he continued.

"You see, it's all about routing and complex computer programs that serve as spies and catch-spies. It works just like it does in the non-virtual world. What good is the spy's information if the target of his spying knows he's been spied on? See what I mean?"

I shrugged. "You haven't answered my question. Let me give you a hypothetical situation. Suppose you wanted to break into a bank's computer system and do a wire transfer without leaving a trace. Could you do it?"

"No such thing as not leaving a trace. The key is to not arouse their suspicions by making the transaction appear as just one in the flow of many. If they red-flag it, they'd be able to trace my break-in through the server and come breaking down the door."

"Sounds risky."

"It is."

"What about government agencies? Suppose you wanted to set yourself up with a US passport, Social Security card and a driver's license from, say, California. Could you enter phony documents into those government files and make them legitimate?"

David smiled and frowned at the same time. "That stuff is enciphered up the yin-yang. I could probably get into the California DMV system, but the State Department? That's treacherous. How did you get fake IDs before?"

I sighed. "Through a lot of hard work." I remembered the countless phone calls to the Social Security Administration and trips to DMVs all over the United States.

Over a few more glasses of hot wine and a mixture of French pop songs and international rock, I gave David Woo, who I'd known one day less than a week, the total lowdown on identity theft. I'd already decided that he was adventuresome and cocky enough to want in. My goal in telling him was to determine exactly how he could help me computerize the crime. The one element I counted on was that through the Internet a lot of time and inconvenience could be saved in a modern identity theft operation. When I was finished, David had some enlightening suggestions.

"All you would need to do is give me the names of people whose credit histories you want to steal," he said. "You don't even need their birth dates and Social Security numbers. If you have access to thousands of names, I can get that information on enough of them to make it worth your while."

"How?" One detail of the operation I had kept from David was the source of the fake identities, the *Marquis Who's Who* reference volumes. That part I would always keep to myself. I surmised that even the FBI and Secret Service investigations, probably at full throttle across the Atlantic that very moment, would never yield that information. They would forever wonder how the ID thieves found so many victims with such bountiful credit.

"Phishing," David said as though answering a simple *Jeopardy* question. "Do you know what spam is?"

"I barely know how to send an e-mail."

"Well, that's what it is. Spam is unsolicited e-mail that goes out to millions of e-mail addresses. Basically it's some company, often in the sexual aids or pharmaceutical business, looking to sell you their products. As a matter of fact, half the spam showing up in e-mail accounts bearing a masculine name hawks potions and pills for penis enlargement. If it's a feminine name, everything they're selling concerns the female parts, not to mention all the weight loss and wrinkles shit." He went on to explain that phishing used spam to deceive people into giving out their credit card numbers, bank account information, Social Security numbers, passwords and other sensitive information. The key was that the e-mails sent looked like they came from businesses the potential victims dealt with: like banks, electric companies and Internet service providers, anything that looked very familiar to people reading their e-mails.

"But how would you get the e-mail addresses of select people?"

"That's not difficult. It's like being able to garner unlisted telephone numbers. I can write a program to troll the Internet looking for the exact names you give me. Naturally, it's best that you give me the least common names. Then the ones with that name who get suckered into sending me the personal info can be sorted by where they bank and what states their vehicles are registered in. Stuff like that. Then you simply compare it to your source material and make the match. If you stick with uncommon names it would be relatively easy."

Phishing was just one of many tricks that David Woo knew then, and that we've all heard of today. There were hundreds of ways skilled hackers could invade sophisticated computer systems and simple e-mail accounts. David told me about a nasty little program they used called a Trojan horse. The name was fitting since the hacker disguised the Trojan horse as another program. He could also disguise it as a video or game. The trick was getting a user to install it on their system. If that were accomplished, the hacker would then have access to all the files on the hard drive, the system's e-mail and could even create messages that popped up on the screen.

And that wasn't even the Trojan's most serious infiltration. As I sat there astonished, David told me that the nefarious program was capable of replacing messages on the screen when a log-in was requested. Users thinking they were logging into the desired system would quite naturally provide their user names and passwords. This information was then recorded on a program and immediately ready for use by the hacker.

I had my fill of David's expert descriptions and virtual demonstrations of how all this worked. I was totally uninterested in the high-tech hacking methods but fascinated by what could be done. What was readily apparent was his ability to actually do everything he described. He didn't admit it at first, but when we met two weeks later at Stanford, he came totally clean with me.

IDENTITY THEFT, INC.

David Woo had been a computer hacker since the age of twelve. He was twenty now, which meant he was already hacking before half the population had ever heard the term "Internet." Now in his junior year of college, he lived comfortably in the off-campus apartment he rented with his online poker winnings. He let me know he had plenty left over for tuition and books.

We sat in the living room, which David called his computer room. He had a half dozen computers and monitors which, he explained, made up his apparatus to fool online poker web sites into thinking they had six different customers when they only had one. David clued me in to his cheating tactic of using six different Internet service providers with six different addresses, so that he could take six seats at online poker tables and gang up on the two or three players unwittingly playing against his silicon army.

We didn't waste much time on the poker. David, at twenty, clearly wanted to move on to bigger and better things.

"So we're gonna start another massive credit card operation?" he asked.

I laughed. If the time had indeed come for David to get into bigger and better things, likewise the clock struck midnight for me. The credit card frauds I'd perpetrated with Bones were passé. What I had in mind was the identity theft wave of the future.

I envisioned David as my man in the cyberworld. I would pull off the scams in the real world. But this second time around, I would strike but a few blows, and hopefully make a big enough bundle to go back into retirement. After David enlightened me at Bettex to the numerous ways hackers used the Internet to swindle banks and credit card companies, I'd spent two weeks thinking how I could come up with the ultimate credit fraud using the web. But before arriving at that stroke of genius, I had to first eliminate the kinds of cybercrimes I did not want to try.

Before flying to California, I'd spent many hours in Internet cafés in Nice. David had given me some pointers to facilitate my navigation of the Web. After surfing its limitless waters, I learned a lot about identity theft and bank and credit fraud online. I saw that I was not going to be the pioneer of identity theft online like I'd been for conventional identity theft. By the first months of 2002, hundreds of scams involving bank and credit fraud had been launched via the Internet. A common one was breaking into banks' computer systems and wiring money from victims' accounts into the hackers'. By that time, most of these illegal electronic transfers were discovered rapidly, if not altogether blocked. Many of the hackers were getting caught and facing stiff sentences for bank and wire fraud.

The more successful lot of hackers ran scams along the lines of what David had said. I read a lot about phishing. Just as he'd explained, people were easily duped into surrendering all the information online that identity and credit thieves needed. Phishing had evolved into pharming, where the thieves created fake web sites similar to those of banks and credit card companies. When consumers not knowing the difference logged in, their account information was sent right along to the hackers. Then the hackers conducted massive skimming operations against thousands of accounts, never taking big sums from individual accounts so as to avoid detection. By operating in that manner, they could make the same illicit fortune once available through large bank transfers.

Then there was a plethora of high-tech equipment geared to turn ATMs and credit card swipe apparatuses into your worst enemy. This stuff was as foreign to me as *The Andromeda Strain*, but if I wanted back into the business I had to learn it. Innocuous-looking equipment was being attached to ATMs that captured your card information, including your PIN, for future use by identity thieves. It was cleverly disguised to look like normal ATM equipment mounted to the front of the normal ATM card slot. Even tiny wireless cameras were in place to catch your fingers stroking the keys. If that were not enough, you couldn't even go to your local service station and pay for gas by credit card without worrying about ID thieves. Every time you swipe your credit or debit card at the pump, your information is sent via satellite to your bank for verification. High-tech identity thieves had already begun hijacking that information by modifying the program that carries out the data transfer so that your credit card number is sent to them at the same time it's sent to your bank. Before you drive away from the pump, the thieves may already be using your credit card.

But as fascinating as all these electronic scams were, I had missed the boat on them. I had always been the innovator of my unlawful activities. I wasn't about to piggyback on someone else's scams. Bones had taught me early on that once you're riding the second wave in the ocean of criminality, you're going to be the first to get caught reaching shore. Therefore, if David's willingness to enter my underworld would result in new riches, my ingenuity would have to be equal to the task.

"Forget the credit cards," I told him. "We're going to do something much bigger. Something you can't read about on the Internet, because it hasn't been done yet."

David Woo smiled broadly. "Just tell me what you want me to do."

"It's very simple, David. I want you to create a whole new person."

His smile did not dissipate. "A whole new person?"

"Yes. But not just any person. You are going to build up the perfect Frankenstein monster to haunt the credit industry, one tailor-made to fit the profile of its most worthy loan-seeker. One no different than all the dot-com multimillionaires who've popped up out of thin air."

David suddenly looked a little perplexed.

"What I'm talking about, David, is creating the next Bill Gates or Larry Ellison, except no one will know who he really is or what he really looks like." My thinking was that it was not difficult to get people to believe the notion of an otherwise average person who had made good in the new Internet economy. The invention of our "dot-commer" and his development would be eased into the proper computer networks. Then I would convince banks to finance his projects, just the way Donald Trump leveraged banks to keep his real estate empire afloat when it seemed ready to crash into the ground like a giant blimp.

Lots of dot-com cash

United States and Europe, 2002-2003

I FLEW BACK TO MENTON, WHERE I SPENT THE SPRING AND summer of 2002 planning the scam I would pull with David Woo. We kept in constant communication. I had been expecting David to get cold feet and back out, but he exhibited nothing other than impatience to get started. After seven months surfing the web, I was pretty sure who my King Kong identity creation would be and what he would do.

I had less than $500,000 in cash secreted away in my vault in Nice when I made the final decision to return to the States. I emptied it out, packed it in a single duffel bag and flew to New York. The money would be used to set up what I hoped would be the last scam of my life. One thing I pondered on the plane crossing the Atlantic was that this scam would either bring me back to France to live the rest of my life or land me in a US federal prison for a very long time.

I thought about Frank Abagnale of *Catch Me If You Can* fame. I had read his book depicting his life as a young criminal posing as an airline pilot to defraud banks and compared his life to mine. Although his scams were much less significant than the frauds I'd already committed, we did have things in common. His crimes had encompassed cities all over the United States, as mine had, and his travels had brought him to live in France. The one thing I did not want to end up sharing with Mr. Abagnale was the time he spent in prison.

Before takeoff, I'd been given the *Wall Street Journal* by one of the stewardesses. There happened to be an article about Donald Trump's latest Manhattan real estate venture. I thought a dozen years back to my first trip to the university library, when I pulled that *Marquis Who's Who in American Real Estate* volume off the shelf. My fingers had gone right to the page containing the information on Trump, above which I found the person whom we used to commit our very first identity theft, Herbert Trumm. Funny enough, Donald Trump was about to make another indirect contribution to my latest ID theft operation.

I would move my dot-com billionaire into the luxurious Trump Tower at the United Nations Plaza in Manhattan. Of course I would not be in the market to buy one of Trump's multimillion-dollar units, but I was keen on finding one to rent. By establishing a residence in Trump Tower, whoever this fictitious person proved to be would transcend scrutiny. A New York address with the name Trump in it was, as Frank Sinatra sang in "New York, New York," the top of the heap. Creditors high up on the financing scale would love it.

After landing, I taxied into Manhattan and visited two choice real estate agencies that handled exclusive co-ops and condos for rent in the city's most prestigious residential buildings. Although there were no unsold units in any of Trump's residential buildings, quite a few of them were for rent. I was informed that for twenty grand a month, I'd have a nice selection of two-bedroom units. For fifteen, owners would lease their one-bedrooms. For twelve-five, I might even find a one-bedroom facing northeast.

The next day I flew to California and handed David Woo $50,000 in cash. For that, he would manufacture a person in the virtual world whom I decided to name Warren Davis. I chose that name firstly because I liked the way it sounded. It stunk of money and prestige, and I was convinced that banks and potential investors would quickly whiff the scent and flock around Mr. Davis with their wallets out. Then I liked it even more because it was a combination of names belonging to two well-known American billionaires: Warren Buffett, the nation's most powerful investor-venture capitalist, and Marvin Davis, the real estate developer and oilman from Denver. The decisive factor in choosing Davis over Buffett as the last name was my appreciation of Al Davis, the highly respected entrepreneur and longtime owner of the Oakland Raiders football team, which played their home games a short drive from Berkeley. Al was a true maverick and, in a way, so was I.

My idea was to do the exact opposite of what hackers and identity thieves had been doing to amass fortunes through the Internet. Instead of using malicious programs like Trojan horses to sucker people into giving away information used to steal their ID and credit accounts, I would have David break into systems and simply add information to them. This information would take the form of names, Social Security numbers, banking records and credit histories. Instead of transferring money from people's bank accounts into ours, we would create our own bank accounts with balances that would be reflected by bank computers, but not activate red flags in the system because the funds would not be transferred. They would lie stagnant deep inside the system so as to not produce any wire transactions that would come under the scrutiny of bank personnel and auditors. As long as the phony funds were entered into the system between monthly financial periods and not moved from one account to another, they would not be noticed and marked as suspicious until one period ended and the next began.

I drilled David on this unerringly. Was it safe? He could not give me a 100 percent guarantee that this theory would hold up, but based on everything he'd researched and instinctively knew about the ongoing war between hackers and security for banks' computer systems, his belief was that a window existed in which detection would be unlikely. He estimated it to be thirty days. I estimated that to be enough time to pull perhaps the biggest short-term fraudulent investment scheme ever. In thirty days, I could bilk banks out of tens of millions. If I were successful, Woo would be paid $1 million for each $10 million I made, with a minimum of a million bucks.

David would see to it that Warren Davis's credit was bountiful and flawless. He would break into the databases of Equifax, Experian and TransUnion, the three major consumer reporting agencies serving the American economy. AAA credit histories would be inserted into their files. Anyone checking into Davis's financial history would have not the slightest doubt that the man honored all his debts, many of which would be seven figures.

Woo's work would not be done with Warren Davis alone. He had several more identities with solid financial backgrounds to create. These would be Davis's shadow investors who owned shadow companies, many based in the

British Isles. When Davis sought his giant loans from financial institutions, he would be able to supply them with groups of upstanding investors from every corner of the world who had already invested in him heavily. Banks felt much better about granting major loans to entrepreneurs who came to them with a following. Thus David would invade several bank computer systems to coordinate banking histories for the investors, and repetitively doctor up the files of the three credit bureaus.

I did not ask Woo how he could manage this. The first few days at his apartment, the only wizardry I witnessed him perform on his computers was to beat the hell out of some online poker games. He gave me a demonstration of his "bot" programs, which played his hands perfectly. When I was not terribly impressed by that, he showed me a program called Peeker that he'd developed with some hacking buddies in a UCLA laboratory. Whatever lack of enthusiasm I displayed for his bots, I made up for when watching him attack online poker with Peeker. This software actually let him see his players' hole cards! If that wasn't enough, he saw the next card to be dealt, too!

Seeing this propped up my confidence that David Woo was, at the age of twenty, a top-rate computer hacker. When I told him this, he informed me that the most skilled hackers he knew were still in puberty, including the one he'd worked with to develop the program for hacking into online poker systems.

However, I still had no way of knowing whether David could successfully implement all I asked of him. In my desperation I had to trust him, and then hope he'd succeed. Of the utmost importance was that he work alone. I didn't want any of his teenage hacking buddies involved in this scam, not even if they were capable of hacking into the Pentagon's early-warning system and programming Air Force computers to launch a nuclear attack on China.

The history on Warren Davis that David Woo carefully planted, nurtured and let blossom on the web seemed like it could have come right out of the *Marquis Who's Who in Silicon Valley*. Davis was born one month prior to me in New York City. He graduated Stanford University in 1978 with a computer science degree. He'd gone to work for a now-defunct software company in the heart of Silicon Valley. In 1984, he left to form his own start-up venture. Like Bill Gates, Paul Allen, Steve Jobs and many other computer-age dot-com success stories, Warren Davis started developing intelligent gizmos in his garage. His first company was called Davis Electronics and a decade later, in 1994, evolved into the Davis Company, with field offices in

England and France. I liked the sound of it immediately. What product did the Davis Company sell? Computer security programs, of course. Warren Davis claimed that his company developed avant-garde software to protect computer systems from hackers!

David Woo worked diligently to make this all believable. After hacking into computer systems of banks, credit card companies and credit reporting bureaus, he manipulated Internet search engines like puppets on a string. Anyone searching "Warren Davis," "Davis Company" or just plain "Davis" would find our Warren Davis and his company at the top of all the lists. He also inserted tons of literature across the web about "one of Silicon Valley's brightest stars." The only thing I worried about was that David might be overdoing it. Perhaps some industry-monitoring entity or curious individuals would wonder who this Warren Davis really was and begin investigating on their own. Then we might have a line of whistle-blowers stretching from one measureless end of cyberspace to the other.

But David told me not to worry. Each time I worried about an Internet facet of the scam, he reminded me that only time was of the essence. As long as the duration of the scam did not exceed one month, there would be insufficient time for his mountain of phony information to collapse on us.

He set up that colossal mountain in three days. On the fourth day, I flew back to New York with a birth certificate and Social Security card in the name of Warren Davis. Both documents David had fabricated with his own graphics program and printer. Their legitimacy was achieved by two computer break-ins, first into New York City's Office of Vital Statistics and then the Social Security Administration. With his talents as a graphic artist, David saved me from having to deal with those agencies to get hard copies of the needed ID documents. As long as the corresponding information was in their computer files, the birth certificate and Social Security card he falsified were as good as any coming from the official agencies.

In the afternoon of that fourth day, I entered a Manhattan office of New York State's Division of Motor Vehicles. As it was now post-9/11, the stringent six-point positive identification system was in use. No problem: I had points to spare and obtained a driver's license as Warren Davis with no hassle.

I hailed a cab to a Madison Avenue real estate agency that had listings for Trump Tower co-ops for rent. I wore an impeccable blue business suit, a Rolex Presidential gold watch and a three-karat diamond on the ring finger of each hand. The heavyset woman on the phone took notice of me before the door shut. I sat before her and waited.

"May I help you, sir?" she said in a rattled voice that indicated time was money.

"Yes, ma'am. My name is Warren Davis. I want to lease an apartment in Trump Tower at the UN Plaza," I said deliberately.

In spite of my attire and jewelry, she was still slightly taken aback.

"That's expensive," she said for some reason, probably involuntary. Then she introduced herself as Rebecca. We shook hands over her desk.

I ignored the comment. "I want it immediately. I'd prefer a one-bedroom; I don't care which side it faces. I'm new to New York, and that's the address I want." Bones had taught me to be very direct and forceful with people in the business world. Doing so made an immediate and lasting impression.

Rebecca did not ask where I was from. In New York's real estate market there was no time for small talk. "I have three units," she said. "The one facing southwest is sixteen-five a month. The one facing southeast is fifteen, and the one on the north side is thirteen. Which would you like?"

I noticed she didn't even bother mentioning that the apartment facing north was on the east or west side. I took that to mean both were on the dark side. "I'll take the unit facing north."

She slid open a file cabinet and pulled a folder. Flipping through its contents, she said, "The owner wants a year lease with three months' security deposit. That's a move-in of fifty-two thousand. He prefers that all utilities, telephone and cable service be transferred to his tenant's name. The tenant is not responsible for any of the association or maintenance costs." After a second, she added, "You do realize, Mr. Davis, that the unit is unfurnished."

"Naturally," I said, though the part about me not putting in as much as a doormat I left unsaid.

Fifty-two grand for a one-month rental! Bones would have turned over in his prison cell.

"The unit is on the seventeenth floor. Not the top of the mountain, but nevertheless, the view isn't bad."

"That's okay." I felt like cracking that I was scared of heights but let it go. "When can I move in?"

Rebecca took a quick glance at her calendar, which had a backdrop of Trump's other residential tower on Fifth Avenue. "You can fill out the application right now, give me a check for sixty-seven thousand six hundred, which includes our agency fee of ten percent of the total lease, which is a hundred and fifty-six thousand dollars. I'll process your application before the close of business today, run checks on your financial position, and you should be able to move in tomorrow. Which hotel are you at, Mr. Davis?"

Wow! Another $15,600 for commission was ten times more than we'd ever paid for a month's rent in any scam house. Davis's apartment in Trump Tower would have to be the "scam palace."

"I haven't checked in yet. How 'bout I write you the check and return tomorrow morning to pick up the keys. I'm sure there'll be no problem with your process and that I'll be approved."

I filled out the rather detailed application with all the information coinciding with David Woo's entries into various computer systems. Before giving it to Rebecca, I attached my business card. It was a handsome platinum card with stylish printing that distinguished me as president of the Davis Company. I wrote out the check against an account I had opened in San Francisco.

As soon as I left Rebecca's office, I telephoned David in Stanford. I told him to be ready to take phone calls on the number I'd furnished on both the application and my business card. Another upgrade to the operation made with David's help was to replace employees formerly needed to answer phones with computerized equipment that supplied any person with any voice he or she wanted. When the phone rang at the Davis Company, it would be David Woo answering, but his voice would be distinctly feminine. If the caller wished to speak with someone else in order to learn specifics about Davis or his company, Woo would adjust the computerized voice and give the information as a man.

I slept in an inexpensive hotel, at least by Manhattan standards, and was up early and ready to roll on the fifth day. After a quick breakfast in a typical Manhattan muffin-and-coffee shop, I taxied over to the real estate office. This would be the first test to determine whether David's computer hacking had held up. I knew that every detail I'd put on the application would be verified. Nobody was getting into Trump Tower without being thoroughly checked out.

Rebecca was all smiles when I came through the door. I knew my tenancy had been approved.

"Good luck in your new residence," she said, handing me the keys. "I'm sure it will serve you well."

"From your mouth to God's ears," I said under my breath. We shook hands and I left. Outside, I did not go to Trump Tower. In fact, I never did go to Trump Tower. Warren Davis was probably the only person in the history of Donald Trump's real estate empire to pay three months' security deposit above a month's rent for a residential unit he never entered. If that wasn't so, then somebody had run a bigger scam than mine.

I rented a car and drove out to the wealthy town of East Hampton, New York, a summer playground for New York's rich and famous. I had an appointment with another realtor there, though this one entailed much more than the rental of a co-op. On the way out, I reflected how by that time I had either carried out, if not conceived, virtually every type of major identity theft-credit fraud available to someone with only human brainpower. Bones used to like to say jokingly that if we hadn't done it yet, nobody's thought of it.

Over the years we had tossed around several ideas on how to expand the horizons of stealing cash by way of credit. We toyed with getting involved in the stock and commodities markets. Buying stocks and options on margin at first seemed very appealing. But upon further investigation, it looked burdensome without proportionate reward, and risked us to the watchful eye of the Securities and Exchange Commission. Another idea was a construction-loan scam. Why not set up a wealthy, creditworthy individual and have him apply to a bank for a loan to begin development of a strip mall or office building? Then upon receiving the loan, we could disappear with the cash without as much as putting a single nail in a piece of wood.

But it wasn't that easy. Researching it, we learned that banks normally did not grant construction loans until the prospective borrower had ownership of the property to be built on. Therefore, we would actually have to go out and buy a piece of land, not a minor outlay of cash. Then, we were pained to learn, construction loans were paid out in stages. You couldn't just borrow five million bucks and walk out the revolving door with the cash. Each step along the way of your project, you had to show the bank where the money was going and how construction was progressing. Banks routinely sent inspectors to audit job sites. If they weren't satisfied, the next stage of the loan was withheld. Thus, in our case, we would only receive the first stage pay-out.

What clouded it even more was the time period between applying for the loan and the bank's decision. Whereas in the credit card scams the cards and identities were all burned up within a month, a construction-loan scam would take longer to pull off, increasing the chances of detection. There was also the problem of the identities. If financial records between the identity's real and fraudulent credit got mixed up, the real person might see our bogus construction loan appearing in his credit reports before we actually absconded with the cash.

But I had come a long way since then. The Internet and David Woo's skill set changed many elements relating to the identify theft business. For one, it greatly reduced the time involved in setting things up. In turn, this got us results a lot faster; the cash flowed readily. So now the construction-loan idea was feasible, but I had formulated an even better one, a real humdinger: home mortgages. And instead of taking them out from banks, I would extract the cash from mortgage companies. This decision was based primarily on my past history of swindling banks. Why go back and fleece them again when I could attain the same result from "virgin" mortgage companies from which I'd never stolen a dime? At that time, I had no idea as to what the fallout had been from bilking millions out of banks and casinos. Whatever it was, I knew it would have no repercussions on mortgage companies.

There were other advantages to using mortgage companies. First and foremost was that they were easier to fleece. Since their primary business was mortgages, they wanted to find prospective homebuyers the money for their dream houses. Their criteria were less stringent than banks' as were their demands on the size of down payments. Mortgage companies were flexible with their creativity in structuring a loan, whereas banks, which lent money on anything under the sun and did not focus solely on mortgages, seldom if ever, deviated from standard-type home loans.

The main negative in dealing with a mortgage company was that its fee for the loan was usually higher than a bank's. I'd gladly pay that difference, knowing that it was insignificant in the overall scheme of things. Maybe I wouldn't have to. I might be able to get the mortgage company to bury its fee in the payments, which I'd never make. I knew mortgage companies generally required the mortgagee to take out private mortgage insurance when the down payment was less than 20 percent, but that, too, was no skin off my nose. I'd take whatever insurance they wanted to secure a loan. In the end, these expenses were just the cost of doing business.

I arrived in East Hampton at the end of the day's business. Although I had never been there, I had expected a "Waspy" village steeped in snobbery, and the town proved me right. The lovely oceanfront mansion Mrs. Thatcher took me to see was indeed owned by old New York money. After my obligatory joke question about whether she was related to "Margaret," the genteel agent said she had no relatives in England and led me through the foyer, out the glass sliding door to a beautiful expanse of sand and ocean.

The asking price on the home was $4.4 million, mid-level range for a beachfront property in East Hampton. Since I had already faxed the financial statements that David had created for Warren Davis to her office, I didn't need to be subjected to any questions to determine if I was a qualified buyer, as upper-crust realtors classified the distinction. The only personal question she asked was if I enjoyed living at Trump Tower. She was not aware that I'd rented that apartment the day before. I told her it had its "ups and downs." Mrs. Thatcher was quite assured that I possessed the means to buy this little palace on the beach.

She was, however, surprised how fast I made an offer.

"Mrs. Thatcher," I said succinctly, "I find this home very charming, and I love its setting on the beach. I do, however, think it is slightly overvalued at four-point-four, therefore, I am prepared to tender you an offer at three million seven hundred fifty thousand." I knew I sounded like a babbling brook of bullshit, but that's the kind of bullshit these realtors loved to hear. I would have liked to just say "Okay, I'll take it" at the asking price, but that was so uncommon as to invite suspicion.

"I will submit it," Mrs. Thatcher replied promptly.

"Thank you. I would like you to as soon as possible, Mrs. Thatcher. Time is of the essence." Of course she didn't know just how much time was of the essence. "These are very busy months for me. I want this home to be available to my family for the Christmas holidays, therefore, if my offer is accepted, I would like a closing within thirty days." Another crucial component of David Woo's work had been to set me up with a family. My fictitious wife's name was Emily. My two children were Sam and Lauren. David had asked lightheartedly if I wanted the cyberworld to know that I had a dog, cat or pet boa constrictor.

"I will get right to it," Mrs. Thatcher said. She added with a smile and in a slightly lower voice, "I think Mr. Adelson will seriously consider your offer."

So, the guy's name was Adelson. I had read that the Long Island real estate market had dipped a bit. I guessed she was telling me that Mr. Adelson might not be receiving higher offers. I did tell her in a very subtle way that I could up my offer a bit if Adelson was not impressed. I gave her my cell phone number, then drove to the neighboring village of Southampton, another beachside bastion of Manhattan summer snobbery.

My appointment with that village's prestigious real estate agency was not until morning. Instead of driving back to Manhattan, I took a hotel room on the ocean, which was not overly expensive during the off-season. Outside, however, it was unseasonably warm, so I took a twilight stroll along the beach. Looking out at the flickering lights of ships lining the horizon, I first thought of France and how I couldn't wait to get back there, then of the scam I was now deeply rooted in. If all went well and I made the millions I'd envisioned, I would not go back to gambling on the Riviera's ritzy casinos. I would live a clean life and hopefully never have to commit a crime again. Even at that stage, I was longing to make the change to become a respectable member of society, though I won't lie and say that I was no longer getting off on big-time scamming.

The mansion I visited on the beach in Southampton was every bit as palatial and gorgeous as the one I'd seen the previous day. Mr. Markson, the agent who showed it, had all the dope on Warren Davis. He led me through its stately interior, informing me that the owner was asking $4.2 million. This house was my backup. Since I could not make two simultaneous offers, I would only make one here if the East Hampton offer was declined. I told Markson I was very interested and would let him know in the coming days if I'd make an offer.

On the sixth day, back in Manhattan, Mrs. Thatcher called. She had indeed acted promptly and relayed my offer to the seller's attorney. It was accepted! For $3.75 million, I could buy the East Hampton mansion. The owner was out of town but due back the following morning. A meeting at his attorney's office could be arranged at ten a.m.

Day seven found me in the offices of Stewart G. Reeser, attorney at law. Mr. Leland Adelson himself showed up, even though he didn't really need to be there. He was curious to see who had made the offer on his East Hampton estate. We sat in a dignified conference room, dripping in mahogany and buttery soft black leather.

Reeser, like everyone else I had come into contact with as Warren Davis, knew who I was. He even had the audacity to say he'd known of my company for many years now and was fascinated by my rise to the top of the dot-com world.

Incredible how people full of shit were even more full of shit when the subject was money. This was the side of human behavior that helped me to shake off any guilt I felt about my crimes.

"So, Mr. Davis," the attorney said. "I understand you want to fix a quick closing to have Mr. Adelson's home ready for you to occupy by New Year's."

"Christmas," I corrected him with a touch of my own practiced snobbery.

Reeser and Adelson exchanged a glance. Apart from the initial introductions, Adelson didn't have much to say. He did mention, though, that he had several friends and business acquaintances living in Trump Tower. I told him I didn't associate with any fellow tenants.

"Won't be a problem," Reeser said. "As I anticipate your finances not to be, either." Then with an invasive smile, "Will you be seeking a mortgage?"

I returned the same smile. "I imagine so, but no matter which option I choose to finance the purchase, I assure you there will be no problems at closing."

"Of course not."

Reeser reminded me of the checklist I would need to satisfy in applying for a mortgage. David had versed me thoroughly on all of it: property deeds, documents pertaining to title insurance and municipal taxes, various inspection certificates and personal financial and tax documents. Thanks to David, I had detailed financial statements relating to my net worth and my company's healthy financial position.

"I'll draw up the contracts," Reeser announced. "Who's your attorney, by the way?"

"James Chan," I responded quickly, the image of David Woo in my head. Then I blurted, "Do you know him?"

"Never heard of him," Reeser said matter-of-factly. "But in any case, I'll have them ready in just a few days."

"I'd appreciate it. Like I said, I'm quite anxious to get to closing."

"I understand."

We all shook hands, and I left. I went back to my hotel room and called Woo on my cell phone. "Everything okay?" I asked him nervously.

"Of course. I'm just hanging out cheating online poker, waiting for our company phone to ring."

"Did it?"

"Not yet."

"Okay, the first phase of the operation is complete. I have to wait a few days for the contracts, then I'll go to mortgage companies. Listen, I have to ask you a favor. Do you trust me?"

"'Bout as much as I'd give you credit." He laughed.

"Well, the fifty grand I paid you up front…"

"You need to borrow it back?"

"I only have four hundred twenty thousand in cash. That's a little short of what we need for the escrow account."

"All right, no problem. I guess we're kind of in this together. Besides, I'm up fourteen thousand dollars in poker."

The ninth day into the scam, Reeser sent a courier to my hotel with four copies of the purchase contract. I had notified the front desk to ring my room the moment the package arrived. It was in my hand at ten a.m. I tore it open, went right to the back page of the top copy. Naturally, I didn't give a shit about any mistakes the attorney might have made. Only one thing mattered: that we had a deal.

Reeser and Adelson had signed them all. I signed on the lines provided, then sent two copies back to Reeser's office with the courier. I rushed outside and jumped into a cab. By ten thirty, I was swinging through a revolving door into the First Fidelity Mortgage Company. It sounded like a bank, but the word "mortgage" was all I had to see. I carried a Gucci attaché case. Inside it were the Hampton contracts and my personal documents, including a tax return in the name of Warren Davis that David Woo had created and sent through the IRS electronic filing system. In a remarkable display of hacking, David had first created a phony portfolio to gain status as an Electronic Return Originator, for which the IRS conducts extensive background checks.

Inside, I was led to Jeff Hausen, the owner of the company, who sat me down in the chair across his desk. He looked over my expensive suit and jewelry while telling someone through the intercom to bring coffee. It got there before Hausen, a slick-looking guy who looked more like a con man than I did, crossed his legs in his swivel chair.

"Where's your property?" he asked as soon as the girl set down the coffees and left.

I laid the contracts and financial documents on his desk. "Further Lane in East Hampton."

Hausen suddenly uncrossed his legs and then recrossed them in the other direction. "That's nice," he said with arched brows. Greedy interest brightened his eyes.

"It's a pleasant summer home, though it's not the size of those 20,000-square-foot monsters selling for twenty mil."

"How large is your new home, sir?"

"It's quite modest, Mr. Hausen. Just a tad under 7,000-square-feet. But it's got quite a view."

"I'll bet."

I had been a little nervous entering the mortgage company, but Hausen seemed completely sold by my front as a dot-com biggie, putting me at ease. He gave me the application to fill out while he went to make a copy of the contracts. When he returned, he said, "I'd say you made a good deal for the house, sir. Anything for less than four million on that street is very reasonable."

It would have been difficult telling him how I'd wished to pay more. I said with a nod, "Yes, I agree. I wouldn't have jumped on the deal so quickly had I not found the terms so attractive."

"What kind of mortgage would you like me to structure?"

Here I had to be careful. Despite the possibility that I may have been a great identity and credit thief, I knew jack shit about mortgages. I had to watch my words. Anything coming out of my mouth that hinted at inexperience, any trace of a slip-up, could blow my cover and the whole scam. David and I had thoroughly researched "everything you need to know about home mortgages," but the Internet could not teach you how to speak and behave while applying for one. I assumed the best approach was to say as little as possible and let Hausen lead me along. As long as he believed in my wealth, he'd find the way to grant me the mortgage.

"Well, first off, I don't think it would be necessary to put more than ten percent down…"

"Of course not, Mr. Davis. A man of your standing would never need to do that." He was fawning. "But I do have to advise you that our company policy is to require all mortgagees to take out mortgage insurance when the down payment is under twenty percent. I'm sorry but…"

"Don't be," I said quickly. "I don't expect you to waive anything for me. I could very well put the twenty percent down, but I'd rather feed the cash into some important investments I've got going."

"Of course, Mr. Davis. I bet you're working on software that's gonna give Microsoft a run for its money."

I chuckled. "You might say that."

Hausen began rattling off different mortgages with fifteen and thirty-year terms carrying different interest rates and payment structures. When he'd finished, he suggested, "I think you should go with a fifteen-year mortgage at 6.2 percent. A man in your shoes doesn't need to spread to a thirty-year deal. Of course there'll be a fee of two points at closing."

I agreed wholeheartedly. A fifteen-year mortgage at 6.2 percent suited

Warren Davis to perfection. I would put up $375,000. The First Fidelity Mortgage Company would loan me $3.375 million. But I didn't want to eat his two-point fee, which amounted to $67,500.

"Can you structure the mortgage so that your fee is included in the payments?" I asked.

"Absolutely. I'll work it in over the first year, if that's all right with you."

"That's fine." Of course there weren't going to be any payments.

"I can have an appraiser out to the place tomorrow. Would that suit Mr. Adelson?"

"Yes, he's assured me that someone will be there to let your appraiser inside."

"Great. Then all we'll need before we make this official is to process the application." This was Hausen's polite way of saying they would check out my banking and credit histories along with my current financial position. "And then we'll have your check at closing," he said with finality.

In preparation for that check, my attorney, Mr. Chan, had opened up an escrow account at Bank of America in San Francisco. We funded it with $450,000, all by legitimate wire transfers from a host of bank accounts we'd set up for that very purpose. The money in the account represented the $375,000 down payment plus a $75,000 reserve for closing costs and attorneys' fees.

But in reality it served only as bait to hook Hausen's $3.375 million. None of our cash would be lost. However, it was necessary to set up real funds in a real bank account. Even though Hausen would have bought my front as a wealthy Silicon Valley businessman, he was obligated to check my banking position to ascertain I had the cash on hand for the down payment on the house.

Hausen called my cell phone at the end of the following business day. He sounded happier than a guy whose dream date just accepted his invite to the prom. "Congratulations, Mr. Davis, your mortgage has been approved. And, I might add, my appraiser just loved your house. You can stop by and sign the docs today if you get here before six."

"I'll be there."

I immediately called Stewart Reeser with the news. He was very accommodating and set the closing at his office in ten days' time. This meant that the total time elapsed from the computerized setup of the scam to its execution and cash dividends would be less than thirty days, just as we'd hoped.

Next I called Woo. "Okay, David, you're now James Chan, attorney at law. Make a reservation for a flight to New York. Be here on the twentieth. The closing is on the twenty-second. Don't forget to practice applying the makeup."

"Wait till you see me with gray hair. I look at least thirty."

"Good. Just make sure you look it when you're here."

This was another problem we had to overcome. At the closing in Reeser's office, my attorney had to be present. I had no choice but to have David Woo play the part. But he was just twenty years old. I couldn't bring a college kid as my lawyer for a closing on a $3.75 million house. At least not a lawyer who looked like a college kid.

So David had gone to a theatrical cosmetics store in San Francisco. An eager salesclerk gave him a brush-up on how to make oneself appear older. With a combination of blushes, makeup tools and hair coloring, David would look like a young attorney with a bit of experience in his briefcase.

Hausen was waiting for me when I came through the door. He took me straight to his office, where the mortgage agreement lay on his desk. As I read through it, he pointed out and explained the salient details. I signed and initialed where required.

"Let me know when the closing is," Hausen said. "I'll bring the check."

Everything appeared to be on the right course, but I still sweated bullets in the interim. Ten days is an interminable wait when you have nothing to think about but getting caught. A myriad of things could go wrong. Wandering the streets of Manhattan, I carried a load of anxiety as heavy as the behemoth steel and glass structures on either side. I kept concocting scenarios in which one thing or another did go wrong.

One unnerving thought was the possibility of David Woo getting busted in California while I was in New York. Would he give me up? He knew my real name. The FBI and Secret Service would surely offer him a deal to help them reel in the big fish. He'd wear a wire and lead the agents to me in New York. Then the whole scam would be caught on audio and videotape. It would be a foolproof case with horrific consequences. If I were caught in this scam, I'd certainly be implicated in the thousands of others involving banks, casinos and department stores. I was not too familiar with the intricate workings of the statutes of limitations pertaining to identity theft and credit fraud. I assumed that they had not run out, at least for a significant number of my crimes. It only took one federal conviction to send you away for a long time.

Then I played the other side of the coin. How could they catch us? I had read that cybercrime was so prevalent and tangled inside the Web that cybercops trying to sort their way through the crooked maze were as frustrated as stymied rats. One article stated that only one in 700 identity thieves were arrested. One in 700! I was pretty sure that my well-coordinated mortgage fraud was a first of its kind, another element that reduced the chances of getting caught.

The vagaries of my thought process were not going to change anything, so by the fourth day I forced myself to stop worrying. What began as trepidation had evolved into impatience. I just wanted the time to pass so I could get my hands on that three million-plus. Another mortgage scam was in the works.

David Woo arrived on December 20. I waited for him in the domestic terminal at LaGuardia Airport. When he walked by, I didn't recognize him! The Asian gentleman with salt and pepper hair wearing horn-rimmed glasses and a charcoal-gray business suit, an overcoat slung over his shoulder, was not someone I knew. But it was indeed David Woo.

"I told you I'd look at least thirty," he said with his handshake.

"*Thirty?* You look forty!"

"You like my suit?" He spread his arms so that I'd have a good look.

"You look sharper than Johnny Cochran. But do you know anything about the law?" I was both kidding and worried. I knew David had accumulated vast knowledge about real estate law in recent weeks. Whatever he needed to know was available on the Internet. Plus the kid was so cocky that if a sticky situation arose in the attorney's office, I had confidence David would smooth his way through it. We had gone over the details of real estate closings. I had telephoned Bim, who'd taken out three mortgages since his cash windfall in Vegas. He went over every step with me. Unless I was thrown a real curve, procedure for closing a property sale would not be complicated.

We arrived at Reeser's office twenty minutes early for the ten a.m. meeting. I'd wanted it that way. I figured it was best that Reeser not have the chance to converse with Hausen before my arrival. You never knew what could come up in conversation that would start people wondering about your credibility. Reeser was already seated in the conference room going over the documents when we were shown in.

"So you're Mr. Chan," Reeser said to David as he stood. We shook hands and took seats around the table, David and I laying our briefcases on the mahogany surface. "Leland should be here momentarily."

"I must be early," I said, looking at my Rolex. "Excuse me."

"Don't mention it."

"Mr. Hausen from First Fidelity will be here at ten."

Hausen came ten minutes early. I guessed he was as anxious as I was. He had his own attaché case, though it didn't appear to be of the designer variety. He laid it on the table and popped it open. Out came the documents. Then my eyes were drawn to a beautiful saw-toothed certified bank check. Unless some cruel joke was being played on me, that check was in the amount of $3.375 million and paid to the order of James Chan.

At ten sharp, Mrs. Thatcher arrived with a younger man I assumed to be her listing agent. She introduced him as Randy. They were there to collect their hefty commissions from the sale.

Leland Adelson stuck his head in the door five minutes late. He was Hamptons-casual and carried nothing. Reeser shot him a "Come on in, Lee" and Adelson skirted the table to sit across from Hausen and me, next to the real estate agents.

The receptionist was back with coffee and an assortment of muffins that looked supreme. But I wasn't hungry. In fact, I felt a little queasy.

After Adelson and Hausen reached for muffins, Reeser passed around original copies of the contracts and inspection documents. I sipped my coffee slowly and tried to stay calm. I stole a glance at David who, incredibly enough, seemed cool as a cat. Hard to believe he was just twenty years old. Perhaps all those years of hacking and cheating online poker made a real daredevil out of him.

"No changes," Reeser announced. "Everything we need concerning the property is here. We have copies of the Town of East Hampton's water inspection report, the Suffolk County Health Department report, property tax records indicating taxes are up-to-date, and, of course, the deeds showing no liens on the property." To David and Hausen he said, "I trust you'd like to take a few moments to review them."

David gave them a perfunctory look-through as though he were an attorney who'd witnessed a thousand closings. Hausen also gave it quick shrift. He was much more interested in my PMI document to assure himself I had insured the mortgage.

As if reading Hausen's mind, David removed the PMI document and slid it along the table to him. Hausen's attention went immediately to it. I watched his lips fold and his head nod slightly in satisfaction. I peeked at the check lying on the table.

Reeser looked at David. "Is everything in order, Mr. Chan?"

"Quite," replied David Woo. "It appears all the terms have been satisfied." He sounded as good as he looked.

"Mr. Hausen?"

Hausen indicated the check. "It's on the table." His manner was kind of brash, as if he'd called a bet in a poker game.

While this transpired, Adelson and I exchanged a look across the table and smiled pleasantly. I got the impression he was silently communicating that this whole business was beneath us, that we were two tycoons wasting time over small potatoes. It was obvious that Adelson was a very rich man, but he was probably thinking I was richer than he. In any case, this closing was no big deal to him. As I understood it, he had his private jet waiting at Teterboro Airport in Jersey to whisk him off to Florida for a round of golf.

Mrs. Thatcher and Randy sat quietly awaiting their checks. Apart from a little small talk with Adelson, they remained silent throughout the meeting.

The moment of truth suddenly arrived. Reeser said, "Okay then. We can transfer the funds."

Each person's eyes lifted off his copy of the contract. Reeser and David gave each other a nod of approval. Hausen pushed his check to me. I looked down at it. For a split second I was mesmerized, frozen stiff. The first thing that caught my eye was the amount in its numeric form: $3,375,000. Then I saw the bold print of it spelled out. The last thing stunning me was to whom it was paid: James Chan. I recognized Hausen's signature. Someone else had signed below his.

Now came my turn. Trying to be as nonchalant as possible, I opened my Gucci case and extracted a check. Like Hausen's check, it was an austere banking instrument: a check from an attorney's bonded escrow account. Like Hausen's check, it had its numeric and bold print forms depicting the value, $3,375,000. Like Hausen's check, it came from a major bank: Bank of America.

But unlike Hausen's check, it was a phony. David Woo had fabricated the check with one of his graphics programs back at Stanford. It was a real beauty with a perfect Bank of America insignia, but had nothing to do with the bona fide escrow account Woo had opened at that bank. When I first saw it, I had the urge to cash it. That's how good it was.

Just like a genuine out-of-state check, a fake one would take longer to process through the banking system, and would take longer to be discovered. It had all been set up so perfectly that no one questioned David Woo's license to practice law in New York. Had the issue arisen, David's wallet contained membership cards to the Bar Associations of New York and California, the state where our escrow account was located. Of course David had fabricated those as well.

I slid the phony check to Reeser. The attorney picked it up, glanced at it only to verify the amount and paper clipped it to his copy of the contract. He next gave Mrs. Thatcher and Randy their commission checks. Finally I was given the deed to that scrumptious Hamptons seaside estate, the inside of which I'd unfortunately never see again.

The handshakes were brief, but firm. Adelson wished me good luck with the house. I assured him it would be hosting a New Year's Eve gala. Hausen informed me that the payment booklet for the mortgage would arrive any day at my office in California. I told him I'd be expecting it. Then came the chorus of "Merry Christmas," and we were out the door.

The race was on. The First Fidelity check for $3.375 million had to be cashed before the gigantic fraud blew up over Manhattan. Figuring that Reeser would deposit the check in his escrow account the next business day, we had to move extremely fast to make sure Hausen's check written to Chan cleared through his bank, Wachovia, before Reeser's bank notified him that Chan's check from Bank of America apparently didn't come from Bank of America.

The holidays and the fact that David's counterfeit check was so good would buy us some time. When it hit Bank of America's processing system, their computers would not recognize any existing account corresponding to the numbers at the bottom of the check. But this would not immediately tell the bank it was a counterfeit. The first suspect would be their own computer system or one of their data-entry clerks who may have erred upon entering the account numbers into Bank of America's database. The fraud, although it would unravel rapidly, still had to be positively identified before bank security set off the siren.

We thus had a few days' head start in the race for the funds. In a perfect underworld, I would simply walk into any Wachovia Bank branch, present two pieces of positive photo identification and cash the check. Then I'd throw the $3.375 million in hundred dollar bills into duffel bags, as I had done when smuggling my cash to France, thank the teller and vanish. But, unfortunately, the underworld is just as imperfect as the regular world, and that swift maneuver in my head would lead to many things, none of which was my safely absconding with the cash.

So coming out of Wachovia Bank with the cash was out of the question. Instead, we created our own banking procedures to rush Hausen's check through the system, moving the funds along a vast network of accounts, and finally turning them into cash.

David and I were both out of breath when we arrived at Citibank ten minutes after departing Reeser's office. We had opened a legitimate checking account at that bank for the sole purpose of depositing Hausen's check. I had David wait for me at a Starbucks next door. There was no reason for his face, even with the makeup and hair-job adequately disguising his true identity, to be caught on camera.

In my case, it didn't matter. By that time, my naked face would have appeared in hundreds of video surveillance tapes. Each time I'd played baccarat in Vegas casinos, where facial-recognition software had been proliferating, I was filmed. There was no use hiding my face. The key to my future security was to avoid having my face tied to my true name until the statutes of limitations ran out on my crimes.

Inside the bank, I notified the head teller that I wanted to submit the check for "collection." Banks generally offered that service for a minimal charge. What it entailed was to place a rush-order on the check so that it received priority while going through the processing system. I was told that a local check put in for collection normally cleared the bank the following business day. The teller stamped the check underneath James Chan's endorsement, and I was on my way.

The second phase leading to turning Hausen's check into cash had already happened. So had the third, fourth and fifth.

The second: A check for $3.375 million written from Chan's Citibank account, emptying it, was deposited by Jonathan Smith into a checking account at Chase Bank. Smith, who of course was none other than James Chan, who was none other than David Woo, who, upon entering the bank, was none other than Glenn Hastings, also put in a collection request on the check.

The third: At a Fleet Bank on Seventh Avenue, Kenneth Adams made an identical deposit with the same rush-order. He was of course an identical triplet.

The fourth: Art Osterwald, who was yet another carbon copy of me, entered the First National Bank of Pennsylvania in Philadelphia and repeated the process.

The fifth: Christopher Lewis joined the list of impersonators when he deposited the same check at a First Massachusetts Bank in Boston.

This chain of events was nothing more than the Domino Theory applied to banks. Since I knew that Hausen's check had gone into collection and would clear his bank, Wachovia, in one business day, I was able to deposit those four checks in four different banks the day before receiving Hausen's. The funds would be available in Chan's Citibank account by the time the second check at the Chase Bank hit the system for collection. Then the third and fourth checks would fall in line to complete the chain that would get the funds to their first "drop off" destination, the bank in Boston. Even if one or all of the four subsequent checks hit the system too soon and were declined payment for lack of funds, no harm would be done since banks automatically submitted returned checks a second time. Thus, the chain reaction of funds skipping from bank to bank could not be deterred.

From the Boston account, a series of a hundred bank transfers totaling $3.375 million were wired to a hundred accounts in banks scattered all over the country. The funds arrived in minutes. Then from each of those hundred accounts, four transfers were wired to four different accounts located at banks in the western and Southwestern United States. The total of those 400 wires was still $3.375 million.

But at that point we finally reached our desired plateau. We controlled 400 accounts in a condensed area of the country, each containing less than $10,000, the amount at which IRS transactions reports were required. Now we could finally withdraw the cash without the scrutiny.

Reminiscent—albeit much more arduous—of my previous sprint across the country emptying safe deposit boxes, David and I frantically took to the yellow brick road making large cash withdrawals. We started in Oakland, crossed the bridge into San Francisco, then worked our way southward and eastward collecting the cash.

For each bank our MO was the same. I would enter while David waited in the car. Thanks to the hundreds of fake IDs he'd secreted into databases of various DMVs, for which he'd also produced the physical driver's licenses and state ID cards, I was able to present the required two forms of ID for cashing the checks. When tellers examined them, they saw perfect laminated facsimiles created by David's computer and low-resolution digital camera. The checks I presented for payment were all made out to "cash." The only questions I was routinely asked were, "Are you sure you want this in cash?" and "How would you like that, sir?" My responses were, "Yes" and "All big bills, please." Nobody became suspicious.

It took two and a half weeks with virtually no rest to get all the cash and then drive it back to David's apartment in Stanford. Since we had done such a thorough job setting up the scam, creating a labyrinth of crisscrossing bank channels set upon by 500 bank wires, the authorities trying to follow were stuck at "go" long enough for us to drain the accounts well ahead of their eventual arrival at the banks. The scam was a true marvel, more to the credit of David Woo than to myself. The precise and laborious hacking he did was probably the greatest overall manipulation of sensitive computer files ever undertaken, at least in fields relating purely to financial and identity databases. It also marked the first time in my identity theft career that no real person's creditworthiness was injured. The only people or entities ripped off were the insurance companies that had insured the mortgage. Leland Adelson was also a victim of the giant sham, but at least he got his house back.

More dot-com cash

United States and Europe, 2003

WHEN THE BIG SCAM WAS IN THE BOOKS, AND AFTER PAYING David Woo his million bucks, my net profit was $2.25 million. It was a great score but not enough for retirement. My goal was $10 million. I figured that ten million non-interest-bearing dollars would be enough to sustain the rest of my life in pleasant surroundings.

But that meant three more mortgage scams, perhaps two if I found bigger mansions to buy. Maybe even one if I fell upon some movie star's Beverly Hills estate. Such was feasible now that we had more than $3 million in potential setup money. But did we want to risk it? If something went wrong, bank accounts could be frozen, and all that cash would be down the drain.

David Woo was all for it. At twenty years of age and a million bucks in his nest, he envisioned nothing but bigger scores. He wanted to retire before he got out of college, not a paltry aspiration. He felt that he could once again invade an assortment of databases, feed them the dope we needed to create more fictitious people, and get out while the cybersleuths were still trying to piece together what happened in the Warren Davis scam.

We decided the second mortgage scam should be far enough away from the first and involve a property in the five to seven million dollar range.

Online, we perused grandiose mansions for sale in America's wealthiest playgrounds. A handful in South Florida piqued our interest. Two were in Palm Beach, one in Boca Raton, not far from a scam house I'd had there with Bones, and the two we decided to check out first in South Beach, just blocks from the estate once owned by the late fashion designer Gianni Versace, who was murdered there.

Basically we set it up as we'd done with Warren Davis. Our new creation, nurtured to life on the Internet three months after Davis miraculously disappeared into cyberspace, was named Kerry Abernathy. Staying distant from the Silicon Valley cover we'd created for Davis, Mr. Abernathy was made to be a Wall Street investment banker who had made millions and never run afoul of the SEC. Again David set up the banking and credit history and ran his electronic tax returns through the IRS database.

I did change my appearance, in case bank surveillance photographs from the Davis scam had been distributed to real estate brokers throughout the country. I now sported longer hair and a beard, the first time I'd grown one. It bothered the heck out of me, constantly itching and catching errant food particles, but these inconveniences were tolerable in the greater aim of stealing millions.

I made an appointment with the brokers handling both houses. They showed me the estates, which were of course gorgeous, and I made a $6.3 million offer on the Ocean Drive estate whose owner was asking $6.8 million. I had been tempted to go ahead and pay the asking price, in order to swindle the mortgage company for that much more money, but I always worried that such brash action would make real estate brokers wary of me. In any case, I knew that first offer would be declined. Whatever price the broker came back with, I would accept.

The contracts I brought into the South Dade Mortgage Company were for a purchase agreement at $6.6 million. I knew immediately by the owner's reaction that this would be the biggest residential loan he'd ever structured. At first I was hindered by it. Perhaps my not going to a major bank, where I'd get better terms, troubled him. Maybe the very fact that I was seeking a mortgage in the first place was suspect to him. Most people with the personal wealth I was representing did not need to take out home loans, unless, of course, they were searching for the tax write-offs.

But it all came down to the setup. Bones had taught me early on that when the setup was right, the end result was forgone. For people in the real estate and mortgage businesses, it was strictly about the cash. They did their background checks on you. If their web of financial information reported that you could afford the house and the mortgage payments, they brokered the deals. If there was one thing that put suspicion to sleep, money was it.

The escrow account David opened at the American National Bank, this time as Stanley Chung, contained $750,000. After David's initial minimal deposit, we launched another barrage of wire transfers to get to that balance. South Dade Mortgage agreed to a loan where I'd put down 10 percent on the estate at closing. The remainder of the money in the account represented additional closing costs, which of course would never be paid.

At closing, David did another commendable job as my attorney. He wore glasses and gray highlights in his hair. It went down as smoothly as it had in New York. The mortgage company check for $5.94 million was made out to Stanley Chung. The check for $6.6 million written to the seller came from David's computer in the name of First Southern Bank. Again, the seller's lawyer only verified the amount of that check before distributing commission checks to the brokers involved in the listing and selling of the property.

Once we had the mortgage company check in hand, we immediately embarked on the same cash-out procedure we'd begun in New York. Only this time it was more demanding if not more difficult. Whereas in New York we had $3.375 million to run through the banks, we now had nearly twice that. Again the second through fifth stages had been commenced before we got the mortgage check. Using two Miami banks and two in Atlanta, and a round trip same-day ticket between the two cities, we deposited four checks totaling $5.94 million with collection orders that would get the funds to their drop-off point in Atlanta.

Just as we'd done from the drop-off bank in Boston, we performed a hundred wire transfers to move the money to a hundred different banks across the country. The total amount remained $5.94 million. Then, in a move that had to set the individual bank wire-transfer record for a twenty-four hour period, David did 600 transfers to get less than $10,000 in 600 different accounts at 600 different bank branches.

This time we used the Midwestern states. There was still no way to speed up the cash-draining procedure, but the fact that Illinois, Michigan and Missouri were geographically much smaller than California, Arizona and Texas significantly reduced the time we had to spend on the road. Distances between major cities were less. We could make more cash withdrawals per day, but we had 200 more to make than during the previous road trip.

David had volunteered to participate in the cash-taking process, to cut the trip in half as each of us could enter the same banks, but I nixed it. "I don't want to totally corrupt a college kid," I told him.

The last laugh was still on the insurers of the South Dade Mortgage Company. It took three weeks to wipe out the accounts and cash out for $5.94 million. In comparison to the first run, it was an optimal performance. We'd hit 50 percent more banks but used only 20 percent more time. It was fair to say that I was a well-oiled machine running through the banks.

We returned our rental car to the St. Louis airport. David and I each carried two heavy-duty duffel bags packed to the gills with cash. Even though there was no federal law requiring you to declare the transport of any amount of money within the United States, we still had to keep it hidden. But David was extremely nervous sending the cash through as checked baggage. I had explained to him that we had no choice. We couldn't take it as carry-on because the TSA agents at the checkpoint would see the cash on their screen as it passed through the X-ray machine.

But he was really shaken. He'd never lost his cool approach to anything before this.

"Don't worry, David," I pleaded with him as we entered the terminal. "The chance of baggage handlers breaking the locks on the duffel bags to look inside is one-in-a-million. First of all, crooked handlers generally break into designer luggage, and most of the time they have porters on the curb who spot elegant people getting out of limos and give the handlers the tip. You and I don't exactly look like two guys who might be carrying six million bucks, do we?"

At that he had to laugh. But I really did know what I was talking about. Years ago, Bones had relayed a story about a baggage-theft ring operating out of New York's John F. Kennedy Airport. He knew one of its participants, who'd told Bones how it worked.

I got David to drink a few vodkas on the flight, which calmed him down. So much so that he even toasted our success with a raised glass and, "Well, if our bags get lost, then we'll just have to go out and do it again. It's just six weeks of work." But when we arrived in San Francisco, the duffel bags were unharmed. We flagged a cab to Stanford. Upon arriving at his apartment, we promptly crashed. We'd been exhausted. The cash-out run had taken its toll.

In the morning over coffee and muffins at Starbucks, David asked me an interesting question, "So how much are you going to pay me?"

It was true that we had never actually discussed his compensation for the second mortgage scam. Initially, I had been counting on paying him a flat million as I had done for the East Hampton scam. But my thoughts on that had been changing. David's value to the operation had dramatically escalated, and he knew it. Without him, I could have never pulled off either scam. Moreover, his innovative powers had become even more potent. The kid was a true genius, and I could see he was now transforming into a true businessman.

"Well, I guess you deserve a bigger piece of the pie," I admitted. "We cleared a bit less than six million. I can't give you half, but how does two million sound?"

"Deal," David said, shaking my hand graciously. "I want to tell you something, Glenn." Suddenly his voice took on an emotional lilt you wouldn't expect from a twenty-year-old computer geek. "I've really enjoyed working with you. I'm grateful to have met you. And if we do another house-scam, I want to definitely do my share cashing out. I mean, after all, it'll probably be our last one. I don't know about you, but I don't think I need much more money, at least not before I'm twenty-one."

I gave the kid a hug, something Bones and I had never done. It was really an emotional moment. Not that I was feeling fatherly towards him, but I was proud of him. And I did want to do one more scam. It would be my last.

"David," I said softly, "we will do a last-hurrah mortgage scam. We'll discuss that later. But first I would like you to do a little favor for me."

David laughed. "Anything. Name it."

I chuckled. "I don't think you're gonna like."

"What is it?"

"Before we start up another scam, I want to return to France. I want to make some arrangements so that when I go back there again, when it's all said and done, I have a home waiting for me."

"Hey, man, that's cool. How 'bout I go with?"

"That's what I was gonna ask you."

He spread his palms. "That's no favor! I'd love to go back to France. Even if I can't go snowboarding in mid-August."

"Sure you can, David. There's a couple of decent glaciers on Mont Blanc. You can go boarding in a bathing suit."

"Great! So what's the favor?"

I wiped the smile off my face and looked him right in the eye. "David, I want you to help me bring back some cash."

Suddenly snowboarding was the furthest thing from his mind.

"If you do it, you get 50 percent of the next scam." Eyeing him now, he didn't look like he'd do it for 100 percent of the next scam.

"Isn't that risky on international travel? Especially with that customs currency-reporting law."

"It's really not risky. We'll do the same thing. Check the bags at the ticket counter and pick them up in Paris."

"Don't they X-ray everything on international flights?"

"No. They have scanning equipment for explosives, but they don't systematically X-ray check-in luggage. They're only worried about terrorism."

"You sure?"

"I've already done it, David. How do you think I got my cash to France the first time, before we met?"

"How much did you smuggle?"

"Five million."

"How much are we gonna smuggle now?"

"Does that mean you're in?"

"Probably."

"If it's more than five million, it won't be much more."

"When are we leaving?"

"Well, we could leave the day after tomorrow. But then we wouldn't get the cheap seats we could with two weeks' advance notice."

David looked at me as though I were half-cocked. "Are you kidding me? We scammed more than nine million bucks together and you're worried about cheap seats?"

"Hey, you gotta be frugal," I said with a straight face. But then I broke out laughing, and he understood I was putting him on.

"Let's go! And by the way, I might just forego my senior year here."

"What would you do?"

"I dunno. Maybe travel the world for a few years. Maybe do a year of studies in Italy. What the hell, there's no rush to get a job when I graduate."

I couldn't argue with that.

That afternoon, David drove us in his new SUV, bought with the proceeds from the first mortgage scam, to a local bank where he maintained a safe deposit box. Now that he had $2 million more to deposit, he had to rent another box to store it. When we returned to his apartment, I began packing up my cash for the trip to France.

The two mortgage scams had netted me $6 million and change. My first thought had been to rent a couple of safe deposit boxes in San Francisco and put half the money in them, bring $3 million to France. But I questioned the sagacity of doing that. There was, of course, always the possibility I wouldn't return to the States—or couldn't return. I didn't want to risk the situation of having half my net worth inaccessible to me. In view of the ease with which I'd transported money internationally in the past, including all the casino runs through the Caribbean, I adopted a policy of taking my money with me wherever I went. I would quit doing that once I was set up in a permanent place.

In August 2003, David and I left his apartment with four duffel bags and two suitcases. Each duffel bag contained $1.5 million in cash. In the suitcases were our clothes and toiletries. We flew from Oakland to Los Angeles, where we met an Air France flight to Paris. During the eleven-hour flight David was fairly calm. We had checked the six pieces of luggage at the check-in counter, carrying only a few bags of potato chips and granola bars onto the plane.

We cleared the first Orly Airport checkpoint without delay. Then, after a five-minute walk, we were in baggage claim. We'd arrived there before the first bags started popping through the chute. As we waited, the throng of people surrounding the carousel built up as expected.

The luggage started coming through in dribs and drabs after a few minutes. Then there was a lapse before it began pouring out the chute. In the first deluge, I spotted one of our suitcases. David hurried to the edge and yanked it off. Thirty seconds later, the second suitcase appeared. David yanked it off. Hopefully, the four duffel bags would soon follow. Despite the early arrival of the suitcases, there was tremendous tension waiting for the bags of cash.

Fifteen minutes and several loads later, none of our duffel bags had hit the conveyor belt. We'd been standing right at the spot where the luggage first appeared outside the chute. We started getting nervous, although there were still crowds of passengers who had not yet spotted their luggage.

But after another fifteen minutes, the crowd was diminishing. So was the flow of luggage making the rounds on the carousel. Not one of the four duffels had come through. David was turning red. The thought that we were standing at the wrong conveyor belt passed through my mind, but it was playing tricks on me. We had already gathered two pieces of our luggage from that belt. I verified the digital display on the façade above it, anyway. Yes, it was the correct Air France flight from Los Angeles.

"Don't sweat," I said, sweating it. "They'll come."

"Our suitcases came a half hour ago. Where're the duffel bags?" Despite the fact it was my money and not his, David was worried sick. Not as much that it had been stolen as that it had been confiscated by customs, and that we'd be arrested for illegally transporting currency.

Just for starters.

"Sometimes bags loaded together at the departure airport get separated on their way to the plane," I said. "Maybe the suitcases were the last items on one truckload and the duffels the first on another." At that point it was more wishful thinking than conviction.

As David grew redder with fear, I felt nausea with anxiety. We had now been standing there fifty minutes. No duffel bags. No $6 million. Virtually every penny I had in the world was missing. All that scamming for nothing. All that planning, hard work, just to be left standing like an imbecile in baggage claim. I didn't want to think about what I would do.

There were just a handful of people gathered around the carousel. They all had that "I can't believe this happened to me" look on their faces. There was a smattering of luggage passing along the belt for the umpteenth time. I had noticed the crew from our plane wheeling their luggage on their way out the door. That was a bad sign.

A worse sign was when the digital display on the façade flashed another Air France flight number that had arrived from New York. This was the nail in the coffin. David and I stared at each other like two jackrabbits lost in a forest. Where the fuck were the duffel bags?

Suddenly an announcement in French filled the area. It was not loud, in fact barely audible. I only heard the names Hastings and Woo. We had of course traveled in our real names, and were now being paged. On the repetition, I made out that we were two people out of six who were being paged to the Air France security counter at the edge of the baggage claim area.

Security counter! Surely we'd be arrested there.

"What do we do?" David asked in a cracked voice after I'd told him where we were wanted.

Well, making a run for it was out of the question. For one reason, you can't run out of an airport when you're on the wrong side of the customs checkpoint. For another, even if you could, we didn't have any money. What would we do on the loose in Paris without cash?

Staring at David, who seemed to have literally shrunk from fear, I surmised that he never looked more like a computer geek than he did now. Gone was that cool cat who'd marched into attorneys' offices to conduct real estate closings. He was now in the pressure-cooker world of foreign airports with foreign customs agents who spoke a foreign language. I don't know if David had ever seen the movie *Midnight Express*, but the image of Brad Davis being searched by the Turkish customs inspectors ran through my head.

"We gotta face the music," I said dourly. "But remember, it's only the money they know about. Just say you came here with me. We brought the cash to gamble at the casinos in Monte Carlo." Another bad image at the *chemin de fer* table passed through my brain.

"They're gonna buy that?"

"You got a better idea?"

We started moving toward the security counter. I felt as though we were walking off the plank of a pirate ship. When we got to the counter, I noticed the same stragglers who'd been standing at the carousel. They were engaged in arguments with each other and with the security agents at the counter. Some of it was in French, some in English, some in broken versions of both.

One of the security agents was saying to an irate woman who'd let the whole world know that her journey had begun eighteen hours ago in Seattle, "Madam, I understand the inconvenience, and if we don't find your bags, you will be reimbursed seven hundred and fifty dollars for each one."

"I don't want seven hundred and fifty dollars for each one!" she screamed. "I want my bags."

"Madam, there is an excellent chance that your bags were loaded onto the wrong flight and will arrive here at Orly later on. If that happens, Air France will be glad to deliver them to you free of charge wherever you will be staying in France."

"I'm not staying in France," she screamed harder. "I'm going to Belgium! The plane leaves in two hours. Now my whole vacation is ruined…"

"Shit!" I said to David. "They lost our fucking bags. I can't fucking believe it."

The color returned to David's face as he realized that this trip to the security counter was not for an interrogation but rather to be notified that Air France had misplaced our bags. The very fact that they knew which passengers had boarded different planes than their luggage told me that they knew where our duffel bags were. But that did not change the fact that they were not in our possession, and that any extra journeys they had to make greatly increased the chances of their contents being exposed and stolen. Who knew what checking they did when luggage mix-ups occurred? It was post-9/11; security alerts were the norm at airports.

"We are sorry, Mr. Hastings," the security man said to me in heavily accented English. I did not bother telling him I spoke French. "We are doing everything in our jurisdiction to locate your luggage. If you will kindly fill out this form and indicate the contents of your bags, I will be able to move along the process."

Next to me, David was engaged with another security agent, this one female. I listened to her tell him that if his two bags were not found, Air France would gladly reimburse him $750 for each one. Great! I thought. If all four bags stayed lost, I'd receive $3,000 for $6 million, some fucking rate of currency exchange. If I ever again heard an American complain about getting ripped off on European exchange rates, I'd kill him!

"When might the bags show up on another flight?" I asked the agent handling my case.

"It could be on the next flight from Los Angeles, or maybe the one after that, or maybe tomorrow or the day after. It's hard to say. It's also possible your bags were unloaded at a connecting airport, so we must trace them."

None of that sounded encouraging, and I cursed furiously under my breath. I just couldn't believe this had actually happened. I'd heard stories about lost luggage, but they'd never really resonated. And now, boom! It happens to me when I'm carrying $6 million in cash.

On the claim sheet were images depicting a dozen types of luggage. One was of a duffel bag of similar proportions to mine. I circled it, filled in the required information saying the contents were clothing and toiletries, and gave it to the agent.

"When does the next flight from Los Angeles arrive?"

"One thirty in the afternoon."

That was in four hours. "Can I wait here by baggage claim?"

"If you wish, *monsieur*. But, like I've said, we can deliver your baggage to your hotel, free of charge." He smiled courteously.

"*Monsieur*," I said curtly. "I don't have enough cash for a hotel."

The duffels did not show up on the one thirty arrival from Los Angeles. Neither did they show up on the next Air France flight arriving from New

York. There was one more flight due in from Los Angeles at eight p.m. We waited for it discussing every possibility as to what might have happened with the duffel bags. Were they stolen? By whom? Were their contents discovered? Were we under surveillance at that very moment? By the time that last plane came in from Los Angeles, we'd been hanging around the baggage claim area for ten hours.

Our duffel bags were not on it.

There were no more Air France international flights landing until the next morning. We could not wait overnight at the airport. Doing so would expose us to scrutiny and possible questioning. So we begrudgingly took a cab to a hotel at the edge of the airport. In spite of my wisecrack to the Air France security agent, I did have a few hundred bucks in my pocket. Not that Air France would have put us up for the night had we been totally broke.

Neither of us slept a wink. I spent most of the night praying that the morning would bring back my cash. About the only solace we got at the hotel was that the door to the room was not broken down by either the French National Police or Interpol agents.

By six a.m. we were back at the airport. We reported directly to airport security and presented copies of our missing luggage reports to the agent. He assigned his assistant to escort us into the baggage claim area. The man brought us promptly to the carousel, and for some reason bade us luck.

The same flight we had arrived on the day before was due in at seven thirty a.m. I knew that the bags showing up might only be a tool of entrapment, but I certainly had no choice but to take the chance. At that point, I had resigned myself to fate. That's usually what happens when this type of catastrophe strikes criminal minds. After a certain point they stop caring. I found myself thinking, "Either I get my money or I don't. And if I don't, going to jail doesn't compound the disaster all that much."

Midway through the parade of unloaded baggage on the carousel, I saw it: an Army green duffel bag unmistakably mine. It was impossible to judge if the contents were inside, but at least it was there. I noticed a distinct red tag with black printed letters on its side. When I grabbed it off the carousel, I saw the same red tag on the opposite side. They were security tags identifying the duffel as belonging to Glenn Hastings from a previous flight. No sooner than I set it down at my feet, a customs official accosted me with a gun in his belt.

"Can I see your passport, please?" he demanded in English. I looked over at David, who seemed ready to bolt.

"Yes." I handed the officer my passport. He flipped it open to the pages containing my name and photograph. The brick I was shitting suddenly stopped when he nodded at me.

"Sorry for the inconvenience, Mr. Hastings. But you will be happy to know that your second bag is coming off this plane as well." Then he checked a list he had in his hand and addressed David. "You are Mr. Woo?"

David breathed a sigh of relief that the agent had to notice. "Yes."

"Passport, please?" After another quick check, he offered David the same apology.

Naturally I was consumed by a terrifying anticipation of opening the bag. But it would have to wait. When I'd pulled it off the carousel, I noticed that the weight seemed right. If we weren't being set up to take a bust after going through customs, then we might be home free.

The three remaining duffels appeared in the chute together. We yanked them off quickly, noting the same red tags on both sides of each bag. We stacked them on a luggage cart and wheeled them through to customs. No one was in line. The three inspectors had nothing to do but watch our approach. The closer I got, the bigger the lump in my throat got.

I went through first, placing two duffel bags on the metal table in front of the inspector. He checked my passport, said something in French that I didn't get, and then suddenly pulled one of the bags toward him.

I shit a yard of concrete. Images of *Midnight Express* and Brad Davis's shirt being ripped off to expose the bags of hashish taped around his body shot through my head. The inspector grabbed the bag with his right hand, his left going for the padlock. Customs officials routinely carried tools to break open locks of many varieties. I guessed that I was about to become the leadoff story on the French evening news. Something like, "Largest Airport Cash Seizure in the History of France!"

Next occurred what to my mind was a miracle, but in reality nothing out of the ordinary. The inspector's left hand stopped short of the padlock, and in a jerking motion tore the red security tag off the duffel bag. He flipped the bag around and ripped off the second tag. He repeated the process with my other bag, and then attended to David's.

We made it through customs, the padlocked bags seemingly intact. All that remained to be seen was whether the cash was inside or someone had gone through the trouble of re-locking the zippers after stealing it. I tried hard to convince myself that the latter could not be the case, but until I had that cash in my hands, I couldn't be sure.

The taxi dropped us off at the same hotel. We were back before checkout time, so we hurried upstairs to the room. When we got there, the hotel maid was making the beds. I excused myself for the intrusion. She hurried up while we stood in the corridor. When she finally left, we poured into the room like a tidal wave, throwing the bags on the first bed.

I reached in my pocket for the keys to the padlocks. Incredibly, they were not there. In our haste to rush back to Orly, I had forgotten that I'd hidden them underneath the bible in the drawer between the beds. Opening it now, I lifted the bible and prayed the keys would be there.

They were.

David looked on like a hungry tiger as I stuck the key in the lock. It snapped open, and I yanked the zipper along the length of the bag. I spread the folds, removed the layer of clothing I'd covered the cash with, and held my breath.

The cash was there! The banded stacks of hundred dollar bills were packed solid, just as I'd seen them before zipping and locking the bag in Stanford.

I opened the next bag as if in a race against impending explosion. The cash was there. The last two bags also hadn't been tampered with. After a huge sigh of relief and grabbing hold of David as if he were the messiah, I found myself thinking not of Brad Davis in *Midnight Express* but of the ballplayer Lou Gehrig in Yankee stadium. Dying of ALS, he referred to himself as the "luckiest man on the face of the earth." He may have been, but at that moment I felt like I had stepped in his shoes.

It was only ten thirty in the morning. I called the front desk and extended the room for another night. I clamped the *Ne pas deranger* privacy sign on the exterior door handle, then bolted and chain-locked the door from inside. I crawled into bed. David was already asleep in his.

We awoke after six p.m. I'd slept like a baby. In fact, I could hardly remember a solid eight hours of sleep that felt so complete. Even with my youthful hangovers partying at Berkeley, I had never slept so soundly.

David looked as refreshed as a newborn computer geek. We decided to hang out in the room, so I called room service and ordered Chateaubriand dinner and a bottle of champagne. For dessert we pigged out on delicious chocolate soufflés. It was totally scrumptious. We ended up ordering a second bottle of champagne, and after polishing it off fell back to sleep.

The next morning we got up with the sun. After a hotel breakfast of crêpes and French coffee, we rented a convertible and drove to Nice. We arrived just after sunset, but not too late to gain entry to the vault facility. I had paid six months' advance rent on my safe deposit boxes before leaving France to meet up with David. I packed them up with the cash, kept $30,000 on my person and hopped back into the car.

"Where to, James?" David cracked from behind the wheel in his best British accent.

"I don't know. Where do you feel like going?"

"How far are we from Italy?"

"Half hour, forty minutes."

"Let's go."

Our jaunt through Italy, Spain, Portugal and Greece lasted a month. We had a ball. Neither of us committed even the slightest misdemeanor. We paid everything in cash. No credit cards. It was all my treat. I wanted to show David my gratitude for his having risked his ass with me. It was the second week in September when I dropped him off at the Athens airport for his flight to Los Angeles.

While traveling breathtaking coasts and serene mountains, including a weekend stopover for sun-drenched skiing and snowboarding on an Italian glacier, we spoke little of future plans. But the night before his departure, we agreed to one final mortgage scam. The plan was that I would meet him in Beverly Hills, California, in two weeks. By that time he would have created the last of our Frankenstein mortgage monsters, with all his bank accounts, credit data and everything else needed for the scam. Since we'd done the first mortgage scam in New York and the second in Florida, California seemed a logical choice for the finale. Not only was it on the opposite coast but it was also my home state. I'd started Identity Theft, Inc. in California. It was fitting that Identity Theft Again, Inc. finalize its business where it all began.

But it was not to be.

Packing it in

France, 2003-2004

AFTER DAVID AND I PARTED WAYS IN GREECE, I FLEW BACK TO Nice and rented another convertible. My mind had been made up to begin a permanent life in France after the last identity theft scam in California. Despite the self-destructive course with which I had run through Monte Carlo's gambling casinos, I still loved the French Riviera and wanted to stay there. However, I decided to find an abode a little farther south.

While living in Menton, I'd never had the chance to see the entire Côte d'Azur. Much of that was due to my preoccupation with gambling. One part of the coast I'd heard raved about was Saint Tropez. Supposedly it had beautiful rock formations along the beach and loads of gorgeous women sunbathing between them.

I put the top down and drove along the Mediterranean. Once outside Nice, the roads began narrowing as they meandered through pretty orange cliffs jutting over the sea. I passed through Cannes, Saint Rafael and Antibes before arriving in Saint Tropez.

It really was magnificent. As soon as I arrived, I knew the place was for me. Along the winding beach were rock-filled crevices that in spots made a casual stroll adventurous. The enclosing structures on land offered an array of bright pastel colors that might have been the inspiration for

Miami's South Beach. Fashionable boutiques and cafés stretched along the shoreline.

I parked my car in a metered lot, took off my shoes, rolled up my trousers and went for a walk on the beach. The topless beauties were as bronzed and shapely as I had imagined. Whereas Menton had old-world charm, Saint Tropez was youthful ritz and glitz, and quite artsy. Standing knee deep in the water gazing at the pretty landscape, I thought how perfect this setting would be for Robin. I hadn't spoken to her since she split Arizona, and I did miss her sometimes, but it was probably wiser not to communicate with her. The possibility that she fell under the scope of a federal investigation always haunted my mind.

Late that afternoon, I checked into a hotel room with a balcony offering a splendid view of the sea. I planned to relax a few days, and then begin the search for my new dwelling. My stash was safely tucked away in the Nice vault. I had no immediate concerns except for the final scam in California. I pondered some alternatives about what I'd do with the eventual cash proceeds. One thought was to leave it in California. Not wanting to undergo another daunting experience like the one at Orly Airport, maybe it was best not to export that money to France. I certainly had enough Eurodollars to live on for an indefinite future.

Juggling these thoughts, I went down to the promenade and found a smart Italian bistro with a glass portico I'd noticed during my afternoon stroll. I ordered a tasty pasta dish with a glass of red wine. I was enjoying dinner when a very attractive woman around thirty entered the restaurant. She wore a white flowing dress that accentuated her tan with laced sandals. I watched her walk to the bar and speak with the man who appeared to be the manager of the restaurant. She looked familiar, and as I continued watching her I was sure I'd seen her before, but I couldn't place her. The bartender was nodding as if in response to her questions. She appeared to be speaking from a position of authority. Perhaps she was the owner.

While I ate, she sat at the bar going through some paperwork and sipping an espresso. We made eye contact on two occasions, though there was no hint of recognition in her eyes. I, however, was certain I knew this woman. It gnawed at me that I couldn't place her. Her attractiveness aside, I had to satisfy my memory.

I picked up my wine and settled on the barstool next to her. I excused myself in French for the intrusion and then told her I was sure I knew her and wasn't coming on to her. She gave me a slightly reproachful look but then smiled faintly.

"Were you studying French in Nice about five or six years ago?" she asked in French?

"*Oui.*" One thing for sure was that this fine woman had not been my French teacher. I would have remembered her. And judging by her French, she had not been one of my classmates, either. She must have read the confused expression on my face.

"And you're German, right?"

"Wrong," I said in English, and she laughed.

"Then you were with some German people when we met."

The woman from the café in Nice! It was six years ago. I had tried flirting with her, but she'd refused me the time of day. "I can't believe you remember that," I said honestly in French. What I remembered was telling myself that if I ever had the good fortune to bump into her again, I would take another shot at that good fortune.

"I see your French has vastly improved."

"When I asked you to have dinner with me that day, obviously my French was not good enough for you to say '*oui.*'"

She flashed a smile, somewhere between fetching and flirtatious. "If you're asking me out again, the requirements are more than just a mastery of the French language. And besides, I see you've already eaten. Was your dinner pleasing?"

"Very."

She raised her glass and we toasted. "I'm glad you enjoyed it."

"Is this your restaurant?" I dared.

"Yes. I just opened it this summer."

"Well, since I've already dined, I would love to have lunch with you tomorrow. I promise not to take you to your own restaurant."

She looked appraisingly into my eyes. This woman was of a discriminating nature, and I imagined that for every credit card I'd ever had, she had been asked out. But I sensed she was presently unattached.

When she didn't immediately answer, I said, "Would you tell me the other requirements for going out with you?"

"Only one, Glenn," she said.

Glenn! Not only had I told this woman my real name six years ago, she remembered it! This was incredible.

"If you can tell me what my name is, I will gladly accept to have lunch with you tomorrow. If not, I won't. Is that fair enough, Glenn?" She was smiling broadly now, thoroughly enjoying this.

One thing she didn't know was that the man sitting next to her had put more people's names to memory than perhaps any other human being in history. Hundreds of them had been my own adopted and discarded names. So right off the bat I had an advantage. Increasing that advantage was that she was French, therefore her name was French, and I had not known but a dozen or so Frenchwomen in the course of my European residency.

I smiled broadly back at her. I playacted that I was stumped and how I would never forgive myself for not remembering the name of such a beautiful woman. She gave me a typical French "*C'est la vie*" and expressed her regrets that there would be no second chance to redeem myself, and I knew she was serious.

But when I said, "I regret it, too, Nicole," she nearly fell off the stool.

And I fell hard for Nicole. Now in my mid-forties, I finally learned about something in life I'd never known: true love. Up until that time, whenever I felt the pull of domesticity, I dismissed it with an "it's too late for me" attitude. I had been a criminal my entire adult life. In spite of the fortunes I had made, I paid a terrible price. That price was the lack of a real, lasting relationship with a woman.

With Nicole it took right off. Starting with lunch at another trendy eatery near hers, we became so enthused with each other that we couldn't stop talking and laughing. The conversation shifted from childhood to intimacy to America to France. The best was that it came so naturally. Of course I didn't tell her anything about my true business, but I didn't have to. That I was an American who could afford himself the luxury of living and loving French culture was enough for her.

That evening walking barefoot on the beach with its intermittent rocky streams, Nicole Coiffet told me of her conservative French upbringing in a small town on the Mediterranean near Toulon. After that, she had tried her hand at modeling and acting in Paris, but instead became disenchanted with the abuses she experienced struggling to make a career. Finally she gave it up and moved to Nice, where she married a restaurateur whose specialty was overpriced menus geared to American tourists. During five years of marriage she learned her husband's recipes. But after catching him in the act with his gay chef, Nicole divorced him and moved to Saint Tropez, where she managed a few restaurants before opening her Italian Bistro, which she named Café Venezia for her love of Venice.

I think I fell in love with her that night when she told me a story about her first love. Her parents were very strict, especially when it came to matters of boys courting their daughter. Nicole had two older sisters, whom she'd watched constantly embattled with their parents over issues concerning their boyfriends. Neither had been allowed to stay out past eleven o'clock at night until their eighteenth birthday. But worse was that their parents refused to allow their daughters to accept any gifts of jewelry from their beaus of high school age. They did not appreciate the significance of such gifts as they represented "going steady," something Nicole's parents deemed inappropriate for their young daughters.

Well, at sixteen Nicole had her first real boyfriend. His name was Bernard and he came from a wealthy family. The fact that Bernard had the means to treat their daughter in style did not favorably impress upon Nicole's hardworking parents. So when Bernard purchased a diamond ring for Nicole's "sweet sixteen," the young girl had a problem in that she couldn't let her parents know about the gift, but at the same time she desperately wanted to wear the ring.

Bernard and Nicole discussed the situation at length. There were several alternatives. One was to just wear the ring and say nothing. If it were noticed on the girl's finger, Nicole would just dismiss it casually by saying it was a gift from a friend who had no romantic intentions. Another was that she simply found it. A third was that she bought the ring for herself. But in rehashing each scenario, they agreed that Nicole's parents would not be duped by any of them. They finally decided that the only solution was that she not wear the ring when at home with her parents. However, that was risky since she was bound to either forget to remove it from her finger or leave it somewhere her mother would find it.

The morning after Bernard presented her with the ring, Nicole sat at the breakfast table with her parents. She'd been awake half the night concocting schemes through which she'd be able to reveal the ring without revealing the truth about who it came from and what it represented. Before finally falling asleep, Nicole thought she might have found the perfect idea.

In the middle of the table sat the boxes of cereal that had been among the first invasion wave of American food products on French kitchen tables. There were Frosted Flakes and Cheerios, the latter being her father's favorite. Since it was, Nicole decided to have Cheerios that morning instead of the usual Frosted Flakes. She opened the box and poured the crispy little Os into her bowl.

"Hey, look, mom and dad!" she suddenly exclaimed. Lying on top of the cereal was a little paper wrapping that had undoubtedly spilled out of the cereal bag. In fact, on the box was advertised a gift that came with the cereal. Nicole eagerly ripped open the wrapping under the curious eyes of her parents. The wrapping fell into the bowl of Cheerios as she slipped the newly discovered ring onto her finger. "Wow!" she hollered with joy. "It's so pretty it even looks real!"

Nicole's parents laughed and congratulated her find, then pouring Cheerios into his own bowl, her father said, "I hope there's something in here for me."

When I heard that story, I knew Nicole was my type of woman. I sensed she had a little bit of Robin in her, though fortunately I would not have to appeal to that side of her. We spent the next week together in Saint Tropez. I continued staying at the hotel while visiting Nicole at her small but elegant home a few blocks inland. She invited me for dinner, during which I learned she was a fabulous cook. I could also see she had done admirably well for herself. She didn't seem to have regrets about giving up her high fashion and acting careers.

We did not make love until the second evening I visited her home. When we woke up to seagulls chanting on the beach, I suggested we take a few days and go to Venice where we could sip champagne while viewing the lights of San Marco Square from a gondola. I was so caught up in her in the moment that I'd forgotten about my impending rendezvous with David. But Nicole said she was too busy with her bistro. She would not be able to leave Saint Tropez until the summer season was over in two weeks.

I had already purchased my ticket for California. As the days wore closer to the departure date, my relationship with Nicole intensified. For the first time in my life, I found myself really hesitant to leave a woman. I began dreading the thought of something going wrong with the final scam. The old saying about "going one time too many to the well" began propping up in my thoughts.

But on the other hand, it was difficult to let it go. I had been in constant communication with David. He assured me that everything was set up and ready to go. He'd even found the target estates in Beverly Hills and Bel Air, both in the $15 million range. We had agreed on a fifty-fifty split; thus my end would be $7.5 million. I could take that money and buy my own villa in the south of France. I mean, *really* buy it.

I was torn, but leaning towards going. Two days before the flight, I lay naked with Nicole on a dark, secluded beach outside Saint Tropez. The air was chilled by *le mistral,* the almost constant gusty wind that whipped the Côte d'Azur in the warmer months. We were wrapped underneath a blanket. I could feel Nicole's body shivering against mine.

"When are you coming back from your trip?" she asked without lifting her head from my chest. Her words came out a little muffled, which made her sound even more adorable.

"It shouldn't be more than a month," I said gently, stroking her long black hair.

She picked up her head. The wind blew the top of the blanket off our naked torsos. "A month! I thought it would only be two weeks."

"When I come back, I'm going to find a house right here in Saint Tropez. I won't have to return to the States anymore."

She fetched the blanket and pulled it over us. She buried her head back in my chest. For a few minutes a tender silence reigned. It was far from uncomfortable. I held her against me while massaging her thin neck. Finally she said, "Glenn, you know I never ask you many questions, but I'm scared."

That's all she had to say. Indeed she had never pried into my affairs. I had never spoken about what I did, mainly because I didn't want to lie to her. Instead I avoided those lines of conversation. I think she sensed that. The woman I was falling in love with was no dummy. She had to figure I was either into something illegal or a lot of money had come my way via inheritance. While living in Paris pursuing a modeling career, Nicole had met her share of lawbreakers, mostly in the drug trade. Despite that, she did not get high, and neither had I since we met. The strange part was that I didn't miss it.

I still didn't want to give her straight answers so I said, "What are you afraid of?" When I said it, it sounded stupid, but she didn't react that way.

"That you won't come back. That you'll never come back."

"Why would I not want to come back?"

"I didn't say you wouldn't want to come back. Maybe you won't be able to come back."

At that moment I knew she knew. She picked her head up. In the faint moonlight I could see she'd been crying. I felt terribly saddened by the thought of not being able to return to France. Much more for her than for me. I realized, too, that for the first time in my life, I had a completely selfless thought of placing someone else's feelings above mine. Nicole was telling me that she sensed my trip was dangerous. I in turn had genuine misgivings about how that danger could hurt her. I knew if I didn't return to France, Nicole would be devastated.

I knew I couldn't go. At least not in two days. I needed more time to think it over. The naturally cynical part of me fought hard to win over against my sudden altruistic tendencies. There was no question that in my own constitution what had started as rebelliousness had turned into greed. I already had millions but thirsted for millions more.

But was Nicole truly any different? I had known her but for a single week. Could I really believe she was for real? That upon peeling away layers of outward beauty, charm and innocence, I would not find a core of self-absorption like I had found in so many beautiful women?

There was also the question of my true destiny. Despite a lifetime of definite choices going against the grain, I was still a believer in destiny. That I had met Bones while embarked on the same scam that he was had to be sheer destiny. I could only conclude that we were meant to join forces along the route to illicit gains. If that was true, then wasn't finding Nicole that second time merely proof of my destiny? Was she not meant to pull me onto the straight and narrow?

I called David the night before my scheduled departure and told him I was delayed due to personal reasons. Strangely, he didn't seem surprised. I said that I'd be freed up by the first of October, a month away. David didn't object.

Neither did Nicole, but she managed to waylay me again. Some unexpected bad weather along the Mediterranean marred the last week of the summer season. Half the tourists booked into Saint Tropez cancelled their trips. Nicole's bistro business suddenly slacked off, and she didn't have to be there that final week. In fact, she pulled a delightful move to let me know.

I was shaving in my hotel room one morning when she showed up unannounced, something she'd never done. She had a suitcase in hand. I laughed. "Are you moving in? Don't you think it would be better if I moved in with you? After all, we'd have a heck of a lot more space."

"No, Glenn, we can talk about living together later. For now, we're going on vacation. That's if you want to go, of course. But I would be very offended if you refused my invitation." She suddenly waved two travel agency packets at me.

I shrugged and smiled. "Where are we going?"

"Someplace you've never been?"

"How do you know? I've never told you every place I've been."

"Believe me, you've never been there."

"Have I ever heard of it?"

"Of course you've heard of it. I'll tell you what. Pack your bag. Our flight leaves in three hours. We'll stop off for some coffee, then we'll take a taxi to the airport. Then I'll blindfold you and put plugs in your ears at the airport and won't remove them until the plane has landed. This way it will be a surprise where we're going, and you won't know where it is until we're there."

"I love the idea, Nicole, but I think it would be easier if I just kept my eyes closed and took a few sleeping pills on the plane. Just tell me one thing, though. For how long are we going?"

"Two weeks."

"Two weeks!"

She frowned. "You don't want to be with me for two weeks at some exotic locale?"

"No, no, of course I do!"

"Then let's go. Hurry up and pack your bag. I'll tell you this much— take only summer clothing. We're not going to Antarctica."

"Got it."

Three hours later we were on the plane. When we landed in Tahiti, I was enthralled. The island was beautiful. I had heard of it before, mainly that the actor Marlon Brando had lived there. The fact that Nicole had arranged this vacation sealed my fate, or rather my destiny.

Two weeks in Tahiti with Nicole was all it took to dissolve more than two decades of a criminal career. Our last night on the Tahitian beach together, again after having made love, she asked, "When are you going to California?"

"You know the answer to that, Nicole."

She smiled warmly, and then embraced me in what became the most delicious moment of my life. I truly wished it could have lasted forever. Maybe it couldn't, but what I knew during that precious time was that I had to be with Nicole for as close to forever as possible.

Today Nicole and I are married and have two children. Tommy is eighteen months, and my baby girl Monique is the most adorable little toddler in France. They both light up my life. We live in Saint Tropez, where not only does Nicole's bistro Café Venezia continue to fare well, but her second restaurant, Café du Matin, has become a popular spot among tourists and locals who live in Saint Tropez year-round.

I have become accustomed to a normal, even conservative lifestyle, thanks to my wife, who has made me capable of enjoying it. I have also been accepted by Nicole's family. Her parents in Montpellier may have been strict with their children, but I've found them to be very warm people with a *joie de vivre*. We make the three-hour drive every four months or so. Her father never fails to give us a tour of his garden and vineyard. The wine he makes is rather good, considering that his region is not well regarded in the annals of French viticulture.

Like her daughter, Nicole's mother is an excellent cook, preparing plates with vegetables grown from her husband's garden. She is especially affectionate with our children. Including Tommy and Monique she now has eight grandchildren, and she makes each one feel special.

Each time we travel to Montpellier, some or all of Nicole's siblings are there. Both her sisters are beautiful like Nicole. One is married to a doctor, the other to a professor at the University of Montpellier. When I met her only brother, Andre, I got a secret chuckle when he told me he was head of the credit department at a branch of Crédit Agricole, one of the largest banks in France. He let me know that if I ever found myself in need of assistance in banking matters, including mortgages, to come see him so that he'd arrange whatever was needed. I thanked him graciously, informing him that the financial arrangements for our house in Saint Tropez had been well undertaken.

The oceanfront house we did live in had been bought for cash in Nicole's name. I set it up that way to avoid complications should something happen to me or should my life end unexpectedly. If ever surprised by the American authorities in my adopted homeland, the last thing I wanted was our house to be seized and my family evicted. I did not know the technicalities of French law but I did know that my crimes were worthy of international extradition, and that the United States indeed had an extradition treaty with France.

As a matter of fact, not too long ago while having breakfast in Nicole's new café, I read a news article about an American accused of killing his wife decades earlier being apprehended in France, where he'd been living with a French wife and child for eighteen years, and shipped off by French authorities to face trial in Philadelphia. The only instance where the French would not extradite, I read, was the case in which the accused faced the death penalty in his own country. My crimes, as distasteful as they may have been, would not be punishable by death. Therefore, I was eligible for extradition. However, that threat would hang over my head only until the statutes of limitations ran out. In the area of identity theft, the interpretation of when crimes actually occurred was somewhat murky. With that in mind, my lawyer advised me to stay out of the US for as long as possible. I may never get a chance to return.

I had also added Nicole's name to the list of persons having access to my vault in Nice. This was done for the same reason I put the house in her name. Should I be caught, killed, or claimed by natural death, I did not want my money bequeathed to the state of France. I did enjoy living in the country, but not enough to make it my heir.

Nicole's parents' names were also included on that list. God forbid anything happen to both Nicole and I, they would have access to the funds, which they would use for my children's benefit.

Nicole never asked about specifics concerning the vault. I told her honestly that I kept my cash there because it had come from income I never reported to the IRS. This obviously was not a lie. What I didn't tell her was how I accumulated the money. The last thing I wanted her to know was that I had been an identity thief. As relationships are built on trust, how could I tell her I'd spent such a big part of my life pretending to be someone else in the pursuit of money? She would forever wonder who I really was and fear that at any moment I might dissolve into another identity. I had trouble living with such evasiveness, but at least it was a deception about my past and not part of the life I had made with her.

The last thing I'd said to Nicole about the vault was that should anything ever happen to me, she would have enough American dollars to raise the family and live comfortably for the rest of their lives.

But still alive, I lived a quiet conventional life with my family. It was the kind of existence I had so revolted against while growing up. But now I was happy being "Joe Citizen" even when living outside the United States. On Sundays, I took my family to church. In the afternoons, I played soccer with Tommy on the beach while Nicole crawled around with Monique. We had a dog and two cats tagging along. I spoke to the children in English; Nicole spoke to them in French. I was proud that they would become perfectly bilingual, and with foreign languages being an essential part of European culture, they would probably learn two or three more. Nicole spoke fluent Italian and very good Spanish, which didn't hurt as a good chunk of her restaurant clientele came from neighboring Italy and Spain.

IDENTITY THEFT, INC.

Naturally there were drawbacks to my new life. While able to adjust to being away from the adrenaline of the adventurous life, I still had to cope with periods of inactivity and boredom that were part of the real world. Sometimes I helped Nicole in her restaurants. During the tourist season and certain holidays when she was short on help, I filled in as a maître d' or table server. When it got hectic in the kitchen, I threw on an apron and expedited food orders. It was satisfying making myself useful, but I still felt out of place among people putting in an honest day's work for a living. I tried to keep that insecurity hidden from Nicole. I didn't want her to know I was struggling with my strange new identity: my own.

It has often been said that the human brain must continually be nurtured and challenged to stay healthy. Not only is this true, but perhaps even more so regarding the criminal psyche. Not to put myself or any other criminal on a pedestal, but many psychological studies have suggested that those aspiring to nonviolent crime are of a superior innate intelligence. Often for these people the everyday challenges of life are not sufficient enough to keep the brain active. They need the constant stimulus, the juice that runs through their veins while they're cleverly doing a number on the system. In my case, nothing could be more accurate. No doubt I flew higher than a kite when launching my scams, especially those against the casinos and mortgage companies. I desperately missed the action. Although my wife and children were enough to insure against any return to my life of crime, they were not enough to take my mind off it.

I had telephoned David Woo after imploring myself not to. What he told me made it even tougher to continue along the straight and narrow: the son of a bitch had done that last mortgage scam without me! He didn't give me the details over the phone, but I bet he made a cool $10 million somewhere in Southern California's exurbs. He did swear, however, that he had retired from the identity theft business and was now starting up his own software security company in Silicon Valley. He even offered me a job. Talk about irony!

As I continued struggling domesticity and pedestrian daily life, I finally decided I had to embark on something that would both occupy my time and be rewarding. I again thought of Frank Abagnale and *Catch Me If You Can*. I had read the book and seen the movie, and been thoroughly entertained by both. As a matter of fact, Abagnale, in other books and seminars he gives around the world, talks about identity theft being the "crime of the twenty-first century." I, for one, not only agree with him, I have proven him right.

A Wild Ride with the World's #1 Identity Thief

If Abagnale's book was the initial exploration of identity theft, I had thought, then why not write the definitive study of it? Abagnale's identity thefts were committed in the sixties, in a crude and elementary, if not totally obsolete, way. I, on the other hand, would be able to tell the world exactly how modern identity theft was accomplished and then used to steal credit and money. In doing so, I would be making a contribution to society in that readers of my story would learn the intimate details of how fraud artists commit these crimes. If I could help society as a whole protect itself from identity theft, then my life as a criminal will have served a purpose to the law-abiding majority of people who are at risk of becoming its victims.

So I decided to write a book about my career as an identity thief. I purchased a laptop and set up a writing table on the veranda of my home on the edge of the Mediterranean. I took inspiration from the sights and sounds of the sea to write my memoirs to the best of my ability. I dutifully wrote every morning from dawn until noon. I was not a natural writer, and I learned that writing a good book is no easy chore.

After several months of what turned into hundreds of pages of disjointed chapters and notes, I came to the conclusion that I needed some help to get the book in order. Immediately, I flashed back to my old casino scam buddy, Richard Marcus. I had heard that he had traded in his chips and taken up writing. His books covered his own experiences in the gambling underworld, but I was sure he could shift gears and help me out. He found my story fascinating and agreed to participate in the organization of this book, for which I am very grateful. He flew to Saint Tropez, which he knew well from his Riviera casino days. Together we set out to get my writings into a viable manuscript. Nicole was incredibly supportive of the project while taking on the double burden of raising our kids and tending to her restaurants. She understood how important the project was for me. She'd realized that I was having difficulties with an unproductive professional life in France.

Naturally, the time had come for me to admit my past to her. Of course we would keep my history away from Tommy and Monique until they were old enough to understand not only what I had done but also what I had done to repent for it. If the book made a big public splash in France before they were of age, we'd deal with it when it happened. For the most part, Nicole was not shocked by what I had done. She'd always suspected I had been involved in shady business dealings. She knew intuitively, however, that whatever I had been doing would cease once we were together. She was content that I was making amends to society.

Thus concludes my story. If you still harbor negative feelings about me, I understand. I have done my best to rejoin society as an honest citizen. I am now truly remorseful for all I have done. I have come to understand that a lifetime of money and self-importance is not worth even a small fraction of what they cannot buy. I will continue living an honest life with my family, and when it's over, I hope I will go down in history not only as the world's first major identity thief but also as someone who made significant inroads to stopping identity theft.

A forward look at identity theft into the future.

What you can do to stop it

WE ARE NOW APPROACHING THE FINAL YEARS OF THE NEW millennium's first decade. As technological advances increase exponentially relative to the passage of time, the efficiency of techniques for using computers and the Internet will advance with the same powers.

What does this mean for identity theft? Firstly, identity thieves are now totally dependent on the Internet. They no longer need libraries or any other information sources. They seldom bother hacking directly into bank and credit card company data systems. These mainstays of the financial world have spent countless millions of dollars to protect their computer operations from talented hackers like David Woo. Nowadays, a high percentage of computer forays into banks and credit card companies are intercepted and defeated, with many of their architects caught and imprisoned in the real world.

Has this caused a significant reduction in the occurrence of identity theft? Unfortunately, not yet. Sophisticated ID thieves have turned to attacking consumers directly. Anyone who carries out bank and credit card transactions as part of their daily lives is a target—essentially just about every adult in the Western world. By using methods such as phishing and pharming, they con millions of people across the world into imparting sensitive information relating to their financial histories. Since these devious programs are capable of sending out literally hundreds of millions of simultaneous e-mails, imagine the tiny percentage of "hits" they would need to arm themselves with enough information to infiltrate the credit world with millions of fraudulent accounts.

Moreover, diverse online hacking scams of recent years have produced combined, more efficient forms of the same scams. An example of this is a hybrid form of phishing, dubbed "spear-phishing," a distilled and more potent version where hackers bait their hooks for specific victims instead of casting a broad, ill-defined net across cyberspace for scores of unknown victims. The bogus e-mail messages and web sites they use not only look like near perfect replicas of communiqués from e-commerce companies like eBay or its PayPal service, banks and credit card companies, or even a victim's employer, but are also aimed at people known to have an ongoing relationship with the sender being mimicked.

But what makes this scarier than ever is how easily today's ID thieves turn this information into billions of dollars. In fact, they don't do it themselves anymore. It's not necessary for them to take the painstaking steps I had to in pulling off my scams. Charades with imposters to set up victims are no longer needed. What the new information age has done for cyberthieves is give them literally millions of available "fences" through which they can sell off their stolen identities, without ever leaving their computer screen.

As India has become the land of outsourcing, the Internet has become the new frontier of ID theft and credit fraud. Once ID thieves have amassed the information needed to open fraudulent accounts, they simply bring it to the online auction block. To see how it's done, just go online. You will come across hundreds of sites offering "dumps." A dump, in the blunt vernacular of the relentlessly flourishing online black market, is a valid credit card number that comes with stolen account information, including the cardholder's name, billing address and phone number. For a hundred bucks, even less, a scheming consumer can buy this information pertaining to Gold Visa and MasterCards. That information alone is enough to commit fraudulent credit transactions via the Internet and telephone. If he prefers, he can marry that information to the plastic and have a perfect counterfeit card produced. With that he can check into hotels, dine in fancy restaurants, rent cars and go on shopping sprees. For a small premium he can buy the PIN number, which would allow him to stop off at the ATM in the mall to pick up some cash. He would have free sway with the card until its genuine account holder is alerted to the fraud by his credit statement. If all this is for sale at such a low price, it's obvious that the purveyors of this information have millions and millions of stolen accounts ready to put on the block, and that there is fierce competition among those purveyors. I would say that the totality of information I had access to from the *Marquis Who's Who* volumes is a mere speck of dust in comparison to what today's cyberthieves can get their hands on.

It gets more frightening than that. Many hackers who started the Internet age of identity theft have taken over both the supplying and selling ends of the business. Whereas hackers previously only gathered the IDs and sold them *en masse*, mostly to Russian web sites, doubly avaricious hackers now create their own sites to unload their stolen information. Being so skilled in cyber-manipulation, they are able to offer new innovative services as quickly as legitimate vendors come up with sales gimmicks. One of them is their "cobs" service. In the black market vernacular, a cob is a change of billing, and it has become a very hot commodity. What these high-tech-low-scruples vendors do is offer fresh stolen bank and credit card accounts along with the ability to change the billing address through a pilfered PIN. In many cases, the vendor selling the cobs will change the billing address himself, as a customer service, just like legitimate businesses often take that extra step to please their customers. That changed address would be a "safe drop," usually an empty apartment or some other locale where goods could be delivered without risk. This is the same principle as the "scam houses" I used. Some sites even offer information on reliable drops. It's not in their interests that their customers get caught receiving property obtained with phony IDs and credit cards.

Although it is rare, large-scale hacker attacks against major financial databases still succeed. The last of these was discovered in June 2005 when MasterCard International reported that more than 40 million credit card accounts had been exposed to fraud through a security breach at a payment processing company in Tucson, Arizona, called CardSystems Solutions, which processes more than $15 billion in payments for small to mid-size merchants and financial institutions each year.

An infiltrator had managed to place a computer program code on the CardSystems network that made it possible to filter information to his own computer, including the three-digit security codes found on the backs of credit cards. The breach was discovered when analysts and FBI officials identified patterns of fraudulent charges on thousands of stolen MasterCard and Visa accounts. The true scope of the damage might not be known for months, even years, until all the statements for the compromised accounts have been thoroughly examined and the fraudulent transactions assessed. What *is* known is that an occurrence like this is tantamount to a radiation leak in a nuclear reactor. Enough credit fallout to enrich cybercriminals to the core.

Can something this large-scale happen again? The likely answer is yes. Visa and MasterCard maintain that their security standards are rigorous, but the truth is that they have been lax in enforcing their rules with their processing companies. Their regulations state that sensitive cardholder information must be rendered unreadable anywhere it is stored, but the fact is that they have made exceptions to these rules for nearly half of all the companies that handle cardholder data, provided other weaker security controls were in place. When rules have not been adhered to, there has not followed any instance of notable suspensions or fines.

Sometimes it's not even the work of hackers when sensitive information is lost. In the same month of June, Citigroup announced that a United Parcel Service shipment of magnetic computer tapes containing nearly four million consumer records had been lost on its way to a credit reporting agency. The tapes were not encrypted nor have they been found. Again an assessment is needed, but the potential loss to ID thieves is alarming. When breaches occur within the financial services industry itself, there is real cause for alarm.

If that's not enough, even the United States government got into the act when it conceded it had lost records containing the Social Security numbers of more than a million employees. Even worse, an employee of the Department of Veterans Affairs took home computer files containing personal data for 26.5 million veterans without authorization, only to have them stolen by a burglar. This may yet turn out to be the most important security breach in history, putting those millions of veterans at risk for identity theft. Similar files have been lost by individual states. One can only hope that these kinds of miscues will be avoided in the future.

But the modern online trade in credit card and bank account numbers, as well as buckets of other raw consumer information, is highly organized and not very prone to mishaps. It is also highly structured like any other active market. There are buyers, sellers, middlemen and service industries to make sure that all the criminals along the spectrum are satisfied. Dishonest people from all over the world converge on this rapidly expanding market. It seems that most of the web sites where they meet are run from Internet servers in Russia and other states in the former Soviet Union, which makes sense as the Russian mafia had always been a pillar of the illegal "hard" credit card trade.

There are site administrators who oversee the entire corrupt industry, much in the fashion of the former mafia commissions that governed the underworld. They make fortunes as they have their dirty hands in every facet of the business, siphoning off percentages of the huge trade. Their key role, and the reason they are needed by identity thieves, is that they control the advertising blocks affiliated with their sites, which by far receive the greatest number of hits. Sites outside the administrators' direct control that get top-billing are the ones selling the whole ID theft package, including the physical credit cards, for which they use algorithms to properly encode the magnetic strips, making the cards usable. These sites have earned the reputation of being at the top of their field. Not unlike eBay's buyer feedback pages, those cybercriminals capable of running the ID theft gamut A through Z receive kudos from other traders who benefit from the influx of business coming to the lead sites. In short, the advertising works in the same fashion as any other legitimate online business. Through widespread linking, virtually everyone with a viable ID theft product thrives on the Internet.

These administrators also review the sites' products, just like Amazon might review a book. They perform actual tests. For example, the trusted "reviewers" might demand a site selling cobs to provide a dozen changes of address for distribution. They then test this service by phone, snail mail or Internet. If a certain number of the cobs prove to be useless, the site offering them risks being removed from the administrators' list of preferred advertisers.

New vendors of credit card numbers must also pass muster with the administrators. They might be required to furnish twenty valid dumps, say ten Visas and ten MasterCards, which would need to be a balanced sample of the various types of credit cards including classics, gold, platinum, business and corporate. The testers then determine the quality of the sites by measuring the percentages of their cards proving to be valid.

Whenever ID thieves meet the rigorous standards of the

administrators, they have the option of paying a fee to peddle their wares on administrating sites' message boards. Banner ads can also be purchased. Through this precisely tangled web, individual ID thieves augment their status in the cyber-underworld. In this fashion, the confidence level of crooked consumers looking to scam credit is kept very high. The administrators let the public know that no one is permitted to post product or service offers in the ID theft business without first having their wares vetted by experts in the field.

Next we come to the question of moving "legitimate illegitimate money" in the online identity theft business. What I mean by that is the money that people intent on buying stolen IDs and credit cards pay in good faith to those who provide them. Contacts among ID theft deal-makers usually move off the message boards and onto ICQ (a play off the words "I seek you"), the instant messaging program of choice among cyberthieves. What ICQ does is offer anonymity that attracts online hackers and thieves the way summer light bulbs do mosquitoes. Because no names, no registrations and no e-mails are required, payments change hands with little regulation by e-gold, an electronic currency that purports to be backed by gold bullion and is issued by e-gold Ltd., a company incorporated on the Caribbean island of Nevis.

Illicit web transactions are also made using WMZs, electronic monetary units equivalent to American dollars and issued by WebMoney Transfer, a company based in Moscow. Whatever form of electronic currency being used in the trading of identity theft and credit fraud data, the banks cannot trace its buyers and sellers through the transactions. That reality makes the whole industry even more delectable to those participating in it. It also makes it extremely difficult for the FBI and Secret Service to combat. To that end, the Secret Service is working hard to get e-currency issuers to address this problem. They will clearly need the help of online financial institutions in their war against credit fraud.

How big is identity theft today in the United States? The Federal Trade Commission estimates that more than ten million Americans have their personal and credit information stolen or misused in one way or another each year, costing consumers and businesses $50 billion annually. In the UK, where identity theft is also running amok, consumers are facing the same staggering numbers in proportion to the country's economy. Other countries have become havens for cybercriminals who have the audacity to post web forms on which they tick off the fields they have to sell or want to buy: everything from Social Security cards to mothers' maiden names. These blatant identity traders are able to slip into the cyber-underground, which in reality means on to Internet servers in regions with lax laws, overburdened, or uninterested law enforcement and no real working relationship with American and Western authorities. Thus the immediate prognosis is rather bleak. To sum it up, authorities have yet to make a substantial impact against identity theft. The criminals are too hard to track and trace, too hard to prosecute, and the information they steal is too easy to use.

Does that mean identity theft will continue expanding indefinitely? In responding to that disturbing possibility, I will draw a parallel to online poker. It seems that, along with ID theft, playing poker on the Internet has become the biggest gambling phenomenon not only online, but in the real world. Internet poker, although a different part of the cybergalaxy, has, like identity theft, become a multibillion dollar business. However, I believe that the poker craze will soon burn out, mainly because of hackers consistently improving their programs to cheat what's becoming a diminishing amount of honest players, who, as they become more aware of hackers, will drop out of online poker games in bunches.

I also believe that identity theft is getting very near its peak. I hope that this book is going to help speed that up and then set the crime of the twenty-first century into a tailspin. Through preventative measures that millions of potential victims are increasingly taking, databases containing the sensitive information needed by ID thieves will become more secure. As that happens on a widening scale, ID thieves will come across less and less usable information online, no matter how hard they search. Trojan and other sneak programs designed to siphon information will suck up fewer marketable personal details. Eventually the ID thieves will find themselves witnessing a drought in bank and credit information that can be sold.

But for this to happen, you, the public, must become more vigilant over your personal banking and shopping habits. The demand for your identities and credit histories will never subside, as there will always be profiteers looking to abuse an imperfect system. But we can reduce the supply of mis-usable information. It might take years to offset the seemingly unstoppable tide of cybercrime now upon us, but with time and diligence it will happen.

The financial havoc identity theft causes is no longer the only reason we must stop it. Criminal use of stolen identities has now become a threat to our national security. Intrusions into our personal records are now precursors of more serious attacks against our very existence. I am talking about international terrorism.

As terrorist organizations such as Al-Qaeda have long relied on the drug trade and other illegal activities to finance attacks against the free world, they now count on forged identity documents to travel through it. As with any other ethnic group or race of people, upstanding citizens of Arabic and Asian descent can become victims of identity theft. What these terrorist organizations do is steal identities belonging to people with Arabic and Asian names, then create identity documents in those names bearing photographs of terrorists whose facial characteristics are in sync with the names. Since the names on these forged documents generally do not appear on terrorist-watch lists, operatives on terrorist missions can move about freely through airports while in possession of them. In carrying American passports, they don't even have to submit to the digital photo and fingerprinting process now in use to screen foreigners at all American airports.

Once the terrorists have the fraudulent documents in hand, they can remain in those IDs indefinitely, or up until the time their mission is completed. Since they are not abusing the credit accounts of the people whose names they have stolen, the victims of the ID thefts are not alerted by credit statements. In the case of suicide bombers, victims would probably never know that their existence aided and abetted terrorist attacks. This is the darkest side of identity theft, and if for no other reason than to preserve our freedom and way of life, we must unite to fight it. While still in the ID theft business, I was not aware of the terrorist connection to the crime, but I am now, which is a big reason why I am urging the public to do its share.

Each citizen must behave in a newly responsible way and watch over every financial transaction he makes, even if it seems utterly trivial. Common sense protective measures almost go without saying. You all know by now not to lend your credit cards to people you don't entirely trust, and not to give anyone personal information unless you're 100 percent sure that the entity receiving it is absolutely aboveboard. Below, I have listed some basic protective measures that when followed, significantly reduce your chances of becoming a victim of identity theft.

Real World Protection

- Always shred personal documents that you no longer need. Discarding them in the wastebasket is not sufficient. Between the garbage bin and the incinerator, someone can collect your documents and obtain your personal information. If you suspect that your information has been compromised, issue a fraud alert to the reporting bureaus. Your credit report will be sent to you.

- Restrict the access to your personal data by signing up for the National Do Not Call Registry. If you do get any solicitous calls, never give any personal information to the caller, especially your Social Security number and your mother's maiden name.

- Never let your credit cards out of your sight. Do not even let store clerks take them away from the counter. If there's a problem during a transaction, they can solve it with you and your credit card in the same place. In restaurants, this might be difficult to do. If you're not familiar with the restaurant or waiter, you can always pay cash.

- Remove your name and address from the phone book and reverse directories as well as from marketing lists of credit bureaus to reduce credit card solicitations.

- Limit the appearances of your Social Security number. Remove it from your checks, insurance cards and driver's licenses. Most DMVs ask you if you want your Social Security number on the license. Say no! Also ask your bank not to use it as your identification number. Never give it to merchants as they have no reason to request it. You don't even have to give it to medical providers. The only time you are required by law to give your Social Security number is when a company needs it for government purposes. If it's about tax matters or governmental agencies like Medicare, then you must give it, but in doing so you're relatively safe.

- Regularly check your credit reports for suspicious activity. Freeze them if that option is available in the state where you live. This prevents anyone from opening up a new credit file in your name. It will not affect your credit rating.

- Curtail electronic access to your bank accounts. Pay bills by snail mail. I know it's a pain in the ass to start licking envelopes again, but that small inconvenience will seem like a pleasure cruise in comparison to untangling abused financial records. Also avoid linking your checking to savings. Use a credit card for purchases rather than a debit card. Customer liability for fraudulent credit card purchases is only $50; for debit cards it can be higher.

- Beware of public computers found in Internet cafés, libraries, etc. Never shop online when using one. Never check your bank account or enter any credit information. Public computers are vulnerable to keystroke catchers, small devices attached to the cable connecting the keyboard to the computer. They have a memory chip that records everything you type. Keylogging programs hidden inside other software are also a threat as they easily infect the machine. They silently copy the keystrokes of computer users and send that information to the crooks, much like Trojans do. Keyloggers stole nearly $5 million from 200 different Brazilian bank accounts within one year. If you go into your bank account at an Internet café, you might find its funds depleted by the time you get home.

- Be extremely vigilant at ATMs. If possible, only use ones located in and around major financial institutions and shopping malls, where the machines get heavy traffic. Outside banks or in their vestibules is safest. Avoid ATMs located in small businesses like bars and convenience stores. While performing a transaction, shield the keys you type. Don't take receipts. Run your finger along the card slot before inserting the card. If you feel any tiny prongs, don't use it. This could be evidence of a data-reading sleeve that has been fastened inside it by thieves. If the machine does not successfully read your card the first time, abandon it and find another one. If the machine swallows your card for any reason, immediately contact the institution that issued it.

- Be careful with hotel room card keys. Personal information is encoded on their magnetic strips, just like on credit cards. Although hotels claim that no sensitive information is contained on the strips, you can't be sure. My advice is to destroy the key cards upon checking out. There is usually no deposit required on the cards. If there is, demand that the clerk clear the computer system of all information pertaining to you.

- Be especially vigilant in the State of Arizona. Maybe it's a coincidence that Arizona played such a big part in the early years of IDT, Inc., but today it has become the identity theft capital of the world. Not only because Maricopa County, which includes Phoenix, is one of the fastest-growing counties in the nation, but it is also home to a heavy traffic in methamphetamine. Users of this drug go on binges that keep them up for days in a row, giving them the time to sort through trash and discarded mail for all kinds of personal information, which they in turn use to scam cash for their habit.

- Some "meth ID thieves" have actually turned their meth labs into ID theft labs as well. They use acetone, an ingredient used in methamphetamine production, to wash the ink off stolen checks, which they turn into their personal financial tools. Then they browse state government web sites for divorce documents listing the parties' names, addresses and bank account numbers. The bonus is that they can lift scans of the people's signatures. With a common software program and check stationery, they can print new checks in their victims' names.

- Finally, the great climate offered by the desert allows ID thieves with laptops to drive around exclusive neighborhoods in comfort, while they search for residents' unsecured wireless Internet connections. Tons of personal information is stolen in this fashion.

Cyberworld Protection

- Protect your home computer with a firewall, especially if you have a high-speed connection. Be just as wary with the computer in your office. Try to avoid doing any personal business on it. *Never* open attachments on any computer unless you know precisely from whom they are coming. Viruses that take over your computer come in attachments.

- Remember that skilled phishers and pharmers use web sites that appear almost exactly like ones you do legitimate business with. Be absolutely sure when conducting online business that you're doing it with the entity you think you're doing it with.

IDENTITY THEFT, INC.

- Do not respond to e-mails with urgent requests for personal financial information no matter what it's for. All those notifications that you've won this or qualified for that are false. They are sent to you just to steal your personal information. You will NEVER win anything online, unless you're playing poker. Remember that real banks and credit card companies will never send you e-mails asking for personal information. Be especially aware of e-mails notifying you of a breach of security concerning your personal or credit information. This is a favorite ploy of thieves to get you to react quickly and divulge it to them. When you see the word "verify" in any of its forms and tenses, treat it as a red flag indicating you're under attack. Anyone wanting to "verify" personal information via e-mail is trying to steal it. In some cases when dealing with a trusted entity, you can give information, but rarely if ever would that entity suggest it is urgent.

- Don't use e-mail links to get to any web page, unless you're absolutely sure about the site you're accessing.

- Never fill out forms in e-mail messages that ask for personal financial or tax information. Instead, telephone the company or log directly onto the web site by typing the address in your browser.

- Always ensure that you're using a secure web site when submitting credit card or other sensitive information via your web browser. You should also install a web browser toolbar to help protect you from known phishing fraud web sites. Ensure that your browser is up to date and has proper security applications.

- Regularly log into your online accounts (protected home computer only) and check all the statements and balances. Ensure that each transaction is legitimate. If you have the slightest suspicion, investigate it. Better safe than sorry.

- All e-mails that you determine are fraudulent should be reported to the Federal Trade Commission, FBI and various anti-cybercrime agencies. Use the Internet's search engines to locate the proper web sites and e-mail addresses for these agencies.

- Lastly, always be aware of the prevalence of identity theft and the role it has assumed in modern times. Its steady expansion through the world's fiscal corridors has reached truly unbelievable proportions. Each of us can only do his or her share to defeat it, and that is to take every feasible action to avoid becoming its victim. If you put in the time and are willing to absorb the inconveniences of watching over your financial life and records, you will become a thorn in an identity thief's side. I cannot guarantee that by adopting these measures you'll never become a victim, but in the greater scheme of things, we will win the war against identity theft despite its victims.

Afterword

Bones was released from prison in early 2004. I have spoken to him one time since, upon which he recounted the story of his downfall in Dallas. He now lives somewhere in the United States under his real name. I cannot tell you what it is.

I'm not sure *I* know what it is.

About the Authors

Glenn Hastings

Glenn is a career "soft" criminal. He has swindled banks, airlines, casinos, insurance companies and hotels. Despite all that, he is college educated and even received a degree in "honest" business administration. This is his first book.

Richard Marcus

Richard Marcus has spent a lifetime cheating casinos at roulette, blackjack, craps and poker. He catalogued his exploits in his first book *American Roulette* (published in the UK as *The Great Casino Heist*), which gave readers a rare glimpse into the underworld of casino cheats. He has been profiled on the History Channel's *Breaking Vegas* series as the ultimate casino cheat. He has also published the definitive study of cheating at poker, *Dirty Poker: The Poker Underworld Exposed.*

disinformation®